A MOST WICKED CONSPIRACY

A Most Wicked Conspiracy

The Last Great Swindle of the Gilded Age

PAUL STAROBIN

PUBLICAFFAIRS
New York

PublicAffairs
Hachette Book Group
1290 Avenue of the Americas, New York, NY 10104
www.publicaffairsbooks.com
@Public_Affairs

Printed in the United States of America

First Edition: May 2020

Published by PublicAffairs, an imprint of Perseus Books, LLC, a subsidiary of Hachette Book Group, Inc. The PublicAffairs name and logo is a trademark of the Hachette Book Group.

The Hachette Speakers Bureau provides a wide range of authors for speaking events. To find out more, go to www.hachettespeakersbureau.com or call (866) 376-6591.

The publisher is not responsible for websites (or their content) that are not owned by the publisher.

Print book interior design by Trish Wilkinson.

Library of Congress Cataloging-in-Publication Data has been applied for.

ISBNs: 978-1-5417-4230-7 (hardcover), 978-1-5417-4229-1 (ebook)

LSC-C

10 9 8 7 6 5 4 3 2 1

For Dad

Contents

Part Four

DEFIANCE

Part Five

EXPOSURE

A gallery of photos appears after p. 153.

CAPE NOME REGION OF SEWARD PENINSULA

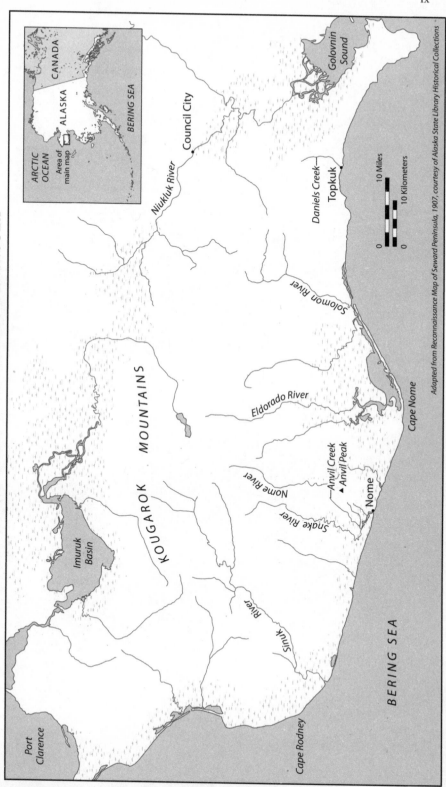

Adapted from Reconnaissance Map of Seward Peninsula, 1907, courtesy of Alaska State Library Historical Collections

Cast of Characters

Pioneer Mining—Wild Goose Alliance

The "Three Swedes"

    Jafet Lindeberg, president of the Pioneer Mining Company

    Erik Lindblom, partner in the Pioneer Mining Company

    John Brynteson, partner in the Pioneer Mining Company

William H. Metson, chief attorney for Pioneer Mining

Charles Sumner Johnson, former judge and attorney for Pioneer Mining

P. H. Anderson, head of Swedish mission

Kenneth M. Jackson, attorney for Anderson

Jo Hahn Tornanses, native of Lapland

Charles D. Lane, proprietor of Wild Goose Mining & Trading

G. W. Price, agent and supervisor for Lane

Samuel Knight, chief attorney for Wild Goose

Fred A. Healy, editor, *Nome Daily Chronicle*

William Morris Stewart, Nevada senator

McKenzie Ring

Alexander McKenzie, boss of the Dakotas, president of Alaska Gold Mining Company

    Mary Ellen, first wife

    Elva, secret second wife

James J. Hill, McKenzie mentor and railroad baron

Arthur H. Noyes, judge, second division, Alaska, appointed over James Wickersham

Joseph K. Wood, district attorney for second division, Alaska

Reuben N. Stevens, US commissioner appointed by Noyes

C. A. S. Frost, special examiner for the Justice Department

Henry C. Hansbrough, North Dakota senator

Porter James "P. J." McCumber, North Dakota senator

Thomas Henry Carter, Montana senator

James Galen, Carter's son-in-law

Milton S. Gunn, attorney in Montana law firm of which Carter had been a name partner

Cushman Kellogg Davis, Minnesota senator

Hubbard, Beeman & Hume law firm

    Oliver P. Hubbard, partner

    Edwin R. Beeman, partner

    Wilson T. Hume, partner

Alaska Gold shareholders

    Robert Chipps

    Kirke Requa

    E. M. Walters

"Captain" Mike McCormack, Alaska Gold director

Dudley Dubose, attorney for McKenzie

Thomas J. Geary, attorney for McKenzie

US Army and Law Enforcement in Cape Nome

J. T. Van Orsdale, major

Charles D. French, captain

O. L. Spaulding Jr., lieutenant

C. L. Vawter, US marshal, second division, Alaska

Cape Nome Miners

Sam C. Dunham, also a poet and US Labor Department analyst
H. T. "Deep Creek" Jones, leader of beach miners collective
Edwin Sherzer, engaged to Clara in Saint Louis
Will and Ed McDaniel, brothers from California

Ninth Circuit San Francisco Group

William B. Gilbert, judge
William W. Morrow, judge
Erskine M. Ross, judge
F. D. Monckton, clerk
E. H. Heacock, US commissioner
Evans Searle Pillsbury, court-appointed special prosecutor
John H. Shine, US marshal for Northern District of California

McKinley Clique

William McKinley, US president
Mark Hanna, Ohio senator, close adviser of McKinley, friend of Hill
and McKenzie
John W. Griggs, attorney general
Philander C. Knox, attorney general, Griggs's successor

PROLOGUE

"Would You Like to Be a Millionaire?"

O NE DAY NEAR THE END OF FEBRUARY 1900, A YOUNG MAN IN HIS twenties set out from his home near Dawson City, in the upper northwest of Canada, on his bicycle. Under a canopy of polar stars, the sun reluctant to appear at this time of year, he made his way along a rough narrow track on the frozen river used by sled dog teams, the trail spotted with the blood of the animals, their nails cracked and paws shredded by shards of ice. Mountainous ice jams halted his progress, forcing him to haul his bike aloft for many yards at a stretch. The wind lashed his face, and the temperature plunged as low as forty-five degrees below zero. The wolves, luckily, let him be as he pedaled across the length of the territory of Alaska, sustained by muskrat stew. Nearly five weeks and a thousand miles later, he arrived at his destination, the settlement of Nome on the Bering Sea coast. His body was badly bruised, his hands and elbows skinned and his left knee nearly fractured from numerous tumbles along the way, and his nose, along with the rubber tires of his bicycle and the oil in its bearings, frozen. But he had made it. The townspeople, accustomed to seeing the occasional dogsledder but never before a cyclist, greeted him with astonishment. The purpose of his journey, though, came as no surprise. Ed Jesson had made for Nome to get a head start on the gold-mining season. His gamble, for which he might have paid with his life, was to reach the town before the Bering thawed and steamers arrived with thousands of prospectors in frenzied search of the glittering treasure.

1

Alaska's gold was the talk and envy of the world. All signs pointed to abundant deposits in the Nome region. Indeed, prime discoveries already had been made, including by foreigners—"aliens"—whose claims some in the United States viewed as invalid. America's gold was for Americans, the feeling went. On the US mainland, tens of thousands of men and more than a few women were making plans to get to Nome, the maddest dash of this kind since the Forty-Niners rushed California a half century earlier. For those afflicted with the fever, the trek was nowhere near as arduous as pedaling a bicycle across jagged ice. From Saint Paul on the Mississippi, getting across the Rockies and the Cascades all the way to Seattle on the Pacific took two and a half days by rail. From Seattle's wharves, the voyage to Nome lasted about two weeks, icebergs permitting. Cape Nome offered "the chance of your whole life," a flier distributed by the Great Northern rail line promised. "Few men become rich by slow economy. Fortunes are made by men of nerve and decision who take advantage of opportunities . . . WOULD YOU LIKE TO BE A MILLIONAIRE?"

Most tantalizing of all, treasure seekers could literally find Cape Nome's gold on the beach, in flakes mixed with the ruby-colored sands stretching for many miles along the coast. Equipped with nothing more than a shovel and a crude, cradle-like wood box, known as a rocker, for filtering out the unwanted materials, a miner could clear $100 in a single day's work, more than enough to cover the cost of the Alaska expedition. Beyond the beach, just a few miles inland, larger veins of gold lay in deposits in the creeks running through tundra speckled with stunted willow trees and covered with snow for most months of the year. And beyond these confirmed discoveries lay a vast and still largely unexplored terrain, containing possibly even more gold.

The idea that "few men become rich by slow economy" was not limited in its appeal to panners and miners. Nome exerted a pull on a class of people seldom disposed to lift anything heavier than a fountain pen. The lure of easy money bred speculative fancies and schemes, as various con artists and conniving lawyers, who were often in on the action, angled to gain control of choice mining properties. Why bother to pan for gold, why bother to sink a shaft into semifrozen ground warmed by a fire demanding constant tending, why brave the wilds at all, when someone else's claim, already yielding the prize in mouth-watering quantities, might be there for the "legal" taking?

Few of these schemes came to anything. But one of them did. The mastermind was a political boss, a maker of US senators, with connections to the Executive Mansion, as the White House was then called, and to the most powerful business moguls in the nation. Alaska's gold beckoned, and he wanted it. Naturally, he planned to cut in his friends. This was, after all, the time in American life known as the Gilded Age, and the bosses operated like lords of the realm, dispensing and receiving favors as a matter of course. The question was, Who would stop him?

Part One

DISCOVERY

Gold "throws off rays that devour the soul. . . . Gold, like passion, makes glands work until the human mind goes berserk."

—*Nome dogsled driver A. A. "Scotty" Allan,*
quoted in Preston Jones, **Empire's Edge**

Chapter 1

ANVIL CREEK

A YOUNG MAN STOOD IN A SHALLOW CREEK, PAN IN HAND, THE CLEAR, cold water rushing by his feet. It was a fairly narrow creek, hemmed in on both sides by dark green brush. In the near distance was a small mountain, ringed by patches of snow, with an eerie-looking pile of large dark rocks, in the shape of an anvil, on the summit. Muskox, a type of wild goat, sometimes could be seen resting on the snow. With two companions, Jafet Lindeberg had arrived at the creek, in a stretch of northwestern Alaska several miles inland from the Bering seacoast, in search of gold. It was late September 1898—seventeen months before cyclist Ed Jesson made his heroic journey across Alaska. Jafet, slight of build and new to the work, did not find panning easy. Scooping sand, gravel, and water and sloshing and swirling the slurry strained the muscles of the hands and arms, the shoulders, neck, and back. Gold, if there was any, was apt to take the form of a fine power, mixed with all the other elements of the sand. The idea was to separate gold particles, heavier even than lead, from the mixture. This could consume twenty minutes or even half an hour for a single scoop of dirt, the pan tilted to let water and unwanted sand escape, refilled to recreate the slurry, a weary finger tapping the side of the pan to get the speckles to move toward the rim. The unpracticed eye might get taken in by crystals of a shiny yellow mineral, iron pyrite, known as "fool's gold." The reward for this effort and aggravation, even in a place known to contain gold, might be little more than a small fraction of a single gram.

But on this day, Lindeberg's first at the creek, the task was easy. Gold abounded, not in a dust but in flakes. Anvil Creek, as the men named this blue ribbon of water, was a spectacular find. The vast majority of prospectors would never stumble upon such a discovery in a lifetime of pursuit. Lindeberg and his two fellow prospectors broke off twigs from what counted for trees in the Arctic tundra—the dwarf willow, standing from three to five feet high—and staked a claim across and along a section of the creek, in the shape of a parallelogram. The men marked each corner stake with a notice written in lead pencil, the notice listing their names, the date of the find, and a physical description of this particular spot. They agreed to share the claim as equal partners, and they called it Discovery.

The men could not know this, but there was gold to be found just about everywhere in these parts. There was gold in many of the creeks, gold in the gulches, gold in the meadows on which prospectors walked, in some places in lodes sixty feet under the ground on top of bedrock, the lodes formed possibly more than four billion years before, in the Precambrian geological era. There was gold in the coastal beach sands, gold beneath the Bering floor, gold embedded in bluffs jutting into the sea. Gold of every conceivable shape and texture—including, in the not-distant future, a seven-inch-long slab weighing 107 ounces—awaited discovery. It might have been supposed the gold came from the seas, spat up on land by gigantic waves. But the truth was the opposite: the gold came from the tundra; some of the accumulated deposits washed into the sea. The gold in the icy streams draining the mountains originated in the veins under the earth, ground down by glaciers, the dust, flakes, and nuggets in time migrating to the water beds and concentrating there in pockets. The gold had lain in wait for eons, noticed by natives as "colors" in the streams.

The dream of gold had led Jafet Lindeberg to leave his uneventful life in Norway. Jafet was from Varanger, in the northeast corner of the country, along the Barents Sea. Born there in 1874, the youngest of twelve children, he was raised to work in the lumberyards, cutting cordwood out of birch. He was just past twenty years old when he heard the news of a sensational strike in the Klondike. Eager to travel there by any means, he signed up for a mission of the US government to transport reindeer from Norway to southeastern Alaska for the purpose of conveying supplies to the miners in the Yukon. He knew nothing about tending reindeer but was hired anyway. He made passage to Seattle and then on to Skagway, on the south coast of Alaska. His task was to find food for the animals, many of whom proved too weak to survive. He resigned his commission and by April 1898 had joined the throngs heading north. Dozens of trekkers had died from snowslides and dozens more from spinal meningitis. Toes and fingers had been lost to frostbite. One adventurer made it over the pass and built a boat to maneuver through rapids only to smash the boat against a rock and lose all his belongings. After retracing his journey from the start, making a new boat, and setting off again, his boat shattered against the same rock as before—at which point the thwarted adventurer blew his brains out. Such stories were known by all; yet still Jafet longed to get through that "storm-locked gate to the golden door," as the trail to the Klondike was called. Fortunately for him, perhaps, an avalanche blocked his path. After helping to rescue the stricken, he returned to Seattle. Again he enlisted in a reindeer mission, only this time the job was to assist native peoples in northern Alaska—the Eskimos—in the development of a sustainable reindeer industry. By government boat he proceeded to Saint Michael on Norton Sound. There he met a medical officer in the reindeer expedition, a fellow Norwegian, Dr. A. N. Kittilsen. The doctor told Jafet that there was no need to risk death by trying to get to the Klondike—there was gold to be found nearby in a new mining district, known as Council, reachable by a boat ride across Norton Sound to Golovin on the coast and a journey inland by river.

In this, a global age of gold, with big strikes not only in North America but also in Australia and Africa, fortune seekers like Jafet might travel thousands of miles to get to the fields. The influx raised a sensitive question of law and politics. The gold belonged to a common earth; yet the earth was divided among sovereign nations. As a legal matter, who was eligible to stake a claim in a given country? While in

Saint Michael, Jafet received a vital piece of information. Even though he was a citizen of Norway, not of the United States, he was nonetheless eligible under the prevailing US law to stake a claim—so long as he first declared his intention to become an American citizen. In July 1898, he formally made his pledge before a judge operating as a US commissioner in Saint Michael. And that act, so he thought, took care of his right to participate in the chase for gold on the promising soils of Alaska, an American possession since its purchase from Russia just over thirty years earlier.

The Council district, as the white Europeans named it, covered a traditional fishing region for the native peoples. There was some gold to be found in the numerous creeks but not, as it proved, a great deal. In the settlement of Council City, on the banks of the Neukluk River, Lindeberg met his future partners, and the three men would soon become known as the "Three Swedes" (also the "Three Lucky Swedes")—even though only the other two were natives of Sweden and they, unlike Lindeberg, were already naturalized US citizens. At the age of twenty-four, Jafet was the youngest of the three. The eldest, Erik Lindblom, forty-one, the son of a schoolteacher, had arrived in California in 1886. A dozen years later, barely making a living as a tailor and entranced by visions of gold, he joined a whaling expedition bound for the Bering Sea. He jumped ship at Grantley Harbor in northern Alaskan waters and found his way to Council City. The third man, John Brynteson, twenty-seven, the son of a farmer, came to America in 1887, one year after Lindblom. Having worked in the copper and iron mines of the upper peninsula of Michigan, he was the only one of the three with any actual mining experience. He arrived in Alaska in the spring of 1898 with the task of finding coal for the Swedish Covenant Mission at Golovin on Norton Sound, but before long he started prospecting for gold.

The "Three Swedes" resolved to head for fresh terrain. At Golovin, known by natives as Chinik, they attached a keel to an old flat-bottomed boat, hoisted a sail, set forth west along the sound, and turned north only to wash up at the mouth of a river in a storm, well short of their destination. To the native peoples, the coiling river was known as the Egoshoruk; white people renamed it as the Snake. From this spot the voyagers came upon what they called Anvil Creek, a tributary of the river about six miles in length. There were other promising streams too, and in addition to staking the Discovery claim jointly, the men marked individual claims for themselves. By power of attorney, they also staked a claim for P. H. Anderson of the Swedish mission. Anderson ran an educational program for Eskimo children, whom he aimed to make good Christians. There was no question of his status as an American: he was an Iowa farmer.

The men sailed back to Golovin to obtain more supplies at a trading post, their sampling of gold, worth about $50, stored in shotgun cases. They disclosed their find to Anderson as well as to Dr. Kittilsen of the reindeer station. Anderson, in turn, confided in a professional mining man in Golovin: G. W. "Gabe" Price, an agent for Charles D. Lane of San Francisco, one of the richest and shrewdest mining barons in America. Lane had fixed his wide-ranging eye on Alaska and tasked Price with scouting the territory for him. So far, Price had found nothing of value.

Although the discoverers were at first reluctant to disclose the location of their strike, Price won their trust and became their adviser. He told them a party had to return to the Anvil Creek area to restake the existing claims with a tape measure to conform exactly to the dimensions allowed by US law (1,320 by 660 feet), properly stake any new ones, formally establish a mining district, and legally record the properties. And with the Bering soon to freeze and become impassable, time was precious.

The missionary, Anderson, who was now a stakeholder, offered to lend them the Swedish mission's huge two-masted schooner on the condition that the miners first construct a schoolhouse at Golovin for his charges. The schoolhouse hastily constructed, the schooner laden with food and mining equipment, the return party set sail.

As Price knew, a minimum of six adults was required to establish a mining district. The three discoverers, along with Price and

Dr. Kittilsen, made five. The sixth man was known as Jo Hahn—his full name in English rendered as John Tornanses. Jo Hahn was a Lap-lander, or Lapp, a people indigenous to an Arctic Circle region of ice and snow encompassing portions of Norway, Sweden, Finland, and Russia. Like Jafet Lindeberg, Jo Hahn had signed up with the American government to come to Alaska to help tend the reindeer. Unlike Lin-deberg, Jo Hahn knew everything about these creatures, for the Lapps were a reindeer people. The reindeer gave them their meat, cheese, milk, and butter, as well as the hides for their clothing and footwear, their bedding and tent coverings. The animal, Jo Hahn and his cohorts found on arrival, was ideally suited for Alaska, finding abundant food in the white lichens that grew on tundra rocks. The reindeer was possi-bly more valuable than a dog, whose food—meat—humans had to sup-ply. But once in Alaska, Jo Hahn abandoned his reindeer job. Just like Lindeberg, he went before the court of the US commissioner at Saint Michael and swore his intention to become an American citizen.

The mission's schooner arrived at the mouth of the Snake in the middle of October. It was already cold and getting darker by the day. The tundra was starting to freeze, the creeks icing up, a thick blanket of snow soon to make mining virtually impossible. The men made it to the Anvil Creek site and declared the creation of the Cape Nome Mining District, the name taken from a bluff jutting out into the Ber-ing. Gabe Price staked a prime Anvil claim for his boss, Charles Lane, and with Price and Dr. Kittilsen as witnesses, Jo Hahn staked a claim, Number Ten Above, meaning the tenth property upstream of the orig-inal Discovery claim. There was gold in the earth around the streams, not only in the beds of the waters, and the men lit fires to warm and soften the ground. Using rockers, they took as much gold as they could in the difficult conditions—about $1,800 worth. By the first week of November, work was no longer possible, and with the schooner that brought them now locked in by Bering ice, they made their way back to Golovin over land by dogsled.

These, then, were the principal stakeholders in the new Cape Nome district as the miners left the area: a Norwegian alien with a declared intention to become a US citizen and a Lapp alien in the same category; a pair of Swedish American immigrants with American citizenship; a Swedish missionary from Iowa who had not staked his own claim; and a US-born California mining magnate, represented by his agent. But what about the native inhabitants, the people known as Eskimos? Why were they not sharing in these riches? Decades later, an interviewer asked Jafet Lindeberg whether Eskimos were "in the neighborhood" at the time of the Anvil Creek discovery. "No, not even Eskimos" were present, he replied. To be charitable, Lindeberg's memory perhaps failed him. Nevertheless, the truth was that the Eskimos were everywhere in the region—and more than that, the Anvil Creek finds might not have been made without them.

An Eskimo elder recorded a story featuring his grandfather, who was in the Sitnasuak village, at the mouth of the Egoshoruk, when the first missionaries arrived:

He saw the first one and said to him, "You come up here for gold too?"
He said, "No."
My grandpa said, "What you come up here for?"
"Oh, I'm up here to spread the good word of the gospel."
"Oh, you're not interested in gold?"
He said, "No."
"Okay, I can still tell you where that gold is, up here."

By one account, an Inupiat Eskimo boy from Golovin, Constantine Uparazuck, steered the schooner that brought the mining party of six to the mouth of the Snake in October 1898. Constantine was a pupil at Anderson's Swedish mission and was baptized there. In the Inupiat oral tradition, Constantine's role in the Anvil discovery was expanded along with that played by a second boy, Gabriel Adams, a standout pupil at the Swedish mission whom Anderson had hired as an assistant. What came to be known within this oral tradition as the story of the two Eskimo boys became a kind of parallel narrative to the standard tale of the Three Swedes as told by white people. By the natives' account, the two boys were, in effect, partners with the Scandinavians.

Whatever the precise truth, the Eskimos were cut out almost entirely from the Anvil Creek claims. The white people presumed falsely that the Alaskan natives were not eligible to stake mining claims in their own names. The founders of the Cape Nome Mining District awarded claim Number Nine Above Discovery to P. H. Anderson as a "trustee," apparently on behalf of the two Eskimo boys, Constantine and Gabriel. But this arrangement became the subject of protracted litigation that in the end yielded very little for the Eskimo boys and their heirs. The encounter between the Eskimos and the white prospectors largely amounted to an exchange of diseases like measles, pneumonia, and syphilis transmitted to the natives and the theft of their boats, dogs, and food.

So far as America was concerned, Alaska was virgin territory, more or less a blank slate. No matter that the word derived from a native expression for "a great land," pronounced as "al-ak-shak" or "al-ay-ek-sa." Human habitation began in Alaska several thousand years before American settlers arrived, with the Inupiat, Chugach, and Yup'ik in the northern coastal region, the Aleuts in the southeast, and the Athabascan Indians in the river valleys of the interior. America tended to overlook, too, the Russian foray into Alaska, dating to an expedition in the 1740s, among its goals "to look for any distinctive rocks and earth in which one might expect rich ores." Alaskan history, in the American eye, began on March 30, 1867—the day that US Secretary of State William H. Seward signed a treaty with the tsarist government of Russia for the purchase of Alaska. The price was $7.2 million, about two cents per acre for an expanse twice the size of Texas. Critics of the acquisition railed against "Seward's Folly" and "Seward's Icebox." They said the land was not worth the cost of maintenance alone. Supporters saw promise. "The treaty is a wise one," said South Carolina's *Charleston Daily News.* "It is very clear that, following

the instinct of proprietorship that is always developed from a plantation to an empire, we intend to own this continent, 'from the center
all around to the sea.'" That was certainly Seward's intention. "Give
me fifty, forty, thirty more years of life," he told a gathering in Boston,
"and I will engage to give you the possession of the American continent and the control of the world."

It took thirty-one years, but with the find at Anvil Creek, the "folly"
seemed redeemed. Seward by then was long in his grave, but posterity
at least could smile on the discovery, which chanced to take place
on the body of Alaskan land named after him, the Seward Peninsula,
appearing on maps as a large thumb jutting out into the Bering, tilted
upward. Such was the power of gold to change, virtually overnight, the
political and economic calculus of men with power and money and the
mood of a nation. And so the jousting began. No matter who laid first
claim to the riches of Alaska, the question remained as to whose hands
the wealth would end up in.

Chapter 2

WHAT'S YOURS IS MINE

I N WINTERTIME, THE LARGE MAMMALS OF THE SEWARD PENINSULA mostly slept—the grizzlies beneath the snow, the humans under their quilts. The ptarmigan roosting in snowbanks and the moose feeding on willows by frozen riverbanks had the land to themselves, along with the fox and the wolf and the furry-footed snowshoe hare. The winter of 1898–1899, though, was different. The report of a big strike near where the Snake emptied into the Bering Sea was making its way through the usual channel of communication in these isolated parts—by word of mouth. From Council City and Saint Michael and from far more distant points in the forests of the interior, dogsled teams raced toward the area to claim the best pickings before they were gone.

Kirke Requa heard the news at her frosty campsite in the heart of the interior, at the mouth of the Tanana River, a tributary of the Yukon. Alaska's highest mountain, Denali, rose in the distance to the south. With her uncle, Requa had arrived in the territory from the American mainland in the spring of 1898, joining a team of workers on a riverbed clearing job to ease navigation on the Yukon. On reaching the Tanana, the crew settled in for the winter. The New Year passed, and somehow word reached of the Anvil Creek strike. A group of nearly twenty decided to head en masse to Cape Nome on dogsleds. They faced a hazardous journey of some seven hundred miles through wilderness, not even a roadhouse along the way at which to stop for food. Carrying her own provisions, Requa left her uncle behind; at age seventy-five he was too frail to make the trip. A white woman on her own was a rarity in Alaska, as white settlers often made her aware. She knew nothing about mining, but that was the least of her concerns.

By the time the journeyers reached the Seward Peninsula, spring was announcing itself on the tundra. The rippling whistle of the male snow bunting was a first sign of the season. Migratory birds arrived from Africa, South America, and Australia. Golden eagles skirted meadows in search of ground squirrels, and rough-legged hawks swooped down from rocky perches to snag songbirds. Tiny wildflowers—glacier avens, mountain harebell, Arctic forget-me-nots—blossomed, dotting the brownish-green turf with splotches of bright purples, yellows, and oranges. Requa and her fellow dredgers arrived in Cape Nome in the first of week of May and found one hundred or so people already on the scene. She was puzzled by what struck her as a distinctly foreign, un-American place. "We called it 'little Sweden' for a while, there were so many Swedes," she later recalled. And there were a number of odd-looking and odd-sounding men who she was told were Lapps: "I could not understand what they said."

Like Jo Hahn Tornanses, the Laplander who rounded out the original set of claimants, these Lapps had come to Alaska on the pay of the US government to tend reindeer. The mining district covered a substantial amount of acreage radiating out from Anvil Creek. Requa found that a fair portion of the district was claimed already. And where it was not, she could not compete with the Lapps, who had devised a system for staking that made adept use of the reindeer in their charge. Small groups of Lapps, three to a team, moved along a sled pulled by reindeer; one fellow would hop out and pace off, as best he could, the length of a claim, a second, a bundle of willow twigs in hand, would plant one at a corner and hammer the stake home, a notice wedged into the stake, and the reindeer procession would continue, never fully halting. After witnessing this display in a spot twenty miles from the tent she had made her home, Requa gave up and trudged wearily back to camp.

THE WORST SIN IN MINING WAS THE CLAIMS JUMP: A LATECOMER TO A PROM-
ising field takes as his own someone else's clearly marked and duly
registered claim. For such a violation, the accused might be put on
trial before a jury of fellow miners, with punishment as severe as death
by lynching—rough justice to warn all others against attempting the
same. Whether a claim truly had been jumped was not always so clear,
though.

One day Requa and two male friends made their way to a river,
running parallel to the Snake to the east, which the settlers called the
Nome. There they began exploring a tributary known by miners as
Dexter Creek, in honor of John Dexter, operator of a trading post at
Golovin to which many miners went for supplies. The ice in the creek
had melted, and the surrounding turf, though still patched with snow,
had started to thaw. There were no other prospectors around, and even
at two o'clock in the morning, there was plenty of light. The trio came
upon small twigs in the form of stakes, but to Requa's eye there was no
orderly pattern clearly marking a claim. Attached to some of the twigs
was a notice in the form of a power of attorney, meaning the claim had
been marked by one person on behalf of another. This practice was
becoming widespread in Cape Nome, even though many prospectors
viewed it as an abuse of the principle that miners should stake their
own claims.

The Requa party quickly found to their delight that Dexter Creek
was rich in gold—easily panned. Requa staked a claim. There was a
"very tattered piece of paper" that might have been a "location notice"
on the spot, she later said, but she disregarded it and officially recorded
the claim in her name. Still, this find, as ripe as it was, wasn't enough
for her. Her heart brimmed with resentment at the foreigners—"the
Swedes" and especially the Lapps—the Lapps making unfair use, in her
mind, of reindeer that were the property of the US government. These
intruders, as she saw them, had a lower standing than real Americans,
and she hadn't trekked hundreds of miles through snow and ice to
leave US gold in their hands. "Mrs. Requa," as she was known around
the camp, wanted a piece of Anvil Creek. She set her eye on Number

Four Below Discovery. Jafet Lindeberg had filed this claim through power of attorney on behalf of John Dexter, the trading post operator. Much revered by miners, Dexter was in failing health, unable to explore Cape Nome on his own. But as Mrs. Requa saw the matter, Lindeberg had done shoddy work—Number Four lacked a proper set of corner stakes. So she restaked the claim in her own name—with the thought of giving the property in clear title to Dexter. Such was the story, anyway, she later told. She may have believed it, but by any definition, she was a jumper.

A claim, once jumped, was likely to be jumped again. A pair of tough-looking men paid a visit to Mrs. Requa at her tent and threatened to put her out of Cape Nome unless she gave up her claim to Number Four Below Discovery. They "could shoot quite straight," they told her. She replied she wasn't going anywhere. The tale echoed through the camp and bolstered her already impressive reputation for pluck. But just as jumping bred jumping, menace bred menace.

Paddy Ryan, a prizefighter known for brawling "like an animal" in the ring, jumped Number Nine Above Discovery, the claim held in supposed trust for the two Eskimo boys by P. H. Anderson of the Swedish mission. Anderson was now actively working the claim, his aspiration to get rich in Alaska trumping his original aim to amass souls for Christ. He was not the only missionary in Cape Nome with a worldly eye cast on gold, and miners tended to hold the missionaries as a group in low regard for failing to minister to the sufferings of the camp. Nevertheless, the missionaries were entitled to their claims. In this instance, Anderson was saved from Ryan not by his fellow miners but by the US Army—the only force strong enough, it seemed, to take on such a brute. Cape Nome was sliding into anarchy, with the new mining district failing to police itself and the nearest court of law, at Sitka, more than a thousand miles away. The army, with a detachment based at Saint Michael, was at best a partial solution to the lawlessness. There were not enough soldiers to keep troublemakers like Ryan at bay, for one thing. For another, some of the troops had caught the fever and were prospecting on the side. They wanted to get rich too.

In the free-for-all, it was inevitable that someone would have the gumption to jump the original claim, Discovery on Anvil Creek, still in the hands of Jafet Lindeberg, Erik Lindblom, and John Brynteson. Into the picture stepped Robert Chipps, a former milkman from Chicago. Chipps had arrived in Alaska in the summer of 1898, on a commission from the London-based Anglo-Alaskan Company, a consortium of investors. According to the terms of his "grub stake," typical of such arrangements, the company paid for his transportation, food, clothing, and equipment. Tasked with exploring for promising mining opportunities, he would retain a one-third to a one-half share in any claims staked. Now, a year later, his contract with the company having ended, Chipps was prospecting in Cape Nome for himself. The grumbling in the camp that foreigners had nabbed the best properties stirred him to file a claim for Discovery. "I located it because I did not think that the people that located it first were citizens," he said. "I knew that they had it staked, but I did not think they could hold it."

IT WAS ONLY A MATTER OF TIME BEFORE A MORE ORGANIZED EFFORT WAS mounted to push "foreigners" off their claims. The initial thrust came, not surprisingly, out of Council City, some seventy miles from Cape Nome, across mountain and river. Council City was the first declared mining district on the peninsula, and its leaders were American citizens born in America. Miners from this district had explored the area around the mouth of the Snake before the arrival of Lindeberg and his companions but had staked no claims. Nevertheless, they took a proprietary interest in the discoveries at Cape Nome and felt especially outraged by the protection US soldiers afforded to claims asserted by Lapps. Particularly galling to them was an incident in late March 1899. A leading miner in Council City, Louis Melsing, asserted a claim to Number Ten Above Discovery, the Anvil Creek plot of Jo Hahn Tornanses, on the basis that Tornanses, as a Lapp, had no right to stake a mining claim in Alaska. In so doing, Melsing defied an explicit warning from US Army lieutenant O. L. Spaulding Jr. that any person who jumped a Cape Nome claim would be arrested and jailed. True to his word, Spaulding put Melsing in the guardhouse at Saint Michael for three weeks. In response, the Council City men formed a group calling itself the Law and Order League, its mission "to prevent crime" and "protect the rights of its members and all law-abiding citizens." The league determined to have its voice heard in Washington, DC. In a letter to President William McKinley, dated May 25, the group recounted the Melsing episode and pleaded for federal judicial intervention to set matters right. The Laplanders, "half-breeds," were in the employ of the US government, the letter writers said. The Lapps, moreover, were "of the Mongolian race" and were "prohibited from claiming and locating the public mineral lands of the United States."

The president may not have received this mishmash; a later search of records by his staff failed to locate the letter. But the sentiments were widely shared by miners now pouring into the region, and not only by greenhorns like Mrs. Requa—known as cheechakoes, or newcomers, a term derived from indigenous language—but also by seasoned miners, known as sourdoughs, for the fermented starter yeast they used to make bread, typically carried in a pouch kept warm against the body. Particularly irksome to the sourdoughs was the practice by which some miners, including but not only Lapps, staked claims willy-nilly, without first doing the hard work of showing that there was gold on the site. In the tense atmosphere, a plot to disenfranchise the "foreigners" was hatched. The bylaws of the Cape Nome mining district allowed for the call of a miners' meeting to discuss and vote on matters of mutual interest. The plotters planned to schedule such a meeting at a makeshift saloon near the mouth of the Snake and then ram through a resolution to annul the claims of "the Swedes" and the Lapps. The instant the resolution passed, a smoke signal would be sent to coconspirators, stationed by the rock formation on the summit of Anvil Mountain some five miles away, who would race to the annulled claims and seize the properties. The plotters figured that the takeover would happen so fast that the targets, likely to be attending the meeting, would have no chance to counterattack.

Robert Chipps—the milkman from Chicago—was among the ring-leaders. Here, he felt, was his opportunity to make good on his Discovery claim. The animus against the foreigners was so widespread, who would vote against a resolution to dissolve their claims and give the mining district a fresh start? The meeting was called for the second week of July 1899, and on the scheduled day nearly five hundred miners crowded into the large tent that comprised the saloon. But just as the resolution prepared by the plotters was being read to the assembly, Lieutenant Spaulding, the bane of the jumpers, arrived. Three of his men, bayonets drawn, stood by his side. Spaulding demanded the withdrawal of the resolution. The reading continued. The lieutenant gave the group two minutes to disperse. No one left. Spaulding ordered his men to use their bayonets to clear the tent, whereupon the miners were forcibly evicted.

Had Spaulding not intervened to prevent the resolution's adoption, bloodshed would likely have ensued. Jafet Lindeberg and his partners at Discovery had heard rumors of the plot, and they were prepared to fight with guns for their property. In hopes of averting a violent confrontation, they had tipped off Spaulding to the intrigue. The aborted meeting, though, hardly pacified the camp. Spaulding was much cursed for his preemptory conduct. The camp was full of discontent: Few miners had much gold in their pokes. Some suffered from scurvy for lack of fresh fruits and vegetables. Conditions were generally filthy. Cape Nome badly needed a diversion, and suddenly it received one, as if sent by heaven.

Chapter 3

"STAR MIST"

THE IDEA THAT THE BEACH SANDS MIGHT CONTAIN GOLD WAS SOME-times talked about in the Cape Nome mining camp in the summer of 1899. But until the middle of July, no one took it seriously. Everything changed when one of Lieutenant Spaulding's men, on digging a well on the beach, found gold. With the confirmation of Soldiers Gulch, as the discovery was called, miners sped to the beachfront. There was room for all, as the beach ran for tens of miles, beyond the mouth of the Snake to the west and beyond the mouth of the Nome River to the east. The finest place to prospect was a strip of rust-colored sand, several feet wide, running parallel with the waterline above the high-tide mark. Iron filaments in the sand made for its "ruby" glow. But there was gold to be found above and below this band, and best of all, the metal lay close to the surface.

The presence of abundant gold in the sands struck the camp as fantastical. Some of the miners were veterans of the Klondike gold rush—survivors, more like it, given the extreme hazards of that trek. Gold by the seashore was unheard of. One miner called the treasure "star mist"—the prospectors, he insisted, were digging up "millions of fine particles" of the metal that had rained down on the earth from meteor showers and collected on the beach.

The beach find immediately lifted the downcast mood of the camp. Gold was currency—to pay for beer to slake one's thirst, for one thing. Sourdoughs and cheechakoes alike could profitably work the beach. A man's last name—his place of birth—suddenly felt less important.

A pan and a bucket for water could be enough to get by, although a shovel was certainly helpful. Rockers could be hammered and nailed together from driftwood. Almost everyone made for the beach.

By general consent, the miners declared the beach a commons. In other words, in this "poor man's paradise," as one newspaper called it, no staking was allowed. A miner could hold a spot for as long as he or she kept at it, whether for four hours or for fourteen. But once the miner left the spot, anyone else could occupy it. Turnover was frequent, as only the hardiest could keep a place for very long. Even in July, temperatures dipped into the forties, numbing the hands after just twenty minutes of work. The winds blew sand into the eyes. A dense fog might cut visibility to twenty paces; a black cloud might bring a cold rain, soaking clothing and bedding. The Bering might be a placid lake one day, a roiling sea the next.

The harsh conditions bred a spirit of fellowship. Miners pitched tents on the beach and established a kind of canvas city in which everyone was welcome to live. As there was no ownership of the beach, there was no landlord to whom rent was due. By the briny mouth of the Nome, pink salmon, on their way to their freshwater spawning grounds, were easily caught. As word of the "golden sands" got out beyond Cape Nome, the first beach settlers were joined by a mini-rush of outsiders, some coming from the Alaskan interior, some from the US mainland. Still, at the height of the summer season of 1899, there were scarcely two thousand miners in the tent city—a manageable number, even if, in some sections of beach, prospectors were so closely packed as to nearly touch shoulders. Those arriving from the mainland often felt a sense of liberation, a feeling of release from the confinements of life back home. They kept the full reward of their labor, for once, and because the beach was a commons, it offered "poor opportunities for that class of men who live on the labor of others," as a miner observed. Indeed, there was a distinct pleasure in knowing that "that class of men"—the bosses of industry—could not have their usual domineering way on this new frontier. A cynic might have said that the fellowship of the beach miners was cheaply earned—arrived at not by some shared high principle but by a rare chance of circumstance that gave material plenty to everyone. But the happiness, no matter its root, was genuine. Many sang songs as they slogged away; an elderly miner, his fortune secured, praised the Lord again and again and again.

It couldn't last. The plenty quickly provoked greed: how to capture these beach riches? For speculators, looking to make a fast profit by buying and then quickly selling mining properties, the idea of the beach as a commons, exempt from the usual rules of property rights, was repugnant. The speculators staked claims starting on the edge of the tundra land adjoining the beach and extending onto the beach itself, all the way to the high-tide mark. This effort took on a more aggressive cast with the arrival on the scene of the Nome Mining and Development Company, a consortium of tundra claims holders, the sort of corporate presence the beach miners feared and were determined to thwart. The company posted notices along the coast, declaring that "its" beach "claims" could be mined only with a permit, available for purchase for fifty cents per day per person. Anyone found working the beach without a permit would be "prosecuted for trespass and larceny," the notice warned. In addition, the company enlisted a half dozen army soldiers to guard the company's "claims" against "jumpers."

Here was a challenge that the beach miners could not ignore. The lawyers among them—and there were a few—believed that the miners were protected by a US law that set aside, as a "roadway" for the public, a sixty-foot-wide strip of beach, above the mean high-tide mark, along every coast in America. This theoretical roadway could be considered part of the commons, the lawyers reasoned, hence off-limits to the speculators and corporations. But it was by no means clear that this law applied to beach mining, and it was difficult to draw an average high-tide line, given the fluctuations in the peaks of high tides.

The beach miners responded with an inspired plan of their own. One of their leaders, Key Pittman, a young lawyer and a future US senator, suggested that the miners defy the warning against trespassing by showing up on Nome Mining company "property" in the hundreds, daring the soldiers to arrest and jail them all. The ploy worked as intended. Nearly three hundred miners were arrested, and each one of them refused bail and demanded a trial. The soldiers could not possibly house and feed such a large group, much less arrange for trials, and the miners all had to be released. For the time being, the commons remained a commons, including the disputed section over the high-tide mark. It was an important victory for the miners, showing their mettle and their capacity for organized resistance. Their fraternal bonds were strengthened as a result of the episode—and they must have felt pleased when a reporter on the scene for the *San Francisco Chronicle* filed a story calling the arrests a "farce" and praising the miners for trying to make an "honest living." But this was just a skirmish: the schemers with their eyes on the beach prize did not consider the matter settled. Surely, they felt, there was another way to seize ownership of the golden sands. And the miners understood the battle wasn't over; even in a poor man's paradise, they had learned, there was always a snake.

THE RICHER CAPE NOME BECAME, THE GREATER THE NEED FOR RULE OF law—which could hardly be assured by roving bands of soldiers, solicited by private parties for one task or another. In August, a federal judge arrived to hold court, the first in the settlement. Judge Charles Sumner Johnson, a Nebraskan, appointed to the bench by President McKinley, had jurisdiction over all Alaska. From his base in Sitka, he did his best. He included Cape Nome on a marathon circuit of seven thousand miles that took three months to complete. His courtroom in town was a large tent; it leaked from steady rain, whereupon the judge donned a yellow slicker and gum boots. Litigants sat on boxes set before Johnson; spectators stood in the rear. The "street" outside the tent consisted of mud, one to two feet deep. In these conditions, those in the jumpers' camp pled the cause of justice, seeking to annul the mining claims of the "foreigners." They asked the judge specifically to rule on the citizenship declarations of Jafet Lindeberg and the Lapps. If Johnson found that such declarations were invalid, all the claims made by aliens could be viewed as tainted, including Discovery. But

Johnson did not give the jumpers what they wanted. He ruled that in a legal dispute between private parties—in this case, the original stake-holders and the jumpers—the citizenship status of a party could not be contested. Only the government of the United States could question citizenship, Johnson said, and the government was not a party to the dispute. The jumpers were disappointed. They had failed in their plot to seize hold of the "foreigners'" holdings at the miners' meeting back in July, and now they had failed again, in a bona fide legal proceeding. Robert Chipps, with his claim on Discovery, and Mrs. Requa, with her claims on Anvil and Dexter Creeks, were no nearer to possessing these properties.

Still, Johnson's ruling did not leave the winners—the aliens—feeling altogether secure. For one thing, the ruling could be appealed. For another, what if, in the future, the US government did challenge the citizenship declarations of Lindeberg and other claims holders in his situation? Congress, which made the laws for Alaska, could pressure the Justice Department to take this step. In fact, Congress on its own could change the law in a manner unfavorable to aliens holding claims. So far as Lindeberg was concerned, he was prepared to fight for the claim, should fresh challenges be mounted. Discovery was a profitable mine, still in an early stage of development as the digging proceeded to the bedrock, and he and his partners could afford legal representation to defend their joint property all the way to the Supreme Court, if it came to that. But Jo Hahn Tornanses and other Lapps felt differently. They had not, for the most part, developed their claims, and the possibility of selling their stakes for cash was tempting. And happily for them, there was an eager buyer: Charles Lane, the San Francisco mining magnate whose interests in Alaska G. W. Price had thus far represented.

"I AM A ROUGH-AND-TUMBLE MINER. I DIG THE GOLD FROM THE GROUND where I find it, having no time for theories. If I fail to find it I move on." So Lane declared around this time to an interviewer from the

Seattle Post-Intelligencer. He was just shy of sixty, but with his thinning hair and his tumbling beard turning white, he could easily be mistaken for a man in his eighties. Of course, at this stage of his career, he was far from a simple miner. He was one of America's premier mining barons, able to raise large sums of capital for his ventures. Born in Marion County, Missouri, in 1840, he crossed the Great Plains in a wagon train with his family, bound for California, in the early 1850s. The Lanes made their new home in Stockton. Charley's mining education began at the age of twelve, with panning and rocking for gold in the streams in and around Stockton, some eighty miles inland from San Francisco. He understood what it meant to work for wages in a mining operation, and he understood what it meant to fail as the owner of a mine, as he had in his late twenties with a quartz venture in Nevada. He had experience, too, of the brute violence of this way of life, waking up one morning in Mason Valley, Nevada, to find his partner murdered. Suspicion, rightly or wrongly, fell on an Indian, who was tracked down by a posse and lynched from a tree limb.

Lane made his fortune late, at the age of fifty, with a strike at the Utica gold and quartz mine in Angel's Camp, California, an abandoned property in ruins when he acquired it for a pittance. Friends called him a "lunatic" for pursuing the venture, and Lane's wife, Sallie, a Kentucky native, told her husband there was nothing in it—but with his "bulldog pertinacity," as an admiring magazine writer put it, Lane ignored the naysayers and plunged deep into debt to finance the undertaking. He kept at his work in wet clothes and boots until others dropped of exhaustion; "there was not an ounce of superfluous flesh on him," the writer marveled. His men dug deep into the earth, a mere two feet a day of excavation, in search of the treasure, and when it was finally discovered, the deepest shaft sunk at two thousand feet, Lane could justly exult to Sallie, "What did I tell you?" It made him a millionaire several times over. But his fortune came at the price of a terrible accident: sixteen men were crushed to death by a cave in. Their fellow workers broke down and wept on hearing the news, but Lane was not blamed. In 1897, six years after this incident, his hometown paper, the *San Francisco Call*, reported an expression popular among miners: "Wherever Lucky Lane goes, fortune surely follows." By then he also was taking a rich harvest in gold from the Fortuna Mine of Arizona. A friend insisted the secret lay in the séances that Lane held on mulling a purchase, a ritual conducted over a sample specimen of the ore, the "spirit medium" declaring yes or no to the transaction.

Alaska was an irresistible lure. But like all of the treasure seekers, Lane confronted the difficulty of just where to look in such a vast, uncharted territory. He launched his first expedition in 1898, in the region of Kotzebue Sound, on the northeastern coast of the Seward Peninsula, a long distance from the area later christened as Cape Nome. He spent an unrewarding summer there with his men. Only by a stroke of luck did Gabe Price, who stayed behind after his departure, happen across Lindeberg, Lindblom, and Brynteson at the end of the year's mining season.

Characteristically, Lane decided to go all in on Cape Nome: no one in the mining world was making a bigger bet on its promise; no one, accordingly, had more to lose. The gold, he believed, had been "belched forth" onto the shores of the Bering and the tundra from deep within the earth, through "volcanic eruption." His geology was wrong, but as usual his gut estimation of the prospects of a virgin mining land was astute. He was willing to accept the risk of buying claims that might be contested. He purchased Number Ten from Jo Hahn and dozens of similar claims, for a total outlay of $300,000. That was a considerable sum for the time—about $9 million in 2020 dollars. Given the risk Lane was absorbing and the investments he would have to make to work the claims, the sellers received a fair price. The Lapps had come to Alaska with nothing in their pockets, and now those among them who had cashed out could return to their native land, if they chose, wealthy.

LANE'S ACQUISITIONS MADE HIM THE SINGLE BIGGEST CLAIMS HOLDER IN Cape Nome. But from the perspective of the jumpers, nothing had changed: if an original claim like Number Ten Above Discovery was invalid at the start, then Lane was merely the holder of an illegitimate claim. The "defect" could never be erased, as this reasoning went, no matter how many times the deed changed hands. The situation was ideal for a new sort of migratory species to flock to Alaska—not birds from Australia or Africa but trial lawyers from the American mainland. The Nome bar, such as it was, consisted of sixteen or so attorneys at this time. The lawyers smelled opportunity in the battling over the gold fields, and none more so than Oliver P. Hubbard, a man with no practical experience in mining but with a sound knowledge of the mining laws.

Hubbard did not make a favorable impression on everyone. "He was a surly, dour man with a shifty eye and the thin, pinched face of a hawk," one acquaintance thought. But a hawk was exactly the sort of lawyer that the jumpers had in mind to litigate their claims. And Hubbard had a proposition for them. His Nome law firm of Hubbard & Beeman would act as attorneys for a jumper willing to take a claim to court—"to commence and prosecute to a final determination" a bid to take title of a claimed property—in return for a one-fourth interest in the claim. Suppose a court awarded a jumper the title to a property that reaped $80,000 in profit in a mining season. Hubbard & Beeman would be entitled to $20,000 of that pot. In return for this interest, the firm provided its services to its clients at no cost.

For Hubbard, just turned forty, formerly a clerk in the office of the attorney general in the Grover Cleveland administration in Washington, DC, the law was a means of enrichment. He cultivated the jumpers, reaching out to them one at a time. In his view, the tool of the law, in the right hands, could accomplish for the jumpers what raw force could not. This was a tantalizing pitch, bound to induce even more claim jumping, considering the alternatives. A miner might accumulate some gold dust from scouring the beach—not the most difficult of work, as mining went, but still tedious, sweaty labor. A miner might head into the tundra in search of gold beyond confirmed places like Anvil Creek, Dexter Creek, and Snow Gulch. There was plenty more to be found; in fact, a rich deposit awaited discovery in a small creek at the southwestern base of Anvil Mountain (and it was found—five years later, in 1904). But the tundra was an enormous expanse—just where to look? A prospector easily could get lost in a fog and spend days wandering around in a circle, the mosquitoes biting, a bear maybe circling, barely anything to eat but rotting provisions. Then there was the Hubbard plan: sign up for no cost and leave the rest to the attorneys. To any of those discouraged by Judge Johnson's proceeding in Nome, Hubbard gave assurance that a new day was dawning. Washington was by now well aware of the gold strikes. Congress was likely to pass a new civil code for the governance of Alaska, subdividing the territory's single judicial district into several new districts, one of them seated in the Nome region, with a new judge appointed to hear cases arising from the disputes over gold properties.

It certainly sounded to the jumpers like Hubbard knew what he was talking about, as might be expected due to his Washington experience and connections. Chipps took the deal with Hubbard & Beeman on Discovery, as did Mrs. Requa, deeding to the firm a one-quarter interest in each of her two claims: Number Eight on Dexter Creek and Number Four Below Discovery on Anvil Creek (the claim she professed to be holding for John Dexter). Louis Melsing, the claim jumper who had brought down the wrath of Lieutenant Spaulding, did the same for Number Ten Above Discovery, now held by Lane. All told, Hubbard was able to gather some one hundred takers for his proposition.

THE END OF THE MINING SEASON WAS SIGNALED BY ICEBERGS DRIFTING down from the north. Their constant collisions created an unnerving din, a low-pitched groaning sound, as if the seas were on their deathbed. Conversations stopped in mid-sentence; it could be difficult to hear one's own thoughts. Eventually the bumping and scraping action in the waters would stop, ushering in an uninterrupted silence—meaning that the Bering was frozen solid, sea passage out of Cape Nome impossible for at least another six months. And so a choice had

to be made—as Alaskans framed it, to stay on the "inside" for the frozen period or to head to the "outside" while there was still time. In the
few months since the discovery of gold on the beach, the settlement by
the Snake had grown to include not only a flock of lawyers but other
professional types, like physicians, dentists, and watchmakers, many
having arrived from Dawson nearly eight hundred miles away. Indeed,
the settlement was now a town, with the official name of Nome and a
young mayor, a leader of the uprising of the beach miners, elected by
the populace. On the dirt road running parallel to the beach, known as
Front Street, there were barbershops and laundries, lodging houses and
a candy store. A pair of newspapers set up operations, the *Nome News*
and the *Nome Gold Digger*. The town even had a celebrity in its midst:
Wyatt Earp, the gunfighter, gambler, and occasional lawman of Tomb-
stone, Arizona, arrived with his wife, Josephine, and, with a partner,
founded a saloon, the Dexter. Never in his life had money been so easy
to make, he boasted to friends.

Still, there would not be much to do in the cold and dark other than
playing cards and finishing off the dwindling supplies of beer and hard
liquor. Most people left; the thousands dropped to a handful. Hubbard
headed out with the rest, with the well wishes of his newfound partners
in litigation, the jumpers, some of whom planned to winter in Nome.
"We all knew that a big fight was pending," Mrs. Requa later recalled.
"Mr. Hubbard went out, invested with authority from his clients to
do all he could to help us." From the mainland, Hubbard planned to
make his way across the Atlantic to London. Apart from his other
interests, he served as company attorney for the Anglo-Alaskan Company, the same consortium of investors that had hired Robert Chipps
to explore Alaska for promising mining opportunities. Hubbard hoped
to persuade the syndicate to invest in the litigation in which his law
firm had taken an interest.

It was characteristic of Hubbard to think big, but there was an in-
surmountable obstacle in his dream path to riches. He was a big man
in Nome, but in the wider world, he was not especially well known.
This was fatally the case, as he soon came to realize, with regard to

the Washington piece of his scheme. He had assessed correctly that Congress planned to draft a new civil code of governance for Alaska. It was also true that depending on the result of this work, a new set of legal conditions might be created that would favor the jumpers' claims, maybe even guarantee them. The difficulty was that he was not the man with the clout to fix this desired result. Hubbard had ties in Washington, but they were of the second order, no better than those of scores or even hundreds of others who came to the capital with the idea of shaping some piece of legislation. He could gain the ear of a US senator, say, for a conversation, but while that was not in itself a small thing, no senator felt any particular obligation to him. That was the crux of the problem. The job of arranging matters in Washington required a man to whom the power brokers felt bound—and what's more, whom they were eager to please. In short, the job required a boss.

Part Two

"ALEXANDER THE GREAT, OF THE NORTH"

"His tactics are: 'Win, no matter what the cost.'"

—*Winnie Pearce, Bismarck friend of Alexander McKenzie,*
in an 1882 letter to her sister Jane

Chapter 4

"HONEST, OUTSPOKEN
AND RELIABLE"

T HE DISCOVERY OF GOLD IN ALASKA COINCIDED WITH THE HEYDAY OF the American political boss, men like Matthew Quay of Pennsylvania, Thomas Platt of New York, and James Clarkson of Iowa. They derived their power, in the first instance, from their control of blocs of votes in state legislatures, typically cemented by the payment of bribes to accommodating lawmakers. The state legislatures, at this time, selected US senators to go to Washington. So, through their control of the voting blocs, the bosses could handpick senators, who, in turn, were beholden to them. The bosses also controlled the state delegations that could make or break a presidential candidate at a party nominating convention. Republican Benjamin Harrison, elevated to the presidency in 1888, credited his triumph to Providence. Matthew Quay ventured an alternative explanation: the willingness of the bosses behind the Harrison campaign to risk prison time to make him president. The bosses also made themselves indispensable to the true titans of the era, the barons of industry and finance. The magnates relied on the bosses to lubricate the wheels of politics—and the bosses gained in prestige from their intimate ties to such figures. Quay, for example, was on the payroll of John D. Rockefeller's Standard Oil. This was how the world turned in the Gilded Age, the period defined in the 1873 novel of that title by Mark Twain and Charles Dudley Warner. Efforts by the so-called robber barons to establish monopolies for their business empires, to corner shares on Wall Street, to manipulate the courts—these were the regular practices of the times, and the bosses were in the thick of the action.

It was the nature of a boss to try to leverage political clout for the accumulation of personal wealth, and this mind-set nourished all sorts of profit-making schemes. One boss was quick to take Alaska's golden potential to heart. Alexander McKenzie, known in political circles as the Boss of the Dakotas and by his friends as Big Alex, had just turned fifty and was at the height of his powers, with a field of ambition that spanned the country. He didn't even live in the Dakotas anymore. His chief base of operations was the Merchants Hotel in Saint Paul, Minnesota, a five-story brick building overlooking the Mississippi set among a row of saloons. The Merchants was a haunt for traveling tradesmen, with games of dice played in the barroom, the occasional knife fight enlivening the competition. Seldom without a gun in his left side pocket, McKenzie felt at home there. He occupied a suite that acolytes called the Throne Room. Legislators from Bismarck, North Dakota's state capital, four hundred miles away, came to seek his advice or ask for a favor. Or perhaps, when McKenzie needed a favor, they were summoned. To ease their compliance, McKenzie was known to offer a rail pass, good for one thousand miles of free transportation on the Great Northern or Northern Pacific, from an ample stack on his desk. Few men could resist such a valuable enticement, but one who did, a young legislator, sensed correctly that to accept the pass "was to obligate myself forever to him."

From the Merchants, a stroll along the northern bank of the Mississippi, departing from the low ground to attain a bluff affording a magnificent view of the winding river, brought one to the estate of James J. Hill, the railroad mogul who presided over the Great Northern. On Summit Avenue, Hill had built for himself and his wife, Mary, a former waitress at the Merchants, one of America's great homes, as befitted one of the nation's wealthiest and most powerful men. Made of red sandstone, the mansion featured a dining room with panels of carved mahogany and Venetian hand-tooled leather on the walls and a ceiling of gold leaf. It was a testament to what the economist Thorstein Veblen, a graduate of nearby Carleton College, memorably called "conspicuous consumption" in his treatise *The Theory of the Leisure Class*, published in 1899—but Hill was not really a man of leisure. His life was business, and that meant time spent investing in important people. President and Mrs. William McKinley had been guests of the Hills at a small reception in October 1899. Hill was McKenzie's most valuable friend, and these two had together helped McKinley capture the presidency in 1896. In the afterglow, Hill told Mark Hanna, McKinley's top political operative, chairman of the Republican National Committee, and possessor of a fortune from coal, iron, and steel, to expect a visit from McKenzie. "His information is better than that of any one else you will meet," Hill wrote Hanna. "You can place absolute reliance upon what he says or does." With Hill's description of him as "honest, outspoken and reliable," McKenzie also had an entrée to Brown Brothers & Co., one of Wall Street's most prestigious banks. Though secretive by nature, McKenzie confided in Hill and, more than that, felt he could rely on the magnate when caught in a jam.

To his critics, McKenzie's interest in any business matter, whether Alaskan gold or Bismarck real estate, augured no good. A federal judge in Fargo, North Dakota, once wrote his friend Theodore Roosevelt a long letter venting on the evils of political bosses, lamenting the maddening "stooping and bowing" to them that went on throughout the land. Winding up, the judge turned his attention to the Boss of the Dakotas: "Alex McKenzie hates everything in Government that you love, and loves everything that you hate." TR dashed off a cryptic reply in two terse sentences: "First as to what you say about Alex McKenzie. I think I understand him thoroughly." While Roosevelt possibly despised McKenzie as venal, he also may have seen in him qualities that he, Roosevelt, deeply admired: physical courage, pluck, and resourcefulness. McKenzie drew many admirers on these grounds, and even detractors conceded such attributes. He was that most American of species, the self-made man.

THE ORIGINS OF ALEXANDER MCKENZIE PROVED IMPOSSIBLE TO PIN DOWN, probably because he shifted his story as it suited or amused him. "His birthplace itself is so obscure that it may never be determined," a biographer who knew him wrote in an unpublished manuscript. He was born almost certainly in 1850 or 1851, definitely in Canada and probably in the backwoods of eastern Ontario. His ancestry, as suggested by the family name, was likely Scottish; he apparently spoke Scots at home. He reliably can be said to have spent little time in a schoolhouse: he was an adult before he learned to write by hand or do basic arithmetic. In any event, he left Canada for America as a teenager, and his legend, in the stories swapped by friends, began with an incident in a railroad construction yard outside Duluth, Minnesota. The young Alex, sixteen years old or so, flat broke, showed up at the yard looking for work. He was well over six feet tall, scrawny, with jug ears, and his clothes were barely better than rags. Mocked for his shabby attire by an older man, he knocked out the fellow with a flurry of right hooks to the head. The foreman promptly hired McKenzie.

America was moving steadily westward, from the Great Lakes region into the Dakotas, a territorial possession of the United States and still a wild frontier. Alex followed the frontier and quickly developed a reputation for dependably performing dangerous tasks. For the army, he carried messages to distant outposts by horseback, "passing through a country infested with hostile Indians," a contemporary marveled. Railroad work often occupied him. He had a natural talent, it quickly became clear, not only as a driver of spikes but also as a leader of men, and he took charge of a work crew while barely out of his twenties. He was a star performer on the baseball diamond, the sort of man, a member of his circle once said, perhaps with a touch of envy, with an intuitive sense for women, able to "read character in their feet, or their tapering legs."

For the caravans of pioneers, the Dakotas, at first sight, could amaze as a wonder of nature, the bluish-green buffalo grass of the Great Plains suggestive of a windswept ocean, the big-sky sunsets of golds, reds, and mauves made for an artist's canvas. Abundant buffalo, elk, deer, and antelope supplied meat for the belly; wild berries and grapes could be eaten raw or cooked into jams. For the romantically inclined, even the desolation of the landscape could exert a strange charm. The sheer variety of the pioneers, many new to America from places like Norway, Sweden, and Denmark; England, Scotland, and Ireland; and the tsar's Russia, inspired a hopefulness about the nation's promise. But the hardships were severe. The future novelist Hamlin Garland, drawn with his family to the Dakotas as a farmer's paradise, nearly froze to death one winter, the blinding blizzard winds howling at seventy miles an hour, no company except for the wolf and the white owl, his supply of coal and nearly all of his kindling taken by a desperate passerby. "No man knows what winter means until he has lived through one in a pine-board shanty on a Dakota plain with only buffalo bones for fuel," he later wrote. He fled to Boston and a less hazardous line of work.

McKenzie, perhaps, had no great romantic expectations to be deflated. Or maybe he experienced the Dakota winter as not appreciably worse than the Ontario winters of his boyhood. He endured. His big break came in 1874, in his midtwenties. At this time, he was living in the rapidly expanding settlement of Bismarck, on the Missouri River, roughly the westernmost line of "civilization," with feared "Indian country" just across the river. He had arrived in town the year before with his soon-to-be bride, Mary Ellen Hayes, five years younger, the daughter of Irish Catholic immigrants in Minnesota. Out on a job, the county sheriff and his deputy fell through an air hole in the Missouri ice and drowned. In urgent need of a replacement, Bismarck turned to Alex, "a tall slim young fellow . . . strong as an ox, with a head to match," in the estimation of an approving newspaper publisher. As the new peace officer, and in fact the only one, McKenzie did not disappoint, repeatedly winning election to a new term of office and serving in the post for twelve years. There was no faster gun in the Dakotas than Sheriff McKenzie, it was said, and hardly anyone better at throwing a catch-rope with a loop. "Alexander McKenzie was absolutely without fear," a Bismarck friend of this time said, the highest accolade that could be paid to any man on the frontier.

Bismarck and thereabouts crawled with all manner of criminals. It was rough country that the sheriff policed with rough methods. He outfitted his home with a trapdoor leading to an iron ring in the base-ment. "When father caught his prisoner he opened the trap door and put him down in the dark cellar," his daughter later recalled. "He sat on the trap door until the prisoner confessed. It was the confession father wanted." McKenzie was open to gentler methods in his deal-ings with the Sioux, who knew him as "No 'Fraid Man." With them, he tended toward diplomacy. Sitting Bull once attended a reception McKenzie arranged. McKenzie's allegiance, of course, was to the white settlers bent on conquest of Sioux lands. He made alliances with the officers at nearby US Army forts, and one historian of the frontier recorded a stint by McKenzie as a scout for George Armstrong Custer, stationed at Fort Lincoln, in the general's campaign against the Sioux.

At around this time McKenzie became known affectionately around Bismarck as Big Alex. Some women found him crude (as did some men); others felt drawn to him and perceived a delicate inner side to his outwardly dominating personality. Volunteers tutored him in the writing of a simple business letter, in the compiling of sums to fill out an expense report. Their efforts were only partially successful; although he had a decent feel for numbers, to the end of his life McKenzie was incapable of writing a letter without glaring misspellings and miscues as in "abel" for "able." His absence of a formal education was a painful embarrassment to him that he tried his best to hide. His friend Winnie Pearce, an early Bismarck settler and a graduate of Cortland College in upstate New York, later recounted his confession that "he would give anything for my education," as he found it "hard to compete in con-versation" with men of schooling. Pearce, though, felt that McKenzie would go far in life on the strength of his magnetic presence: "His keen features, well developed physique, dark skin, eyes and hair, attracted attention, as he towered above any ordinary group of people." (Esti-mates of his height, possibly exaggerated by those of smaller stature, ranged as high as six feet, six inches.) And "in his bosom," she felt, "beat a heart full of kindness," as shown by his generosity in helping "many a young family to its daily bread."

Alexander and Mary Ellen produced two daughters, but his hopes centered on his son, John Alexander, born in 1875. The son, the father vowed, would be raised with a formal education. But at the age of eight years, twenty-seven days, as recorded on his small gravestone on a hill in Bismarck, the child died of diphtheria. Known as "the strangling angel of children," diphtheria was a dreadful scourge. The disease often presented as a common cold; before long an awful-smelling pus discharged from the nose; then the neck started to swell so that swallowing became difficult, followed by coma and at last death. Alex and Mary Ellen for days sat alone at home with the corpse of their dead boy, no one calling on them for fear of the disease. Finally Winnie Pearce and a friend took pity and went to the home to prepare John Alexander for burial, a kindness that Alex never forgot. "He never seemed to recover fully from the loss," Winnie felt.

McKENZIE'S AMBITIONS EXCEEDED HIS ROLE AS SHERIFF. THE JOB, HE realized soon enough, could be a platform for wider opportunities. To think this way was to think as a great many public officeholders were wont to do all across the country. The idea was to use the position, itself not especially remunerative, for some manner of gain, not necessarily in illegal ways. An obvious prospect for McKenzie in Bismarck was real estate. The growing town needed to construct schools, businesses, and housing. The sheriff knew the landscape as well as anyone and began purchasing lots, often in combination with partners. In one instance, he sold to the board of education, for the building of a school, a plot of land with a sunken area that filled with water after a heavy rain. There were grumbles, but the school was built anyway. He was also a founder of the Bismarck Water Company, a profitable holding for him for many years.

Inevitably he began to play an active role in political matters. At first he was a Democrat, but as his personal business interests grew, he switched to the Republican camp and stayed there for good. The reason, as a senior Dakotas politician once explained to James J. Hill, was pure pragmatism, as McKenzie felt the switch was "necessary to protect his holdings" in the Bismarck area, with the Republicans the ascendant party in the Dakotas.

While still serving as sheriff, he made his reputation for nimble po-litical maneuvering with a feat that endeared him to the railroads and Bismarck while, not coincidentally, inflating the value of his properties. The episode began innocently enough. In 1882, McKenzie journeyed to the capital of the Dakotas in Yankton, on the southeastern fringe of the territory, on a mission to persuade the territorial legislature to choose Bismarck as the site for a new penitentiary. A severe blizzard trapped everyone assembled in Yankton for nearly three weeks. The great question before the legislature was whether to remove the capital from Yankton, an undesirable location for the railroads, and if so, how to select a new site. McKenzie managed to secure for himself a spot on a commission established to decide the matter of a new capital. It was now in his enterprising mind, and also in that of the Northern Pacific railroad—though in few others'—to set the capital in Bismarck.

One requirement for the commission tasked with deciding the new capital was to hold an official meeting in Yankton. This stipulation boded poorly for McKenzie, as Yankton still aimed to keep the capital where it already was. As the months rolled by, with the question of a new capital still unresolved, there was talk that Yankton partisans might barge in on a commission meeting, keep its members from con-cluding their business, and tie up the matter in courts. Anticipating these hostile steps, McKenzie arranged for commission members to board a special train in nearby Sioux City. As dawn broke on an April morning in 1883, the train rolled into Yankton. The city limits pene-trated and Yankton in slumber, the commission "met" for a few min-utes, unbeknownst to the Yankton partisans. The train then exited the town, a blast of the locomotive whistle the only signal that the meeting had taken place, unperturbed by the disruptions that the Yanktonites had hoped to visit on it. Through this masterstroke, McKenzie won the great prize for Bismarck. "To him we owe all honor," the *Bismarck Tribune* crowed. "He never fails." Among the outmaneuvered was the territory's own governor, who had hoped to place the capital in a new city bearing his name. Losers of the competition fumed over the result but still paid grudging homage to "Alexander the Great, of the north," as a newspaper in the southern portion of the territory called him.

In a letter to her sister Jane, Winnie Pearce tried to explain why she was so sure her friend Big Alex would "go far in the political world," despite his lack of education. "He seems to know how to pull the political strings," Winnie wrote. "His tactics are: 'Win, no matter what the cost. The rich will pay the bill.'" By instinct, through trial and error, McKenzie honed a playbook on how to thrive in this unforgiving domain. A first rule was never to write anything down. "Walk across the state if necessary, but never write a letter," he advised friends. "Sure, what you say goes up in smoke, but what you write is before you always." Even in conversation, he sometimes chose to say little, "appreciating the power the listener had over the one who did the talking." If it could advance his aim, he didn't mind playing the dupe. A Dakota politician once bragged of taking McKenzie's money at poker, not realizing that McKenzie had rigged the game that way. "X is an honest man," McKenzie told a friend, "you can't give him money, but you can lose it to him." And his physicality, he understood, was one of his best assets. "His brawny right arm encircled my body and I was fairly lifted out of the crowd of delegates and bustled to a more secluded environment," a Dakotas newspaper publisher once wrote of the McKenzie style. "His hand rested caressingly upon my shoulder and occasionally my knees were affectionately stroked, after the manner of stroking the fur of a cat with whom you desire friendly relations." Should caresses fail to work, McKenzie also was capable of bald threats, and as seen in a separate episode involving yet another publisher with whom he had testy relations, he apparently could go beyond threats. A gang of men broke into the office of the Bismarck newspaper run by this man, smashed the presses with sledgehammers, and dumped the refuse into the Missouri. Possibly the thugs were acting on McKenzie's direct orders; possibly they were doing what they thought he expected of them.

HIS MARK MADE, "ALEXANDER THE GREAT" HAD CHOICES. AN OBVIOUS one was a higher post, beyond sheriff, in elected political office. Innumerable tenders came his way, as he appeared to be a cinch for nearly any office he desired. But what would he do with it? In 1886, Theodore

Roosevelt, not yet thirty, gave the honorary peroration on the occasion of the Fourth of July celebration rites in the town of Dickinson, directly to the west of Bismarck. At the time, TR was living in the wild country known as the Badlands, hunting and ranching while still trying to get over the loss of both his mother and his wife on the same day two years earlier. In expounding on the "duties" of all American citizens, for "none can escape them," Roosevelt might have been speaking directly to McKenzie. "We are the pioneers," he said, and "the first comers in a land can, by their individual efforts, do far more to channel out the course in which its history is to run than can those who follow after them." But if you "cast your weight into the scales in favor of evil, you are just so far corrupting and making less valuable the birthright of your children," Roosevelt warned. "Like all Americans," he allowed, "I like big things; big parades, big forests and mountains, big wheat fields, railroads—and herds of cattle too; big factories, steamboats and everything else. But we must keep steadily in mind that no people were ever yet benefitted by riches if their property corrupted their virtue."

TR was mustering his countrymen to stand against the worst features of the Gilded Age. Perhaps McKenzie was there in person to hear the future president speak; in any case, he could have read the address, in its entirety, in the *Dickinson Press*. He may even have heard a message of this sort directly from the irrepressibly talkative Roosevelt, who performed a stint as a deputy sheriff in Billings County, in the Badlands. Their paths crossed, possibly first in Bismarck, on TR's arrival in the Dakotas. But unlike Roosevelt, Big Alex shied from an outward role in the public arena, never seeking a station beyond county sheriff. Even on North Dakota's becoming a state of the Union in 1889, with Bismarck, thanks to him, as the capital, he balked at the opportunity to go to Washington. Instead, he chose to become a backroom political boss.

As his critics saw it, he opted to become, in effect, the well-paid tool of the railroads and the grain elevator operators, the powerful businesses determined to shape North Dakota, South Dakota, and beyond to their liking, often against the interests of farmers. There was something to that assessment, as could be seen in his close bond, both personal and professional, with J. J. Hill. Their link was forged in the mid-1870s, when Hill, in his midthirties, a dozen or so years older than McKenzie, was assembling his railroad empire. The story passed down to a daughter of McKenzie was that the two men split rails together. Hill was short of stature, with one eye lost to a childhood accident, but an impressive physical specimen nonetheless, with a massive leonine head and muscular shoulders and arms. He must have seen in McKenzie something of himself. Born in rural Ontario to a Scotch mother and Irish father, his schooling halted by the death of his father, Hill also headed to America to make his way, arriving in Saint Paul by riverboat at the age of seventeen and finding work as a shipping clerk. He combined a dominating will with a fixation on detail and could find fault in seemingly everyone and everything, once instructing the house gardener, in a crisp note, on how to tend to a common hose. But he made an exception: "One man never disappointed me, and that man was McKenzie," Hill told a Bismarck friend. His faith extended to what was perhaps most dear to him, money. "Be sure Alex McKenzie has twenty or twenty-five thousand dollars," Hill once wired his son Louis, without saying what the money was for. Hill advised McKenzie on "proper" appointments of government officials for the Dakotas; McKenzie advised Hill on the expansion of the railroad as a matter not just of heeding geography but of locking in political support for the building out of the line.

Their collaboration was not, of course, between equals, as Hill turned the Great Northern into one of America's premier railroads and became a peer of the likes of J. P. Morgan. For McKenzie, Hill served as a mentor, perhaps the only true mentor he ever had. From the more senior man, for example, McKenzie might have taken a lesson in how to profit from speculations in land. Hill held personal stock in a land development company that benefitted from the growth of new towns in the Dakotas, happily created by Hill's own rail lines. The pair conferred frequently in Saint Paul, and Hill, who considered himself a visionary, conceivably put the idea of an Alaskan venture into McKenzie's head. "Alaska awakens the imagination of men," the magnate once said. He saw William Seward as a prophet for arranging Alaska's purchase, and he saw the sharp-elbowed contest playing out for the gold prize as the sort of competition by which vigorous civilizations bettered themselves. "Men in our day move towards their material advances principally through the struggle for wealth," he believed.

UNDERNEATH ALL HIS CLEVER MACHINATIONS AND THE VOUCHING BY HIS powerful friends for his character, who was Alex McKenzie? In truth, he was not "honest," as Hill assured Brown Brothers & Co., but a habitual and skilled liar. When it fit his interest, he was capable of intricate fabrications, as shown by how he extracted himself from his first marriage. Whether because of the strain of young John Alexander's grisly death or for other reasons, the marriage between Alexander and Mary Ellen failed, and misery reigned in the McKenzie household. On an April day in 1890, the marriage in its seventeenth year, he slipped into Fargo, a few hundred miles east of Bismarck on the border with Minnesota. There, in Cass County district court, he filed a complaint for divorce on the grounds of "extreme cruelty"—of his wife toward him. His complaint asserted,

> That for more than five years past defendant [Mary McKenzie] has been almost constantly intensely jealous of plaintiff [Alexander McKenzie] and has repeatedly and many times charged him, without any foundation in truth therefor, with infidelity with other women. That she has for the same period of time been constantly in the habit, without cause or provocation therefor, of flying into violent passions at plaintiff, and calling him vile and indecent names. . . . That she has at diverse times, and when in the heat of her frequent violent and unreasonable passions, used personal violence upon the plaintiff, and has thrown missiles at him. That she has on diverse occasions locked him out of their joint bed room, and locked him out of their house. . . . [T]hat the plaintiff has no home in fact, and no home comforts, and that his peace of mind and happiness has been destroyed.

It was an astonishing complaint, all the more so because, seven months earlier, McKenzie had been in correspondence with his lover, Elva Crapper, about the negotiations he was actively conducting with Mary Ellen on the terms of their divorce. It was the rare occasion when he committed frank business matters to paper. "She is willing to take $15,000 but I declined to give it to her," Alexander apprised Elva, vowing, "I will never give her more than $10,000," and maybe, he said, not even that much. "I am awful lonesome," he closed. "I love you more and more every day." He had taken up with Elva in Bismarck, where she was a schoolteacher, likened by especially ardent admirers to Lillian Russell, the popular blond, full-figured stage actress. Elva also was married—to a gunsmith. It was a ticklish situation all around.

Mary Ellen got her $15,000, worth more than $400,000 in 2020 dollars. The judge awarded her that sum, along with (unchallenged) custody of the two daughters, notwithstanding his "findings of fact" that Mary Ellen had inflicted on Alexander "the most grievous mental suffering." For the children, McKenzie supplied an additional $15,000, lodged in an investment trust. In August, four months after the divorce, McKenzie wrote to Elva of his eagerness to see her and "the babies." She must have conceived and given birth to at least one child before the divorce, a material fact not disclosed to the court of Cass County. A few months later, McKenzie was addressing Elva as his wife. She had secured a divorce from her husband, and the two were married secretly, probably in upstate New York. Elva soon had a third child, another son.

McKenzie kept his second marriage and his children from it a closely held secret for the remainder of his life. It was a remarkable deception, requiring constant lies to friends about his whereabouts. Elva and the children, in the first decade or so of the marriage, were comfortably stashed in Manhattan. Mary Ellen lived in Saint Paul, dying there in 1897, seven years after the divorce; McKenzie kept in touch with his two daughters from Mary Ellen, but by his design, neither of his two sets of children knew of the existence of the other. But one person was in on the secret, a man whom Elva told her children she knew quite well in the early years of the marriage. The ruby ring she wore on a finger was his gift—a present from "Mr. Hill."

Chapter 5

THE NOME PROPOSITION

B Y 1900, MRS. ELVA MCKENZIE, WITH HER THREE CHILDREN— Jeannette, the oldest; Alexander Jr., known as Sandy; and Thomas, the youngest—were living in an apartment at No. 1 Hamilton Terrace in Harlem, thirty blocks above Central Park and across from an Episcopal church. Even when he was in town, McKenzie preferred to take rooms at a hotel, his favorite being the Everett House, a first-class establishment on Union Square, named for the Massachusetts senator Edward Everett and known for its rosewood furniture and velvet carpets. From his suite at the Everett, McKenzie conducted his business, taking meetings in the privacy of his quarters. Wall Street was a short ride away by horse-drawn carriage. "I have been so busy all week I could not get up to see you and the children," he wrote to Elva on January 13, the letter postmarked in the city. "I am to work on the Nome Proposition, and I think I am going to get a lot of property."

The phrase "Nome Proposition" indicated the boss had a name for his budding Alaskan venture. For the first stage of the plan, he told his wife, the idea was simply to acquire mining claims. McKenzie had in mind jumpers' claims, of the sort in which the Hubbard & Beeman law firm had invested, as well as speculative claims for sections of the beach that the miners regarded as a commons. On the afternoon of January 8, five days before he wrote Elva, four men called on him at Everett House. Each held a claim on Cape Nome property. A fifth visitor also was present for the first part of the meeting—a distinguished-looking man in his fifties with an ash-gray moustache, an unwrinkled oval face,

53

and a carefully parted head of hair. This was Henry C. Hansbrough, a US senator from North Dakota. He was far from a national figure, and McKenzie's other guests probably knew next to nothing about him. His appearance was arranged by McKenzie to demonstrate that he, McKenzie, had important political connections in Washington. The conversation with Hansbrough was restricted to the "situation of the country," one of the claims holders recalled. Perhaps there was mention of a front-page story in that day's New York Tribune on the reputed ambition of New York's impatient governor, Theodore Roosevelt, to join the Republican ticket as the vice presidential running mate for William McKinley's reelection bid in the November election. Hansbrough departed, his purpose served, and the remaining men got down to the fine points of their business.

McKenzie was an interested buyer; they were interested sellers—the question was on what terms. The meeting broke up without agreement and resumed in McKenzie's suite on the following day. Now McKenzie found promising bargaining ground with one of the men. E. M. Walters, a speculator, not a real miner, had acquired a number of beach "claims" in the summer of 1899. His plan all along was to sell the claims, but he had yet to close a deal. McKenzie suggested that a deal might be had, but first a larger number of claims needed to be gathered into the pot to make the venture worth pursuing. Walters said he knew of a man in Chicago with more claims for sale. McKenzie deputized Walters to go to Chicago, all expenses paid, to track the fellow down. "He told me to go ahead and act for him, the same as if I had a million dollars to buy property with," Walters later recalled. Walters found the man and returned with him to New York to resume the bargaining at the Everett.

McKenzie had no intention of writing checks for $1 million or so. He proposed to pay for claims not with cash but with certificates of stock—in fact, not even with the certificates themselves, for none yet existed, but with promises of shares in a company still to be formed, the claims serving as it "assets." With his influence in the worlds of politics and finance, McKenzie vowed, he would be able to make these paper shares worth a lot of money. At first glance, the proposition might have seemed preposterously thin. Then again, how much was a beach claim, say, really worth, given that the miners working the beach had so far successfully defended their commons? Walters agreed to deed his claims to McKenzie in return for a promise of stock shares, listed at a face value of $475,000. Walters's Chicago friend also agreed to exchange claims for shares.

Through Walters, McKenzie learned that Oliver Hubbard, the claim jumper–backing attorney, on behalf of Hubbard & Beeman, had acquired an interest in a basket of jumpers' claims. Fortunately for the boss, Hubbard was holding a weak hand. The Anglo-Alaskan Company had turned down his request to invest in the claims. So Hubbard & Beeman had a stake in claims the firm had promised its clients to litigate to conclusion—but unless the litigation was successful, the claims were worthless, both to the clients and to the firm. From Hubbard's perspective, the McKenzie connection was a piece of good luck—assuming that McKenzie had the means, through high-level political connections, to make the claims worth something. The two men conferred at Everett House. Hubbard felt sufficiently intrigued by the meeting to board a train to Chicago to talk to his most valuable client, Bob Chipps, the jumper of the Discovery claim, who had left Alaska for the off-season, about the fresh opportunity available to them. Hubbard "thought McKenzie was a smart man, a man of ability, and that he had looked him up the best he could, and found him to be all right," Chipps later said.

Hubbard saw that McKenzie had pull in Washington—far more pull than the lawyer had. The tie with Hansbrough, for example, was not a casual one. The bond was forged back in 1891, when Hansbrough, as a member of the US House of Representatives, a native Virginian with a background as a newspaper publisher and a postmaster, sought elevation to the Senate. McKenzie produced the votes in the legislature in Bismarck to make it happen. The newly crowned senator served as one of the boss's "most trusted and useful aides" for years afterward, in the estimation of a McKenzie admirer, and the Bismarck legislators aligned with McKenzie reelected Hansbrough as senator in 1897. At that time, writing of "the gang that today controls the machinery of the Republican Party in North Dakota and disgraces the state at Washington," the *Grand Forks Herald*, an anti-McKenzie newspaper, declared that "the relationship and the ties between them all, from the thugs at Bismarck to Senator Hansbrough at Washington and Alexander McKenzie in Wall Street, New York, are going strong and divert political power for private plunder." Of course, that sort of criticism was precisely what Hubbard and Chipps hoped to hear. "Political power for private plunder" was what they needed.

Then there was the question of McKenzie's close ties with moneyed men. Besides Brown Brothers & Co., McKenzie had a connection to a second prestigious banking firm, J. Kennedy Tod & Co., at 45 Wall Street. The principal, Tod, owner of an estate on Greenwich Point on Long Island Sound, was a director of James J. Hill's Great Northern railroad. He also was the nephew of Hill's longtime personal financial adviser, John Stewart Kennedy. Hubbard, then, could feel assured that McKenzie had the ability to arrange the flotation of shares of stock tied to Alaskan gold claims.

Chipps heard enough from Hubbard to agree to make the pilgrimage to Everett House to meet McKenzie. Hubbard, too, was there for the meeting; McKenzie was interested in acquiring not only Chipps's jumper claim on Discovery but the one-quarter interest in the claim that Chipps had given to Hubbard & Beeman. In fact, McKenzie wanted to purchase all the interests the law firm had acquired from the jumpers in Cape Nome. It seemed, though, that the boss wasn't offering enough, at least for Chipps, as he returned to Chicago without a deal. Perhaps Chipps had qualms about McKenzie: as he was less than scrupulous in his own dealings, suspicion came naturally to him. Hubbard remained in New York and continued the negotiations.

Soon enough, Chipps came around and returned to Everett House. McKenzie gave him $750 for his claim to Discovery, along with a promise of $300,000 in stock. Hubbard, too, came to terms for his law firm's interest in jumper claims. The bargain was for cash (of an amount kept confidential) and $750,000 in stock—with the deal conditional on acceptance by his partner Edwin Beeman in Nome and a third partner Hubbard had invited to join the firm.

AMID THIS DEALMAKING, A NEW FIGURE ENTERED THE PICTURE, SENATOR Thomas Henry Carter of Montana, who arrived at Everett House with Senator Hansbrough to join the discussions. Carter's involvement suggested that the senators were there not merely as showpieces for McKenzie but as active collaborators in the scheme taking shape. Unlike Hansbrough, Carter was one of the reigning powers in Washington. A former chairman of the Republican National Committee, he was a friend of President McKinley's, a fellow native of Ohio. The *Washington Post* considered him "a Republican leader of the very first magnitude." At an energetic forty-five years old, Carter also was chairman of the Senate Committee on Territories, the panel with jurisdiction over Alaska. This put him in a prime position to shepherd though his committee and the full Senate the legislation that Congress was crafting for a new civil code for the governance of Alaska. That code was expected to address the treatment of gold mining claims in Alaska. And unlike Hansbrough, Carter was a true expert on mining law. Mining was a leading industry in Montana, to which Carter had moved in the early 1880s to practice law, and in a stint in the US House of Representatives he had chaired the Committee on Mines and Mining. He could hold forth on the Senate floor on mining at great length, without reference to notes, without an aide whispering in his ear. As for his relationship with the boss, he had known McKenzie since the late 1880s. The two were neighbors of sorts, with McKenzie's political reach in the Dakotas extending into Montana. Like McKenzie, Carter, the son of Irish immigrants, was a self-made man. Raised on a farm, he worked on the railroads and as a schoolteacher before entering the law and politics. An admiring sister recalled him as "plumb & strong & full of pluck, adept with his fists on the school playground." He viewed politics as an arena for combat, and perhaps he needed to, for any Republican was on treacherous ground in Democrat-leaning Montana, where Carter had powerful enemies determined to drive him from office.

Behind his back, though not in an unfriendly way, McKenzie's new associates called him the "old man." They found him mysterious. There was the matter, for example, of the cash McKenzie had in hand to pay Chipps for Discovery and Walters for travel expenses. "It was not his own money," Walters felt sure. The sole hint of a source of the funds was a man who took up residence in the Everett and had a private line to McKenzie. This was Mike McCormack, "the Captain," as he was known, an old McKenzie friend from the Dakotas, thought by Walters to be in contact with a banker in Saint Paul. McCormack had a long-standing relationship with J. J. Hill as the skipper, years before, of a steamboat for the Red River Transportation Co., by which Hill made his first fortune. Walters considered him sketchy and wanted nothing to do with him, but McKenzie insisted that McCormack was essential to the project, without explaining why.

On January 20, McKenzie took a moment to write Elva with regrets that he had been unable to find a moment to see her and the children. "I never had so much to do," he said. As to the Nome Proposition, he was feeling a mounting optimism: "if I get it through I will make a lot of money." A week later, the Engineering and Mining Journal, published out of offices on Broadway, came out with a long article, titled "Some Notes on Nome, Alaska," intended as a primer for miners seeking to make their fortunes there in the season to commence in the spring. Nome is the "new Eldorado," the piece proclaimed, and could be expected to yield at least $5 million in gold in 1900 alone. But difficulties abounded: "Practically it is always winter at Nome. It is wet and foggy at all times, and to go tramping over the country in the slush of melting snow, with never a dry spot to rest on, is anything but pleasant or healthy," the article warned. "Comparatively few will succeed in this country, for not many are physically capable of enduring the hardships attending this work." If McKenzie happened to come across "Notes on Nome," no doubt he had a good chuckle, for if all went according to his plan for achieving success in Alaska, he would never break a sweat.

Chapter 6

"WHERE THEY WILL
DO THE MOST GOOD"

THE KEY TO MCKENZIE'S PLAN TO "MAKE A LOT OF MONEY" FROM HIS Nome Proposition turned on the Alaska Gold Mining Company, the name the members of the ring arrived at for their enterprise. The idea was to make good on the sketchy mining claims held by the company by exploiting the investing public's lust for gold. It was a matter, really, of financial alchemy. Suppose one of the jumpers represented by Hubbard & Beeman filed a lawsuit in the Alaska court to wrest the claim from the original holder. Suppose the judge, friendly to the ring and guided by a new Alaska code as passed by Congress, found for the jumper. The jumper then would have clear title to the property, with Hubbard & Beeman taking its one-quarter interest in gold—with that gold actually belonging to the Alaska Gold Mining Company as the ultimate owner of the law firm's one-quarter interest. Suppose a sampling of the gold was shipped to New York, amid great fanfare, as tangible proof of the lucrative assets held by the Alaska Gold Mining Company. In the excitement, the original shareholders—the members of the ring—would sell their shares to the public at enormous profit. All of this could be accomplished, McKenzie figured, by the fall of 1900—before a higher court had a chance to reverse, on appeal, the decision of the friendly Alaska judge, a reversal that could sink the market value of the shares.

As for other possibilities for inflating the worth of shares in the Alaska Gold Mining Company, the ruby sands of Cape Nome beckoned. Suppose a provision could be tucked into the Alaska code to change the standing "come one, come all" practice for prospecting on the beachfront, so that beach claims like those held by E. M. Walters, but now belonging to Alaska Gold Mining, could be made good. In the discussions at Everett House, according to Walters, North Dakota senator Henry Hansbrough agreed that Congress should "have the laws fixed" to "shut out" the all comers and put an end to the beach commons. There was, too, the possibility for Alaska Gold Mining to purchase additional claims on arrival by McKenzie in Nome for the mining season. The mining camp could be canvassed for fresh recruits to the ring, willing to trade their claims, disputed or not, for promises of stock. As far as the Everett House schemers were concerned, the bigger the pool of claims, the more impressive the eventual showing on Wall Street.

The plan was bold but not, from a practical standpoint, unworkable. A company like Alaska Gold Mining, with assets that might look dodgy even on cursory scrutiny, would not be out of place at a time when stock gambits of every variety were regularly visited upon investors. Gullible speculators—gamblers—were in plentiful supply, with mining ventures a popular lure. According to an adage credited to Mark Twain, who lost money speculating in gold stocks and just about everything else he invested in, "A mine is a hole in the ground with a liar standing next to it. The hole in the ground and the liar combine and issue shares and trap fools."

State laws barring the issuance of fraudulent shares in mines or other ventures were toothless, and Washington was decades from creating a federal agency that would require the offerers of a new listing of shares, an "initial public offering," to disclose the nature and purpose of the enterprise, the composition of assets and liabilities, the roster of shareholders, and the risks faced by investors. An investment bank underwriting an issuing of shares could disclose as much or as little as the issuer—in this case, Alaska Gold—chose about the venture.

Publicly traded mining companies rarely issued an annual report. The stock market itself was frequently prey to manipulators vying to corner large blocks of shares, pump up their value on rumors, and then dump the shares in a rush. Through such gambits, millions could be won by insiders—company executives and directors, share underwriters, favored friends of all these people—and millions lost by the suckers who knew no better. Yet, despite warnings in the financial press that mining shares in particular were unfit for the small investor—they could be expected to result in a loss ninety-nine times out of a hundred, with no dividends ever paid out—enthusiasm for them showed no signs of abating. Once issued, stock in Alaska Gold Mining, puffed up by reports of the fabulous treasure already taken from Cape Nome, could be advertised in the Sunday papers, popular magazines, and promotional circulars. Shares could be sold in "bucket shops"—makeshift trading parlors in cities all over the country, devoted to "coppering suckers' bets." The bucket shops typically dealt in stocks listed on an official exchange, the prices displayed on ticker tape printed out by a telegraphic device. A listing for Alaska Gold Mining might be obtained on a regional exchange, from San Francisco to Hartford, or perhaps even on the preeminent New York Stock Exchange if a firm like J. Kennedy Tod & Co. underwrote the shares. Then, too, mining shares often were traded on the unofficial "curb market," operating outside any established exchange, in which the "broker" might also be a bookie taking wagers for horse races and boxing bouts.

As disreputable as this all seemed, the popular longing for immense quick wealth was a fervent conviction of the times, approaching religious gospel. Baptist minister Russell Conwell preached that greed was good in a lecture titled "Acres of Diamonds," delivered thousands of times in halls across America. Conwell, founder of Temple University in Philadelphia, related a fanciful tale of a California man who shamefully failed to realize that his ranchland contained gold "for the mere taking." Desire for the fast buck sprang not from the seed of sin but from the yearning for self-improvement, Conwell told his flock: "I say that you ought to get rich, and it is your duty to get rich."

ONE COULD NEVER ACTUALLY VISIT THE ALASKA GOLD MINING COMPANY.
McKenzie did not subscribe to the concept of a fixed headquarters. His
itinerant lifestyle had him living out of suitcases in hotel rooms and
train sleepers, and Alaska Gold had no office—although he did station
a secretary in his suite at Everett House, "a thin, worried little man,"
as described by one visitor, who also encountered the boss himself, "an
enormously big man with crag like eyebrows and humped shoulders."
But on paper the company had a definite structure, with McKenzie as
president, Oliver Hubbard as secretary, and Robert Chipps and "Captain" Mike McCormack among the directors. An attorney brought
in by McKenzie drew up articles of incorporation and filed them in
the territory of Arizona (not yet a state of the Union)—at least, the
boss told the others that such articles had been filed in Arizona. The
enterprise was given a nominal value of $15 million in stock, with a
controlling 51 percent bloc of shares in the hands of McKenzie and
the remainder reserved for those assigning mining interests to the
company in return for promises of shares. Chipps filled out a stock
book with certificates listing the shareholders and the value of promised shares. For McKenzie's 51 percent, Chipps made out a certificate
for shares assigned a value of some $7.65 million. The certificate was
drawn in McKenzie's name only, but "he said it belonged to himself
and others," Chipps later recalled, adding, "He did not mention their
names." Chipps deposited the stock book with J. Kennedy Tod & Co.
for safekeeping.

Who were the unmentionables, the unnamed holders of Alaska
Gold Mining stock, the list composed in McKenzie's mind but nowhere written down? His confederates might have had the wayward
thought that the "old man," full of bluff, was only pretending to have
powerful men backing the venture. But no one really believed that.
For one thing, he needed funds, tens of thousands of dollars, just to
purchase mining equipment to ship to Alaska to work the beach he
planned on controlling. J. J. Hill, with his faith in McKenzie, was an
obvious source for such funds—presumably in return for shares. J. Kennedy Tod's firm was a second obvious source; Chipps assumed the

banking house was an investor in the project. On the political side, McKenzie's associates assumed that he had promised shares to both Hansbrough and Thomas Henry Carter—why else would the senators take an interest in the venture? To entice prospective shareholders to sign claims over to the company, Hubbard told them that Hansbrough and Carter were vested participants in the scheme.

As for other names, the associates could only guess. And that, of course, was how the boss wanted it. He was hardly the first power broker of the era to hold shares, as a kind of trustee, in a secret slush pot. The established practice was to distribute the shares "where they will do the most good." That was how a Massachusetts congressman, Oakes Ames, memorably described his method in a letter to his associates in a scheme undertaken three decades earlier. In that episode, Ames, a member of the House Pacific Railroad Committee, sold colleagues shares in a railroad construction company at a price far below market value. Sadly for all concerned, the affair came to light, and the House formally censured Ames for his role in what was known as the Credit Mobilier scandal, so labeled for the name of the construction company. Credit Mobilier was the first great swindle of the Gilded Age. Had he paused to consider the example, McKenzie surely would have dismissed Ames as a fool for making the elementary mistake of putting his plans into writing. Probably, though, he didn't give Credit Mobilier a second thought. His disposition was to look forward, not back, and he had his eye cast on Washington.

Chapter 7

"TURNING ALASKA OVER TO THE ALIENS"

ON MARCH 26, A CHILLY DAY IN THE NATION'S CAPITAL, WITH THE temperature dipping below freezing, the gas and electric arc lamps soon to be lit on the streets, and the Senate about to adjourn, the senior senator from North Dakota, Henry C. Hansbrough, approached the desk of the presiding officer with a short amendment to the bill pending on civil government for Alaska. The secretary read the proposal aloud. "Aliens," it began, "shall not be permitted to locate, hold, or convey mining claims" anywhere in Alaska. What was more, any claim *already* made by an alien was to be deemed invalid, and any claim *already* purchased from an alien, even if the buyer was a US citizen, also was invalid. The floor manager of the legislation stepped forward. "I think the amendment is a meritorious one," Thomas H. Carter of Montana said. This was a striking statement, given that the bill his colleague was seeking to amend had been approved by his Committee on Territories three weeks earlier with language that expressly allowed "any alien" both to acquire and to transfer mining claims in Alaska— and did not speak at all to claims that already had been made. This provision had not been a point of controversy in the committee's crafting of the bill, and Carter had not shown any sign of being dissatisfied with it. And yet now he was embracing a raid on the richest claims in the gold fields of Cape Nome.

It was a surprise attack by the McKenzie forces. Hansbrough's proposal was written to benefit the Alaska Gold Mining Company. If enacted, the amendment would invalidate the original Discovery claim of the "Three Swedes," Jafet Lindeberg, Erik Lindblom, and John Brynteson, since Lindeberg was an alien when the claim was made. The amendment would invalidate Charles Lane's holding of Number Ten Above Discovery on Anvil Creek, since Lane acquired the claim from Jo Hahn Tornanses, an alien. The many other claims Lane purchased from the Lapps also would be invalid. The way would be clear for jumpers like Robert Chipps to win their claims by lawsuit, and in that event, the property, including the interest held by the Hubbard & Beeman law firm, would belong to Alaska Gold. In coordination with Hansbrough, Carter, and Oliver Hubbard, McKenzie had spent weeks plotting the maneuver, arriving in Washington near the end of February, his base of operation now shifted from Everett House in New York to the Raleigh Hotel on Pennsylvania Avenue and 12th Street, a few blocks from the Executive Mansion. He shared certain details of the Alaska venture with a friend from North Dakota, a Fargo politician, who, perhaps to McKenzie's surprise, boasted with gusto to the *Bismarck Tribune* of the boss's project. "He is moving among the big men of the nation," the man told the paper. "He is the manager of a syndicate investing $15,000,000 in Cape Nome. He is buying machinery by carloads and looking after details of shipments, as well as purchases, with that wonderful energy ever characteristic of him." There was no $15 million investment—that was simply the notational value of the stock of the Alaska Gold Mining Company—but the report of the machinery purchases was accurate.

The *Tribune* item put Washington on notice that one of the country's most powerful political bosses had designs on Alaska's gold fields. Of course, that was not how Carter, Hansbrough, and other senators in the McKenzie camp publicly framed the matter in the bid to annul alien claims. The strategy was to inflame nativist sentiments by characterizing foreign interlopers as thieves, more or less, of a treasure that rightfully belonged to America and bona fide Americans only. The national political mood seemed receptive to this message. A sense of imperial destiny was sweeping the country, with William McKinley waging a war to subdue the former Spanish colony of the Philippines, the goal, he told a delegation of Methodists, being to "uplift and civilize and Christianize" the Filipinos, numbers of whom were violently resisting US Army forces deployed to put down an insurrection. As the Senate took up the Hansbrough amendment, a thousand-plus fresh recruits shipped out from New York aboard the *Sumner*, the vessel carrying five hundred American flags for distribution to the natives in Manila. Advocates of Hansbrough's proposal warned that Alaska, even closer to the mainland than the Philippines, was imperiled by an inferior race of people. Carter had the Senate secretary read out loud the letter that the Law and Order League of Council City had written to McKinley the previous year, alleging that "secretly and clandestinely," a party including Laplanders, "or half-breeds," had conspired to organize the mining district in Cape Nome and take the gold for themselves.

In tandem with this presentation, the senators aligned with McKenzie presented a new narrative—a counternarrative—for the discovery of gold in Alaska. This origin story credited the finding to American miners, specifically to a small party from California led by a Mr. H. L. Blake, a US citizen, in the summer of 1898, before Jafet Lindeberg and Jo Hahn Tornanses set foot on Anvil Creek. "These Laplanders" and "these Scandinavians from Northern Europe" were not the true discoverers, Senator Richard F. Pettigrew of South Dakota told his colleagues. Pettigrew put into the record a "statement of facts" from a former constituent who had gone to Cape Nome as a prospector, the statement decrying the "treachery" of the "men who had robbed Blake of his discoveries" and then spent the winter "comfortably around the fire" eating succulent reindeer meat provided by the US government. These were flimsy assertions. Even if a Blake party was the first to come across what was later called Anvil Creek, the weavers of this new narrative offered no evidence that Blake or any members of this party had put so much as a single twig into the earth to stake a claim. Nevertheless, the fulminations against the "aliens" rang loud in the Senate. "I believe that the American miner should be protected and the American prospector should be protected," Pettigrew declared.

The "America First" rhetoric (as it might have been called in a later era) scaled a cynical peak in an alarm raised by Carter on the Senate floor:

> Mr. President, Dutch Harbor, the common inlet to Bering Sea for shipping, is only about 400 miles farther from Yokohama than from San Francisco. Suppose we give notice to the forty-three or forty-five million people of Japan that they, without disturbing their relations to the Japanese Government, or changing their relations to our own Government, may proceed to Cape Nome and . . . the whole of that Alaskan coast and there participate like our own citizens in the benefits which accrue to the locator of mining claims. It would be equivalent to turning Alaska over to the aliens who might desire to come there from all over the world. Now sir, I do not think this policy ought to be embarked upon.

Japan was a rising naval power. In a few years' time it would shock the world by vanquishing the Russian fleet in the Battle of Tsushima in the Korea Strait. Still, the threat of a Japanese invasion of Alaska was very far down the list of concerns of the War Department, as Senator Carter well knew. He was stooping to public fearmongering on behalf of a project of private enrichment. Did he believe his words even as he spoke them? Just a year later, he showered praise on Japan, to which "the world is indebted for the rapid and peaceful growth of commerce on the Pacific Coast," at a banquet in Seattle to honor the Marquis Ito Hirobumi, a prominent Japanese statesman. Colleagues with long memories could recall, too, that Carter had made his mark in Washington as a passionate defender of the rights of all "pioneer miners," including aliens, to stake claims to America's bounty. In his very first speech in Congress, on the floor of the House in April 1890, he noted, "Mines are ordinarily discovered by poor men. . . . The law gives the exclusive right to citizens or those who have declared their intention to become such to explore the public domain for hidden treasure." Now, it seemed, the "pioneer miner," that "stout-hearted and hopeful man who . . . goes forth to prospect and labor alone for days and weeks, perchance for months and years," as he said in his maiden speech, had disappeared from the senator's field of vision and interest.

THE MCKENZIE FACTION WAS NOT WRONG IN PERCEIVING A SWELLING OF American pride in Alaska, coupled with a lust for the territory's gold. Washingtonians themselves were besotted with gold. The "Hard Pan List," a register of the town's elite, used by the McKinley Executive Mansion for awarding invitations to social events, owed its name to the gold craze. Capitol Hill was part of the frenzy. "Gold, gold, gold! Its quest pervades the minds of individuals, corporations and nations," began a mid-April "Special Washington Letter" on "the Alaska fever" in the pages of the *Cameron County Press* of Pennsylvania. The dispatch noted that "committee clerks and congressmen are talking of going there" for prospecting, although "the congressional elections this year will probably keep them at home." But the McKenzie crew overplayed their hand. Calculated to win sympathy, the nativist jabs also served to provoke offense among members of both parties. The result was a protracted debate over Hansbrough's proposal—just what the boss hoped to avoid, lest its true purpose be exposed. "I am somewhat acquainted, Mr. President, with the Swedes and the Norwegians and the Finns. They are pretty thick in the Western country" and "are good, law-abiding citizens," Senator Knute Nelson of Minnesota said. "Why should we resort to a species of retroactive legislation," he asked of the Hansbrough amendment, "that we would not have the hardihood or the cheek to invoke against native-born citizens? The spirit of the United States of America, ever since it became an independent nation, has been contrary to all such notions."

Nelson was speaking on behalf of large numbers of his own constituents, Minnesota being a haven for immigrants from Scandinavia, and in a sense he was speaking for himself as an example of how thoroughly natives from that region had assimilated into the American way of life. Born in Norway in 1843, he came to the United States at the age of six with his mother, fought for the Union in the Civil War, and served as governor of his adopted state before being elected to the Senate in 1895. But the senator did not limit his defense of the "alien" to his fellow Scandinavians. After listening to Hansbrough complain of the unfair advantages of Laplanders as prospectors in Alaska, how they had "the benefit of reindeer to bring them into the country" whereas "the American citizen was obliged to drag his sled over the ice and snow by hand," he responded sharply, "I desire to say to the Senate here and now that a great deal of prejudice is sought to be created because these men were Lapps." He provided his colleagues a lesson on the geography of Lapland, "a dreary waste of icebergs and snow," and the settled habits of the Laplanders. The Norwegians, he noted, treated the Laplanders as second-class, in the same way that whites in America treated the "colored people down South." Still, the Lapps were not an "emigrating people," he said, and came to Alaska only at the urging of the US government. Colorado's Henry Moore Teller, a former mining attorney, joined in the defense of the Lapps, saying he had been informed on "good authority" that "they are the men who opened up that rich country, the men who went in there and found gold; and perhaps it would never have been found if they had not gone there."

From a defense of the rights of aliens to stake claims, opponents of Hansbrough's amendment pivoted to the argument that the proposal would serve to reward jumpers. In pointing this out, they also shifted the debate to more favorable political terrain for their side, given the scorn Americans widely felt for jumpers. "In ninety-nine cases out of one hundred when a man puts his claim on another's, he is a blackmailer and a thief," Colorado's Teller said. "It has been the curse of the mining camps ever since we have had a mining camp. . . . Mr. President, if I speak with a little warmth on this subject, it is because I have seen the evil of it." Even warmer on the topic was Senator William Brimage Bate of Tennessee, a former governor of the state who had once commanded armies for the Confederacy as a major general and who took particular umbrage that the "aliens" provision had never been discussed in Carter's committee, of which he was a member. The jumper, he said, might be likened to the jackal "that follows in the wake of the lion to get his prey." Then, too, he continued, inspired by his analogy, there was the cuckoo bird: "whenever another bird makes a nest, the cuckoo bird comes along, takes the nest, lays its eggs, and hatches its young. . . . [T]hat cuckoo is a jumper."

"That is good," Nevada's William Morris Stewart said in compliments to his Tennessee colleague. No senator stood stronger in resistance to the Hansbrough amendment, and that spelled trouble for the McKenzie side. An elder with piercing blue eyes that flashed with anger and a long white beard tumbling down to his chest, Stewart could be formidable on any matter, and on mining issues in particular, no senator, including Carter, possessed greater expertise. Now in his seventies, Stewart was a child of Jacksonian America, born in a log cabin in a small town in upstate New York in the mid-1820s, his grandfather a soldier in the Revolutionary War. Adept at mathematics, he enrolled at Yale and, on the discovery of gold in California, sailed to San Francisco to join the Forty-Niners. He promptly contracted Panama fever in the mountains and might have died had his fellow miners not nursed him back to health, fashioning a dipper so he could drink fresh water while lying on his back. In Nevada, he got a "good claim," only to meet with challenge from a jumper: "I choked him and took up a rock" and threatened to "knock his brains out," he recalled in his *Reminiscences*. Trusting his impartiality, his fellow miners on one occasion made him an umpire to settle a dispute over a claim, the loser firing a bullet that whizzed past him. Unfazed, Stewart applied his energies to keeping "the boys" from hanging the miscreant. He developed a practice in mining law, entered politics as an elected district attorney, and made the rounds of miners' meetings with a pair of Texas derringers in his side pockets. First elected to the Senate in 1864 to represent Nevada, newly admitted to the Union as a state, he was now, in 1900, in his second stretch of service in the body, having logged twenty-three years of service altogether.

Stewart shared the visceral animus toward jumpers felt by colleagues like Teller and Bate, but this sentiment was only one aspect of his stand against the Hansbrough amendment. In his mind, the proposal invited chaos in the gold fields. "Now, the question," he said to his colleagues, "comes right down to this: Is the Senate to legislate one man's property into the hands of another?" Stewart was for the orderly development of Alaska. He had once run a quartz mill and could see matters from the perspective of an entrepreneur, risking capital to build a profitable enterprise. There was nothing wrong, in this view, with a large operator buying the stakes of small claims holders, so long as the transactions were voluntary. In these terms, he defended Charles Lane's purchase of claims from Lapps, putting into the record a letter from Mrs. Lane declaring that her husband, beyond the $300,000 he had already spent to acquire these claims, was planning to invest an additional $500,000 for needed infrastructure projects for the development of the Cape Nome mining district. Hansbrough's proposal, Lane said, would scuttle such beneficial investments.

DEBATE SLOGGED ON FOR WEEKS, SANDWICHED BETWEEN OTHER SENATE business. Sensing victory, opponents grew bolder, insinuating that a corrupt purpose lay at the heart of the Hansbrough amendment. Not once was McKenzie's name mentioned on the floor of the Senate, but Hubbard and Hansbrough were called out. At one point, Stewart produced an affidavit attesting to Hubbard's presence in a committee room of Senator Hansbrough. The implication, left unstated by Stewart, was that the two men were collaborating on a nefarious scheme related to the amendment. In response to this barely veiled challenge to his integrity, Hansbrough submitted to the Senate an affidavit sworn by Hubbard. In that document, Hubbard blandly identified himself as an attorney on behalf of mining litigation in Nome. He omitted that he was also the secretary of the Alaska Gold Mining Company and had made a deal with a political boss to sign over to the company his law firm's interest in mining litigation. He left out, too, that he had been engaged in private discussions of this matter, for months, with both Hansbrough and Carter. But by this juncture, the opponents of the Hansbrough amendment knew, if not every detail of these machinations, the broad thrust. "They have a jumper on this side of the amendment," Tennessee's Bate told his colleagues, fingering Hubbard. "This man has jumped four or five thousand miles, all the way from Cape Nome, and lit down into the committee room of my friend the Senator from North Dakota, for the purpose of doing what? Why, of helping those jumpers who are at Cape Nome to take that which does not belong to them and put out the man with the pick and the spade and set up for themselves there and make a fortune out of this interest. That is a long jump and an adroit one."

The vise tightening, Hansbrough insisted that there was no truth to a newspaper report suggesting he had "a personal interest" in jumper claims on properties claimed first by aliens. "I have no interest in any of these Laplander or alien claims in Alaska, immediate or remote, direct or indirect, contingent or otherwise. That is my answer to that," Hansbrough said to his fellow senators. Not believing a word of this statement, Bate now directly confronted Hansbrough about the provenance of the North Dakotan's "adroitly written" amendment. Beneath its "innocent look," Bate said, the proposal was a "serpent coiled beneath that rose, a dagger behind that smile." Hansbrough was forced to respond, "What is the information the Senator from Tennessee desires?" Bate replied, "The Senator can tell exactly how this came about. He presented it. It is his bantling." By "bantling" Bate was using a derogatory term for a young child, as in a bastard. "I have named it in a certain way as your bantling, and I think it deserves the characterization," Bates continued, "but I know the Senator will make an explanation here, which no doubt will be satisfactory to him if not to the Senate." Hansbrough, rattled, shot back, "I think the Senator will be satisfied with my explanation when I make it."

Bate, though, wasn't done with his needling: "Of course there were some inducements—honorable inducements, I mean to say"—that brought Hansbrough's amendment, the illegitimate bantling, to the

Senate. Now the old general had more or less accused his colleague of taking a bribe. Hansbrough smoldered over this charge for more than a week and finally burst into flames. In fact, he told his colleagues, "there is a monster conspiracy afoot to grab the richest gold region on the face of the earth, and . . . a few men in command of a great many millions of dollars are the conspirators, and . . . they are using this half-civilized people, the Laplanders . . . to further their nefarious schemes." He was referring to Lane's purchases of Lapp claims. But it was a desperate argument since Lane, far from hiding his interests in Alaskan mines, had brought his holdings and his business plans to the attention of the Senate. The only "monster conspiracy afoot" was the scheme of McKenzie and his associates.

Rather than suffer an outright defeat on the Senate floor, Carter, on May 1, withdrew from consideration the bid to repeal alien claims. Stewart, in his declared "funeral oration" for the proposal, said the lesson was plain that "a retroactive law is always obnoxious." McKenzie confessed his frustration to his hidden wife. "I never worked so hard in all my life and I have got so little money for it," he told Elva in a letter. There remained hope that the House might accomplish what the Senate could not. On May 22, the matter was brought to the House floor, a fresh effort to repeal "alien" claims, and yet again the predations of the foreigners, the Laplanders in particular, were inveighed against, although with a bizarre twist. Alaska's gold fields had been invaded and illegally captured by a "horde of Chinese" from the northern part of China, Henry Dickinson Green, of Reading, Pennsylvania, informed his colleagues. This was gobbledygook, on a par with Carter's nonsense about a Japanese plot to seize Alaska. And like the Senate, the House did not swallow the bait. "We desire the gold and silver, which nature has given us in such abundance, taken from the earth and used for the enrichment of all," said William Henry King, the at-large representative for Utah. "It is not so material who takes it from the ground." Proponents of the repeal language demanded a call of the roll and were soundly defeated, with only twenty ayes in favor of the amendment and fifty-two nays.

Notwithstanding Hansbrough's assurance in the discussions at Everett House that the Alaska code could be written to end the practice of miners using the beach as a commons, that effort failed too. Having defended the right of aliens to stake claims, Congress was in no mind to take away the commons, especially with thousands of Americans actively preparing to go to Cape Nome to try their luck in the golden sands.

"IT COULD PROBABLY BE SHOWN BY FACTS AND FIGURES THAT THERE IS NO distinctly native American criminal class except Congress," Mark Twain said, in still another of his quips on the character of the Gilded Age. Many Americans agreed. In the popular mind, Congress was corrupt, craven, complacent, worse than worthless, a blight. Yet in this episode, Congress failed to conform to caricature. The Boss of the Dakotas, a protégé of James J. Hill no less, had distributed the shares "where they will do the most good," in the manner of Credit Mobilier, and fallen short of his objective. Not all legislators were on the take; some had a clear-eyed view of the scheme and called the schemers (if not the boss by name) on the shenanigans in the full glare of public debate. Nor was Congress easy prey for demagoguery: lawmakers were not roused by talk of a foreign invasion of Alaska. Even "half-breeds"—the Lapps—found a stalwart defense. So the beach commons survived, and the claims made by aliens were not repealed.

Chapter 8

"BUT THE CHAIN'S MCKINLEY GOLD"

Y ET NOT ALL HOPE WAS LOST FOR THE BOSS AND HIS CLAN. THE ALASKA bill, as it headed toward final passage in Congress, then to the Executive Mansion for the president's signature, established a new judicial framework for the territory. Instead of a single district for the whole of Alaska, the existing impractical arrangement, there would be three districts, the second of these encompassing the Seward Peninsula, Cape Nome included. Each district would receive a federal judge, a US attorney, and a US marshal, the nominations to be made by the president. The Republican-controlled Senate was likely to confirm whatever choices President McKinley made. The second division, as it was called, was the prize, with its jurisdiction over the gold fields, and McKenzie, as he shuttled back and forth between Washington and New York awaiting completion of the Alaska legislation, aimed to secure these appointments, most importantly of the judge. He strove for nothing less than to control the legal and law enforcement apparatus of the Seward Peninsula on behalf of his company.

That was his ambition—and he was confident he could achieve it, he told a visitor to his suite at Everett House. His guest was Wilson T. Hume, the attorney whom Oliver Hubbard had invited to join Hubbard & Beeman as the third partner. A former district attorney and state legislator in Oregon, Hume, just over forty years old, had a practice in Nome representing claim jumpers and had staked his own claim to a section of the beach. At Hubbard's urging, he had come east from his off-season lodgings in Seattle to gain an understanding of the scheme on which Hubbard had embarked and to meet the principals. First he conferred with Senators Carter and Hansbrough in Washington and now he was meeting McKenzie for the first time. Sensing Hume's wariness, the boss tried to allay his concerns. Everyone was going to get rich, McKenzie said, because he "controlled" the appointments for the second division and because those officials, once installed, "would be friendly" to the interests of the Alaska Gold Mining Company. McKenzie added that "a large number of wealthy, influential, and prominent men" stood behind the company (as usual, he didn't provide names) and arrangements already had been made with prominent stockbrokers on Wall Street to handle the sale of Alaska Gold's stock in the fall. Hume need have no fear, McKenzie said; the attorney simply needed to do as instructed.

McKenzie was promising a bird not yet in hand. The appointments had not yet been sewn up. He knew that, because he was in the thick of the scrum underway in Washington for these positions. His candidate for the judgeship was not necessarily the favorite, and the president had yet to make up his mind.

ALASKA MATTERED TO MCKINLEY. WHEN THE FIRST DISCOVERIES WERE made at Anvil Creek in the fall of 1898, his presidency was in its eighteenth month. While the McKinley administration could not take direct credit for the finding of gold in Alaska, nonetheless, this was a good news story about the undiminished bounty of America in which any president could bask. McKinley needed such stories, for he wasn't the sort of figure to generate excitement on his own. Fifty-seven years old, a former Ohio congressman and governor, short and stocky, the customary cigar soothingly in mouth, he had a plodding style and could seem less the master of events unfolding during his presidency than their beneficiary—or victim. Alaska and the Philippines vied for headlines, and now, two years after Commodore George Dewey's electrifying sinking of the Spanish fleet in Manila Bay in May 1898, the news from the islands was bad. Even fellow Republicans tore into

McKinley as the papers reported on bloody ambushes of US troops by Filipino guerilla bands. South Dakota's Richard F. Pettigrew called him a "puny President," a tool of "the imperialists." The cause of Alaskan gold, though, unified the Republicans, all the more so because the party, which not only controlled both the House and the Senate but also had won the presidency in eight out of ten presidential elections starting in 1860, had welded its political fortunes and the health of the US economy to gold. In March, McKinley had signed, with a gold pen, the Gold Standard Act of 1900, defining gold as America's official means of payment and the only metal for which paper currency could be redeemed. The bill passed the House without a single Republican in opposition and with only eleven Democrats in favor and more than one hundred against; it cleared the Senate with all but two Republicans in favor and all but one Democrat against. The law was a forceful rebuke to "free silver" Democrats led by William Jennings Bryan. He had been McKinley's opponent in the 1896 election and was now the leading contender for the Democratic nomination to take on the president in November. Most Republicans, especially businessmen, viewed the coinage of silver, supported by struggling farmers as a means to pay off their debts, as a recipe for inflation. James J. Hill, once a backer of Democrats, went over to the McKinley Republican camp largely over his disgust at the Democrats' embrace of silver. In the spirit of the times, the McKenzie children by Elva could recite by heart a jingle from pro-Republican newspapers:

> My Papa's watch is Big and Fat,
> The hands are hard and cold—
> Its face looks like a Democrat,
> But the chain's McKinley gold.

But in rejecting sliver as currency, the Republicans now had to make good on their promise of a steady, reliable supply of gold, and Alaska was vital to that promise. The "treasure land of Alaska," a Republican power broker in the state of Washington confidently declared, "will make the free coinage of silver sink into insignificance." That vow could not be fulfilled, though, if the disputes over the claims at Cape Nome were not resolved in an orderly and a peaceful manner.

The most qualified choice for the gold district judgeship was James Wickersham of Tacoma, Washington. Wickersham had experience as an elected county probate judge, a city attorney for Tacoma, and a state legislator. Forty-two years old, he was an outdoorsman, fond of hunting and hiking, with a robust physical constitution well able to handle the rigors of the Seward Peninsula's climate. He had faults, notably a hot temper, and eleven years earlier he had been convicted on a charge of seducing a teenage woman, but his accuser later recanted her damning testimony. Wickersham also was known for making enemies. But tellingly, his enemies tended to be of a certain type—the grasping political power brokers and the predatory business moguls who attracted so much public derision in the Gilded Age. Wickersham had two sterling character traits that recommended him to the Alaska position: independence of mind and fearlessness. He made his name in Tacoma by winning a spectacular $1 million refund for taxpayers from a utility he took to court for defrauding the city. The case, a distinct long shot at the outset, went all the way to the US Supreme Court.

Championing Wickersham's candidacy for the judgeship was his home-state US senator, Addison Gardner Foster, a Republican whom Wickersham, as a state legislator, had helped bring to the Senate. Foster mounted a vigorous campaign, organizing testimonials for Wickersham from dozens of prominent figures in the state's legal community and personally lobbying McKinley for the appointment.

McKinley's naming of Wickersham would have stopped McKenzie's Nome Proposition dead in its tracks. The boss, on a larger scale, was exactly the sort of person of whom Wickersham had made bitter and enduring enemies in Tacoma. Wickersham despised the system of graft that McKenzie embodied and would never have participated in a scheme to use a federal court in Alaska for private enrichment. With his pugnacious temperament, he probably would have relished a fight with McKenzie on this matter. McKenzie's choice for the job, not surprisingly, was a man of a quite different type. This was Arthur H. Noyes, an attorney in private practice in Minneapolis. Unlike Wickersham, Noyes, now in his midforties, had no public experience to his name—not on the bench, in a municipal office, or in a legislature. He was a corporate lawyer whose clientele included railroad companies. A native of Wisconsin and a graduate of the state university law school at Madison, he moved to the Dakotas as a young man and opened a practice in Grand Forks. There Noyes met McKenzie, just starting his ascent as a political boss in the territory. "I knew him intimately in Dakota," Noyes later recalled. "I think generally his intimate friends were my intimate friends." Their mutual friends included Hansbrough, also at that time based in Grand Forks. And when McKenzie shifted his base of operations to Saint Paul, Noyes was a regular visitor to the Throne Room at the Merchants Hotel.

Loyalty, of course, was an indispensable requirement for McKenzie in any relationship. But the boss was surrounded by loyal men who might have suited for the judgeship. Noyes's defining feature was his pliability. He had an inviting softness, suggested by his plump cheeks and the girlish locks that tumbled over the back of his shirt collar. As harder men found on first acquaintance, Noyes disliked confrontation and affected a cordial desire to please. Underneath the smooth surface was a jangle of nerves. He frequently drank, perhaps as a form of self-medication, in public settings as well as in his office. He was aware that he had a serious problem with alcohol and once confided to a superior that emotional strains invariably drove him to the bottle. From McKenzie's perspective, the habit probably was another recommendation. The boss was not looking for an agile and alert legal mind; he planned to do the thinking for the second division's new judge.

Happily for McKenzie, Noyes was afflicted with the Alaskan gold bug. In 1899, he joined a company, as treasurer and a shareholder, organized to dredge gold out of the Bering off the shores of Cape Nome. There were many such ventures, and dredging was a more difficult operation at which to succeed than it generally appeared to the hatchers of these ventures thousands of miles away. Noyes, though, was not easily dislodged from his enthusiasm for Alaska. On hearing of Washington's intention to create a judgeship for the Cape Nome region, he wrote to his old friend Hansbrough inquiring as to the possibility of his getting the appointment. He thought of Alaska as "a new country," a place for a fresh start in life with his wife, Nancy. Perhaps in his desire to get away, he felt a sense of not measuring up to his father, who had come home from the Civil War minus a right foot, lost at Antietam. A federal judgeship would be a pinnacle in a career that had scaled few summits and an enviable status symbol, making him one of the most important people in Alaska. Noyes cared deeply about social status, another feature of personality that made him vulnerable to manipulation. His mother was the granddaughter of an officer in a Massachusetts regiment of George Washington's Continental Army, a line of descent that gave Arthur his proud membership in the Sons of the American Revolution.

As pliable as Noyes was, McKenzie may not have felt the need to ply him with shares of the Alaska Gold Mining Company. The boss, after all, aimed to practice thrift, not largesse, in the doling out of treats; he was not in the custom of buying subservience when no outlay was necessary. Surely, though, Noyes had an inkling, and probably a good deal more than that, of the scheme that McKenzie aimed to execute in Alaska and the role that he would be expected to play from the bench in facilitating it. He journeyed to Washington to confer with McKenzie on his candidacy, and the boss arranged for him to meet with Robert Chipps at the Raleigh Hotel. Noyes later said that he thought he was merely being introduced to an "Alaskan miner," but that statement was hardly credible. If all went according to McKenzie's plan, Chipps soon would be filing a lawsuit in the court of the Honorable Judge Arthur Noyes to take ownership of the Discovery claim. Certainly as Chipps understood the encounter, he was meeting with a new recruit to the McKenzie ring.

First, though, McKenzie had to win the judgeship. Just as Wickersham had Senator Foster pressing McKinley for the appointment, Noyes needed a champion in the Senate. Hansbrough wrote to the president, vouching for Noyes as "a gentleman of strict integrity," but the leader of the campaign was Cushman Davis of Minnesota, the state's senior senator, a Republican, the chairman of the Foreign Relations Committee, and a close ally of Carter. Through his Saint Paul law firm, Davis combined business and politics. The *New York Evening Post* in the mid-1890s accused him of using his political clout for the benefit of his interest as a stockholder in a Minnesota syndicate granted concessions by the government of Venezuela to develop coffee plantations and gold mines. Davis spoke to McKinley on behalf of Noyes. On the principle of distributing the shares "where they will do the most good," McKenzie must have seen the senator as a deserving target for shares in Alaska Gold Mining, and Davis was later named in a newspaper report as a participant in McKenzie's venture. But it seemed that more than mere shares in a fledgling company of uncertain value was needed to build momentum for such an undistinguished candidate as Noyes. An associate of the boss later testified to McKenzie's complaining about having to spend $60,000 in hard cash (nearly $2 million in 2020 dollars) on behalf of the judgeship. "If he did" spend that money, Noyes later said of McKenzie, on being asked specifically about sums devoted to "bribing" senators to back the appointment, "it was in a way unknown to me."

NOYES, THEN, WAS A MEDIOCRITY, WHILE WICKERSHAM WAS A GOOD DEAL better than that. Of course, from just about the beginning of the republic and not only in the Gilded Age, presidents had sent bumblers to the bench, a practice used especially for openings in territories yet to be admitted as states. This was a time-honored way for the chief executive to gratify senators and other operators in the greasing of the wheels of political commerce. Such judges could usually be forgotten about, but the judge for the gold fields would be in the spotlight; reporters, not just prospectors, were headed to Cape Nome, and the papers could be expected to train a sharp eye on the jousting for claims as the mining season got underway. Was McKinley really going to appoint a milksop to the position?

He was. On June 6, the Congress at last passed the Alaska bill. McKinley signed the legislation and immediately sent his judicial nominations to the Senate, which promptly ratified them. Noyes received the second division, with Wickersham, as he remarked ruefully, "shunted to an obscure place in the Yukon wilderness," the third division, based at Eagle City, in eastern Alaska by the Canadian border. "Tremendous pressure" won the prize for Noyes, Senator Foster told Wickersham in a consoling wire.

The boss, with whom Noyes met on the day after the Senate confirmed the nomination, had mounted an impressive campaign on behalf of his man. But the appointment also had to be seen not simply as the result of political pressure exerted on McKinley but as an act of presidential will. McKinley could be plodding, but he was not dim-witted, and he seldom allowed himself to be maneuvered into a choice he didn't want to make. He had a quiet cunning. In favoring McKenzie with this appointment, he was, in the first instance, redeeming a political debt. With Hill, McKenzie had done yeoman's work on behalf of the 1896 McKinley presidential campaign in bringing Minnesota and North Dakota (though not South Dakota) into the Republican column. A boss like McKenzie did not undertake such work without expectation of tangible reward. It undoubtedly pained McKinley, in some higher region of his being, to acknowledge this side of politics. He didn't create the oppressive boss system, but he surely didn't have it in him to overthrow it. Besides, in 1900, his reelection bid underway, he again needed men like McKenzie. The Republicans would be gathering in Philadelphia in mid-June for their nominating convention, with McKenzie attending as the head of the North Dakota delegation. It was an ideal time to feed McKenzie a plum.

A darker explanation also could account for the appointment of Noyes. A half century later, decades after McKenzie's death, an old friend from Fargo said that, as he had understood the arrangement, McKenzie and McKinley had formed a "partnership project" on the Nome venture. Without doubt, McKenzie had the brass to offer an inducement to a president, any president, if he thought an enticement might work. If he was promising shares in the Alaska Gold Mining Company to US senators, then why not to the country's highest official? It was his nature to think along these lines. There was little, though, in McKinley's background to suggest receptivity to a bribe, apart from an incident in the early 1890s, during his tenure as Ohio's governor. McKinley had cosigned loans for an old friend, and with his friend teetering toward bankruptcy, McKinley found himself on the hook for an amount on the order of $130,000, well in excess of his personal wealth. A group of wealthy friends with an interest in McKinley's political career offered to bail him out: "My purse is open to you," one said. In the end he accepted an arrangement immediately cancelling his debt in return for regular repayments to his rescuers to retire the obligation over time. He had not taken a bribe exactly, for he had not promised to take any particular actions in return for this assistance. But he could be fairly expected to remember with gratitude those who had come to his aid in an hour of need. McKinley must have sensed that McKenzie had some sort of pecuniary interest in the fervent pursuit of an Alaskan judgeship for a nondescript Minneapolis lawyer. Why else would the Boss of the Dakotas care so much about this faraway land? Perhaps he deemed it best not to inquire of the details, preferring to be ignorant rather than implicated. Maybe he figured that satisfying McKenzie could buy political peace on the Alaska front. Sometimes a president can do no better than to try to calm the waters of the moment.

McKenzie got his judge—and he got his district attorney too. McKinley nominated, and the Senate confirmed, Montana's Joseph K. Wood for the position. Wood was a neophyte, just over thirty years old, with experience as a lawyer in private practice in Grand Forks and as an assistant district attorney for Missoula County, Montana. McKenzie had known his parents, before Wood was born; Wood knew of McKenzie "by reputation." Montana senator Carter, "my political backer . . . my principal friend," made a "personal appeal" to the president for the choice, Wood later recalled. Wood knew where his obligation lay, just as Noyes did—with the boss. McKenzie was delivering on the vows he made to Hubbard's skeptical law partner, Hume, in their meeting at the Everett. The Washington end completed, the McKenzie band made haste to go to Alaska. The group was behind schedule, for the Bering ice already had melted, thousands of treasure seekers had arrived in Nome, and a great many more were en route. The Alaska gold rush of 1900 was on.

Part Three

NOME, 1900

"The main street is a motley mob of people of all conditions & classes, but all free and equal, all bent on getting the Almighty Dollar by any way they can."

—*Nome miner Edwin Sherzer in a letter to his fiancée in Saint Louis, quoted in Kenneth J. Kutz,* **Nome Gold**

Chapter 9

"TENTS, TENTS, TENTS"

T HE FIRST PASSENGER STEAMER OF THE MINING SEASON OF 1900 arrived in Nome on May 23. The *Jeanie*, of the Pacific Steam Whaling Company, left port in Seattle on May 2, sixty-one ticketed voyagers aboard. The schooner had smooth passage until encountering gigantic blocks of ice just south of volcanic Nunivak Island, three hundred miles south of Nome. The bergs were a mortal threat, capable of shunting a vessel onto a coastal mud flat, the ship then vulnerable to a violent storm that could smash it to pieces. The *Jeanie*'s passengers were on the whole fortunate. Captain P. H. Mason skillfully guided her through an opening in the floes, although he did have to retreat temporarily in the face of a thick fog. The ship made good time, reaching Nome, a voyage of twenty-three hundred miles from Seattle, in twenty-one days. There was little for cramped passengers to do on these trips; holding down the dreadful grub slopped on plates by the crew was more than many stomachs could handle. "Eat, sit, walk, sit, walk, eat, sleep, with a little conversation, lots of gossip, some cards, etc. thrown in," a bored adventurer, just six days on the water, wrote in a letter to his wife back home. Suspicious types on one ship swore that overworked Chinese cooks in the galley were spiking the food with soap to keep passengers from eating.

Close behind the *Jeanie* were ten passenger steamers out of Seattle and four out of San Francisco. The *Robert Dollar*, out of Seattle, stuffed four hundred ticket payers into its warrens. A throng of well over one thousand clambered onto Yesler's wharf to see off the party, the cheers subsiding only to mount for the next vessel making its leave. On a busy day, as many as ten thousand well-wishers might visit the Seattle docks. Construction materials were en route too. A barge, the *Skookum*, was hauling one million feet of lumber. Other vessels were carrying the spigots, pipes, glassware, screws, nails, dice, mattresses, and all else for quick-to-assemble saloons, restaurants, and hotels. Beef steer, whiskey, and cigars also were on their way. Tugboats, three-masted sailboats, ocean liners—virtually anything that could float and trampers that could just barely—bore down on Nome.

The townsfolk, the hardy nub that had eked out the nearly seven-month winter stretch when Nome was sealed from the outside, saw much to scoff at as the steamers discharged their passengers. With Nome lacking a proper wharf, the newcomers clambered onto small craft that took them through the surf to the beach. It was obvious at a glance that this contingent was not as seasoned as the group that had made it to Nome the year before: probably nine out of ten had never been near a mining camp in their lives. They were more or less properly outfitted for the job, with their shiny picks and shovels, gum boots and all-weather pants and jackets, acquired at the port in Seattle or San Francisco or earlier by mail-order catalog, but that didn't make them miners; they were the very definition of cheechakoes. Many brought along newfangled gadgets for working the beach or a creek, but they had no idea how to use them—assuming the devices worked as advertised. More than a few had no work experience other than office desk jobs, the sort of exertion that kept one's fingernails clean. Their biceps were flabby and their hands uncalloused and ripe for blistering. Their lack of fitness showed as, for $1.50 per hour, some accepted jobs off-loading supplies from the barges moored offshore. The townsfolk hooted as these recruits clumsily negotiated the narrow wooden gangplanks stretching from the barges to the shore, the greenhorns buckling under the weight of the boxes and bales in their charge.

But weak flesh did not make for weak spirit. The pioneers were not lazy; slack muscles could acquire fiber and raw hands a hard shell of protection. Having unloaded freight from the boats, the materials now piled in heaps on the shore, the tenderfoots turned to carpentry. Nome rang with the sound of hammers—without stop through the bright nights. Soon went up the Golden Gate Hotel, four stories high, bay windows across the front, the "only first class hotel in Nome," the proprietors claimed, even as guests grumbled about the flimsy construction—so efficient at carrying sound, one complained, "you can hear a man kiss his wife in the fourth room down the hall from yours." Few, though, could afford the Golden Gate's daily rate of $1 per day. The vast majority of those arriving in Nome pitched a tent along the coast and called it home. "Tents, tents, tents extending along the shore as far as the eye could see," a visitor said of his first glimpse of Nome from his incoming ship in mid-June.

FROM TWO THOUSAND OR SO INHABITANTS THE SUMMER BEFORE, THE TOWN now swelled to some twenty thousand. Nome in a matter of weeks became the single-largest general delivery address in the US postal system. The twenty-three clerks stationed at the town's lone post office needed five filing boxes just to sort letters sent to those with the last name Johnson. The vast new population changed the atmosphere of Nome. Front Street in places was nearly impassable, inviting pushing, shoving, and jostling to make one's way forward. With just about everyone, it seemed, carrying a loaded firearm, frayed tempers and free-flowing alcohol led to disputes settled by shoot-outs. The traditional etiquette of the sourdoughs—in a well-functioning mining town, a fellow could leave his poke unattended and expect to find it there on his return— was not honored. Hustlers of every variety abounded. Several hundred prostitutes established a base of operations behind a row of saloons on Front Street. The "good time girls" had heard the news that Nome was the place to be in 1900. Although their trade was illegal, the law was seldom enforced. Business was so brisk that a dedicated worker could turn tricks for enough gold to return home after a few weeks, her purse full and her season done. Dance halls and gambling parlors took in gold just about as fast as miners could sift the dust from the beach sands. Bettors wagered on cockfights and boxing bouts, at times between professional brawlers, at times between amateurs capable of little more than a prayerful roundhouse right. The ladies of the dance halls also knew how to use their fists—on each other. They formed a union whose members asserted an exclusive right to work the floors for customers, who paid for the women's time as dance partners and for any other services mutually agreed upon. A woman tried to breach this rule—only to be pummeled by a member of the collective, on the spot, and thrown out of the hall. The number of saloons rose to over sixty, still not enough to keep Wyatt Earp from turning a big profit in his second season at the Dexter. A seasoned traveler cast a practiced eye on the revelries of Nome and assessed them as wilder than anything "in the worst days" of Montmartre in Paris or State Street in Chicago.

More than a few veteran miners looked on in disgust: to them Nome had become an unbridled circus, not a proper mining town. Dawson City in the Yukon never had a spectacle of this magnitude, even at the height of the Klondike boom. But the first-time prospector from the mainland, with no good idea of what to expect from a mining camp or from Alaska, was prepared to endure the hazards and hardships of Cape Nome—the risk, say, of contracting dysentery, as some did, for failing to boil drinking water—as the price of the chase for riches. The beach was a daily reminder of the possibilities, its vast quantities of gold still barely tapped, and so was Anvil Mountain in the distance.

The prospectors participating in the new season's gold rush for the most part regarded the original discoverers, "the Swedes" and the Lapps, without bitterness. They saw the miners who had come before them more as examples to emulate. Nor was there talk, as on the floor of the US Senate, of an imminent invasion by the Japanese. The riches, it was generally thought, would go to those willing to work hard to obtain them, and there were plenty of cheechakoes able to resist the faro table and the soft warm arms of a "good time girl" and go out on the tundra for a thirty-mile expedition, braving the mosquitoes and the bears.

Typical of these determined prospectors was a young miner, Edwin Sherzer, who arrived in Nome in mid-June, the end point of a journey that had started more than three thousand miles away in Saint Louis. He was there to join his brother, who had staked a tundra claim the previous season and stayed the winter in Alaska. Three days after landing in town, Edwin wrote a letter to his sweetheart, Clara, back home. "Well, here I am safe and sound in the famous Nome mining town," he began. "I don't look anything like I did when I left Home. I wear a flannel shirt, a suit of old clothes, bicycle cap & rubber boots." There was not much to eat besides bacon and bread, he wrote, and to obtain fresh water, he had to visit a swamp "that comes up to your knees in places and it is no fun, in fact everything here is work, work, work and the hardest kind too. . . . I don't see what all the people here are going to do, there will certainly be a lot of suffering & disappointments." But he was hardly ready to quit. "Brother says that this is no place for a man but when he thinks of going back to the life of a common slave in a Railroad office," Edwin told Clara, "he prefers this." After all, "here he is free & independent & acknowledges no man as master. I feel about the same as he does and will stick it out with him God willing. I don't want to come home unless I can afford to get married." A week later, his optimism intact, he wrote Clara of the hopeful masses on Front Street, all vying for the "Almighty Dollar." He couldn't possibly have known that the threat to his dream was not so much the tundra swamp or the whims of the divine but a political boss with designs on just about every gold nugget and speck of dust worth possessing.

And indeed, the predator already was in his midst—not McKenzie himself, not yet, but an advance party sent by the boss, which had landed in Nome several days before Sherzer's arrival. This group, traveling on the *Tacoma* out of Seattle, was led by "Captain" Mike McCormack, McKenzie's buddy from the Dakotas and a director of the Alaska Gold Mining Company. It included Senator Carter's brother-in-law James Galen and E. M. Walters, the speculator who had traded his beachfront claims for promised stock in Alaska Gold. Also on board was an engineer in charge of the machinery purchased by McKenzie, stored in boxes in the hold, to work the beach. Walters assumed that Carter's brother-in-law, a "kind of bookkeeper and cashier," was there to keep tabs on the senator's financial interest in the venture. It soon became evident that the boss also planned to use Jimmie, as Galen was known, as muscle to keep the beach sections McKenzie intended to mine free of "trespassers." While McKenzie aimed to use the mechanisms of the law to achieve his aims in Alaska, he understood that other means might be necessary. Cape Nome was a rough place, but no rougher than the Dakotas frontier of his days as a sheriff and rising power broker. Violent methods were never his first resort; nor were they to be ruled out as a last one.

NOME WAS TWO TO THREE WEEKS BEHIND IN NEWS FROM THE MAINLAND. As June turned to July, the town learned that Congress had approved a new code of governance for Alaska. A federal judge and district attorney, along with lesser officials, were due to arrive, with rooms awaiting them at the Golden Gate. "It is to be hoped that the establishment of a court of competent jurisdiction will relieve a situation that at times has been strained to the breaking point," the *Nome Daily News* said. So it was hoped—but when would the officials show up? That was an especially urgent question for jumpers like Kirke Requa, who had retained Hubbard, Beeman & Hume, as the law firm was now called, to litigate their claims. Some of the targeted properties were being actively and profitably worked—a prize nugget weighing 8.75 ounces had been taken from a Dexter Creek mine sought by a jumper represented by the firm. The discovery, reported in the *News*, could only provoke worry among the jumpers that there would be less gold left for them once they seized hold of "their" mines. They were impatient for the judge, impatient for their cases to get moving. Although Edwin Beeman and Wilson Hume were in Nome, the firm's lead partner had not been seen in town since the previous year, before the Bering froze over. What was keeping Oliver Hubbard?

Chapter 10

"ALERT, AGGRESSIVE, AND BUSILY ENGAGED"

T HE HOLDUP WAS THAT MCKENZIE FIRST NEEDED TO ATTEND THE Republican National Convention, which opened in Philadelphia on June 19. His leadership of the North Dakota delegation, as the state's Republican national committeeman, meant a great deal to him, not just because of the entrée it afforded to him to national party circles but also because it conferred prestige. McKinley, as universally expected, won the party's nomination for a second term, and the convention selected Theodore Roosevelt as his running mate. As always, TR, outfitted in a cowboy hat for the length of the convention, stood out in a crowd; perhaps he received congratulations from his old acquaintance from the Dakotas. Talk of gold was on the lips of the delegates. With the discoveries in Alaska, US Senator Edward O. Wolcott of Colorado declared in a floor speech, "this country can better afford than any other to enter upon the contest for commercial supremacy with gold as its standard."

Gold bonded the Republicans and bonded, too, the members of the McKenzie party, as they now made haste to get to Cape Nome. It was a motley band that converged in the "Gateway to Alaska," as Seattle, its merchants and transport haulers enriched by the gold rush, promoted itself. There was the hulking "old man," largely a mystery to his fellow travelers, accompanied by a young associate, known to all as Burns, a professionally trained nurse who functioned as the boss's manservant. There was McKenzie's longtime operative from the Dakotas, the attorney and former state legislator Reuben Stevens, for whom the boss had in mind a special, undisclosed mission in Alaska. There was Oliver Hubbard, his beady eye cast on the gold fields that so far had eluded him, and by his side the equally grasping Robert Chipps, his chronically mistrustful client, consumed by anxieties that the boss would divert for personal gain the riches that were due to all shareholders in the Alaska Gold Mining Company. There was Joseph Wood, the young Grand Forks lawyer whose appointment McKenzie had secured as district attorney of Nome. The boss already was buying him expensive dinners. And there were Mr. and Mrs. Arthur Noyes. The proud new judge had taken his oath of office back in Minneapolis before boarding the Great Northern for Seattle, solemnly swearing to "administer justice without respect to persons and do equal right to the poor and to the rich." His dredging venture had come to nothing, and he had virtually no money to his name; yet still he harbored a dream of somehow finding gold in Alaska and becoming fabulously wealthy. He was accompanied by his chief clerk and deputy clerk and their wives. Of the two assistants, Noyes trusted only the deputy clerk, the brother of a man well known to him. The appointment of the chief clerk had been forced upon him. This fellow, a stranger to Noyes, also nursed hopes of becoming a gold millionaire, but he was of Scandinavian descent and unsympathetic to any scheme that preyed on miners of his heritage. His presence was an indication that not even the boss could control every facet of this sprawling operation.

McKenzie arrived in Seattle on June 29, dashed off an "all OK" letter to Elva, and settled into the Butler, an upscale hotel favored by wealthy businessmen. Noyes and his wife checked into the lower-class Rainier-Grand by the docks. James Wickersham, the man who had lost the Alaska judgeship to Noyes, was also about to depart for his remote posting in the Yukon. He met the McKenzie entourage at a get-together arranged with Noyes to fix boundaries between their respective judicial divisions. The convivial gathering reminded Wickersham of his pain at not gaining the prime judgeship for himself, as people in Seattle "stood open-mouthed about those bound for Nome," the "great Nome gold camp" the only topic of conversation, as he recalled in his memoirs. "On comparing the Nome group with the Eagle City group," he wrote, "it seemed to me that my companions were rather unimportant and probably blessed with only moderate ability. Members of the Nome group were alert, aggressive, and busily engaged in planning huge mining ventures." Wickersham qualified this assessment, though, with a cautionary observation about Noyes: "The judge appeared to be an agreeable man, though . . . immoderately fond of the bottle."

THE SEATTLE POST-INTELLIGENCER REPORTED ON JULY 6 THAT THE Democrats, meeting in Kansas City, had nominated William Jennings Bryan to stand for the presidency against McKinley in a rematch of the 1896 election. Bryan aimed to run against imperialism, against what the party's chairman called an unwholesome American empire "founded on gold, grandeur, greed and glory"—which was to say, against the very pursuits leading so many of the candidate's countrymen to Alaska. It sounded like a noble campaign plank but not a winning one. At midnight on July 8, the boss and his cohorts set sail on the *Senator*, the general solicitor of the steamship line extending "the courtesy of transportation" to the McKenzie party, that is, free passage, with Noyes and his wife deposited in a stateroom. For this VIP group, far from steerage, there would be none of the foul conditions that plagued the voyage for so many other travelers to Nome that summer. Noyes brought along law books and office supplies; McKenzie, a case of port.

The boss now had time to reflect. He had lost the battle in Congress over the Hansbrough amendment but had won the contest for the gold-district judge and district attorney. He had secured Hubbard as part of the venture but not yet the attorney's two partners; that would be a first order of business in Nome. As for the objectives of the Alaska campaign, at the outset there were two principal ones: to seize control of the beach and to take custody of the disputed properties in which the Alaska Gold Mining Company had an interest. The beach, he decided, could wait. As for the properties, first in mind was Discovery, followed by the other prime Anvil Creek claims.

In talking over the matter, McKenzie and Hubbard concluded that a tool of law known as a receivership could serve their purpose. A receivership was a kind of guardianship for a distressed holding, the device dating to sixteenth-century Elizabethan England and imported to the American colonies. In the case of a struggling company saddled with debts, its assets tied up in litigation, creditors might petition a judge to appoint a receiver, some private person, knowledgeable about business matters, to preserve and protect the assets until the dispute was resolved. This would prevent the managers of the company from making off with the company's valuables for themselves, leaving nothing for the creditors. An essential quality, then, for a receiver was neutrality between the parties in a dispute. A receiver was supposed to conserve the assets for the length of the legal proceeding and above all not help himself to them—there could be no greater violation of duty. Once again the Gilded Age displayed a core attribute of its character in showing how a tool intended for good public use could be abused for private gain. The financier and speculator Jay Gould manipulated receiverships to take control of railroads that owed him money, using the instrument as a weapon for forcing workers to take pay cuts and even depriving them of their right to strike. In the hands of a robber baron like Gould, one labor organization said, the receivership was a hammer wielded by "contemptible and blood-sucking organizations and their governmental allies."

McKenzie well understood the opportunities afforded by receiverships, for seven years earlier he had served as a court-appointed receiver for a number of branch lines of the Northern Pacific, his office lasting for a year, amid James J. Hill's bid to take control of the ailing railroad. He understood precisely what a court demanded of an honest receiver; therefore, he must have known exactly how his plan—to become the receiver for disputed claims secretly in the cupboard of Alaska Gold—would violate those standards. He knew, too, that young gold mines, many prospering rather than failing, were strange candidates for court-imposed receiverships. But this was of no concern to him, because he regarded the Noyes court, with good reason, as his to command. He was on the threshold of becoming Alaska's "King of Receivers."

Chapter 11

BIG ALEX ENJOYS A MEAL

THE *SENATOR* HAD AN EASY PASSAGE, ARRIVING OFF THE SHORES OF Nome early in the morning of Thursday, July 19, only eleven days after leaving Seattle. Judge Noyes and his wife stayed on the ship while McKenzie and the others climbed into skiffs to get to land. And there the Noyeses stayed, in their stateroom, for another two nights, leaving the vessel only on Saturday. Perhaps the reason, as Noyes later said, was that Mrs. Noyes was indisposed, and when she started to feel better, the surf was too rough to go in. The likelier explanation was that McKenzie urged the judge to stay behind to delay the opening of the court until papers were drafted for his signature. Noyes knew that Robert Chipps planned to file a lawsuit to take possession of Discovery because they briefly discussed this matter in a conversation aboard the *Senator*. The judge said he "supposed" Chipps would seek the appointment of a receiver in the matter, Chipps later said.

McKenzie came ashore at an especially frenzied moment for the town. In front of the Horseshoe saloon, a small boy with a fire shovel had extracted, from a ditch being dug for the laying of a water main, a mound of ruby-colored dirt that panned out for gold. "Nome's Streets Paved with Gold," the *Nome Daily News* blared on its front page, only partly in jest. The *Nome Gold Digger* reported on its page one that a sourdough arrived from California had proclaimed that the potential of the region was on a par with California in 1849, with gold "in paying quantities" to be found well beyond Cape Nome, along two hundred miles of seacoast extending to the interior for fifty miles or more.

Perhaps this story planted the thought in McKenzie's mind that he might expand his vision of conquest to a larger swatch of the Seward Peninsula. He took a room with District Attorney Wood at the Golden Gate and, wasting no time, proceeded two blocks down the street for a conference at Hubbard, Beeman & Hume.

The firm's offices consisted of three small rooms on the second floor, over a store, of a wobbly building on Second Avenue, parallel with Front Street. Taking command of the meeting, McKenzie asserted himself immediately over Wilson Hume, about whom he had doubts arising from their first meeting back at the Everett in the spring, and over Edwin Beeman, whom he had never met. The boss said he needed both men to sign off on the deal tentatively agreed to by Hubbard: $750,000 in stock in the Alaska Gold Mining Company, shared by the three partners, in return for the firm's interest in jumper claims. With Hubbard quietly looking on, McKenzie told the two that if the firm desired to have its cases heard in the Noyes court, they would take this deal. If they refused, he would crush them. After all, he had devoted time and money to this venture and was not about to see his investment go down the drain.

Hume and Beeman had expected to hear as much and yielded. But there was more: McKenzie said they must make Wood a silent partner in the firm, with a one-quarter interest in its business. The two men felt uneasy about this unanticipated and unorthodox demand, and yet, once again, they agreed. Still the boss wasn't done. Now he placed his two big hands on Hume's knees and demanded for himself a one-quarter interest, same as Wood's, in Hubbard, Beeman & Hume. This was at last too much for Hume and Beeman, and they cried foul. Why should McKenzie get a cut? How could he be given, in effect, a partnership in a law firm when he wasn't even a lawyer? McKenzie intimated that his quarter interest would be held as a consideration for Noyes to keep the judge in line. Hubbard urged the two to accept the arrangement, but they refused, and an hours-long row between McKenzie and the other partners ensued. Finally McKenzie said he would take an answer from the pair in the morning—if they came back to him with a yes, he would make them rich; if not, they might as well get out of Alaska, because there would be nothing for them there.

Beeman and Hume had a lot to think about. Was McKenzie truly the power he said he was? Could he really destroy their ability to operate in Nome? The answer, they reluctantly concluded after sleeping on the matter, was yes. "We were compelled to submit to Mr. McKenzie's plans and accepted whatever he dictated," Hume later testified under oath. He added, "We believed that we were under the wheels of a political machine that would grind us and our clients if we did not acquiesce." Still, while Hume had given way to the more powerful man, he was now a member of the ring, dealt in for a cut of the profits. He understood that McKenzie desired a kind of seamless bonding between the legal apparatus of the new second division court and the law firm, all working for the same objectives, and in this spirit he also agreed, as McKenzie insisted, to serve as the deputy district attorney under Wood, an appointment that Wood now duly made, notifying Washington of his choice in a letter written nearly three weeks later. With his experience as a DA in Oregon, Hume could be of help to the younger man in the job. Still, to be squeezed in this fashion rankled; McKenzie had bound his interest but not, should anything go awry, his loyalty. The pact between the principals was put in writing and locked in a safe.

The boss, caring nothing for Hume's bruised feelings, felt satisfied. Within twenty-four hours of landing in Nome, he had organized his ring, flattened all resistance to his demands, and established himself as the only voice that mattered going forward. The work of the law firm now proceeded feverishly. McKenzie ordered the roundup of every available stenographer in town, demanding haste in the preparation of legal papers that, once completed, could be brought to Judge Noyes. He showed the typists no mercy, working one of them until her fingers were raw, the keys "smeared with blood," as she later recalled, noting that "in these low-ceilinged, cramped rooms, he loomed above everything else like some great animal which paced back and forth in its cage." Nome suited him fine. The muddy streets, the ramshackle housing and squalor, the raft of petty criminals and hustlers—it was not unlike Bismarck in its infancy. Most important to him was the battle for Discovery—the case that the Hubbard firm was assembling of Chipps against Jafet Lindeberg, Erik Lindblom, and John Brynteson, the defendants in the lawsuit about to be filed in the Noyes' court. Other cases also were being prepared, but Discovery was the grand prize, McKenzie declared, the claim worth as much as all the rest of them put together.

On the morning of Saturday, July 21, with this work still in progress, Noyes at last came ashore, accompanied by his wife. A reporter for the *News* caught up with him, "a large man of distinguished appearance and of suave, easy manners." The couple took a room at the Golden Gate, next to the room occupied by McKenzie and Wood. McKenzie parked himself at the Hubbard firm's office and, when not torment-ing the stenographers, cut deals for his company. Two men known to Hubbard came by the office and agreed to McKenzie's offer of $50,000 in shares of Alaska Gold in return for their beachfront claim. Their "property," a strip about a mile in length, was being worked by unin-vited miners with rockers—illegal squatters, in the view of the claims holders—but that was now McKenzie's problem to handle. In a con-versation with the beach "claim" speculator E. M. Walters, who by now had been back in Nome for a month, the boss exuded confidence, explaining that he was about to take charge of Anvil Creek. He offered Walters a job shoveling dirt on Discovery for $5 a day, but Walters, in-sulted, declined, saying the Swedes would pay more for the same hard physical work. McKenzie took no offense; he figured, correctly, that he would have no problem assembling a work crew for "his" mines at the wage he set and not a penny more.

The drafting of the legal documents continued through Sunday and spilled over into Monday. McKenzie remained in the office nearly every hour of every day, frequently inspecting the papers himself. Wood as-sisted his new partners with the work, his district attorney duties put on hold for the more urgent task. McKenzie hoped to cloak his maneu-vers in secrecy, but disguise in Nome was impossible to maintain. A mixture of gossip, rumor, and innuendo, speckled with truth, coursed through the town like muddied water through a sluice box. Sharp eyes and keen ears were everywhere—among the newspaper reporters and editors, the lawyers and merchants, the dance hall girls and the prospectors. Townspeople noticed an unusual sight in Nome: a team of horses, hitched to a wagon, stationed outside the Hubbard firm's office. Horses were difficult to come by in Nome; yet by the afternoon, a second horse-and-wagon team had been added to this first. Something was clearly up, as suggested by the large man, not yet known to Nome as the boss, beating a path between the Golden Gate and the law firm. There was, as yet, no court in session; Noyes was keeping to the hotel. The papers were not finished until nearly six o'clock in the evening. Hume, the designated emissary, hustled over to the Golden Gate, bundle under his arm, and found the judge sitting on the front stoop. It was their first encounter. Noyes suggested they do their business in his bedroom, but finding Mrs. Noyes there, they installed themselves in the adjoining room taken by McKenzie and Wood.

McKenzie, it seemed, had prepped the judge well, for Noyes's first question to Hume was whether the attorney had brought the Chipps case. Hume had. In fact, he had brought five cases: five lawsuits filed by jumpers against claims holders on Anvil Creek, the Hubbard firm representing all the plaintiffs. The "complainants," in the first instance, were asking for the appointment of a receiver for the disputed properties. And there for the judge to review was a draft order for "Alexander McKenzie, of Nome, Alaska" to be made receiver, "hereby authorized and directed to take immediate possession" of the Anvil Creek claims and "to manage, mine, and work the same." As for the defendants, the order barred them "from interfering in any manner whatever with the possession or management of any part of the said property over which said receiver is hereby appointed." The wording was everything McKenzie could have asked for—which, of course, was no surprise, since he had more or less dictated it.

As for McKenzie's obligations as a receiver—as a supposedly neutral protector of disputed assets—the decree instructed him to file with the clerk of the court a "proper bond with sureties" of $5,000 on each of the claims. In plain language, this special type of bond, a standard feature of any receivership, was a guarantee against misconduct by the receiver, for which the receiver ultimately could be held personally liable. Suppose a receiver stripped the assets, worth $10,000, of the property he was supposed to protect and held a surety bond in the same amount. The insurer issuing the bond would have to make good on the loss—but could then seek full reimbursement from the receiver. In this circumstance, though, McKenzie had arranged for his bonds to be worth many times less than the value of the Anvil Creek claims. Discovery alone was producing $10,000 worth of gold in an average day of extraction. Thirty days work at that rate would produce $300,000 in gold. Yet McKenzie's "proper bond with sureties" for the property of $5,000 was just under 2 percent of that total. By this wondrous math, he could make off with 98 percent of the take after reimbursing the issuer of the bond in full to make good on his personal liability. It was not, in fact, his intention to quit Alaska with the gold while Discovery and other properties were in receivership; the plan was to work the mines while the lawsuits were heard by Noyes and to make off with gold only after the plaintiffs won the lawsuits, as he knew they would. Nevertheless, the lowballing of the bonds showed just how thoroughly he had stacked the deck in his own favor.

Surely this pile of papers contained much for the judge to consider—requiring hours of his time, were he to read from top to bottom. An inquisitive mind might have paused, say, over the provision of the orders directing the receiver not only to take possession of but also to work the mines. Why? If the goal of a receivership was to protect the assets, and the assets, as in this case, were buried safely in the ground, unable to take flight on their own, why not just halt work at the site until the legal dispute was calmly adjudicated in court? But Noyes was in no mood for consideration or consultation. When Hume began to read from an affidavit from one of the plaintiffs, the judge told him that was not necessary and asked for the orders pertaining to the receiverships. Hume launched into a testimonial for McKenzie as the right man for the job, and Noyes said that was not necessary either: "he had known Mr. McKenzie a good many years. . . . [H]e thought he was a very good man, a capable man; being a stranger in this country, he would prefer to appoint some person that he was acquainted with." With that, Judge Noyes went back to his bedroom, returned with pen and ink, signed the orders, gave them back to Hume, and told the attorney to move along, their business done.

NOW MCKENZIE HAD IN HAND HIS PRECIOUS ORDERS, THE RIPE FRUIT OF his labors since landing in Nome, stamped with the full authority of Alaska's federal district court, the first act of the new second division, despite this court's never having actually met, despite the target of these orders having no notification of the signed decree, which had been made, in legal parlance, ex parte, without input from the opposing party in a controversy. It was time to move out for the wagon ride to Anvil Creek with his "boys"—a dozen or so men he had assembled and kept on hold, the length of the day, for this very moment. "Just as soon as the judge can sign these papers I will want you; don't go away; just keep in touch with me right here," he had instructed. One fellow, especially desired by McKenzie for the mission, had balked, saying he was about to go to Siberia with a French count for $15 a day, all expenses paid. Never mind about that, McKenzie replied: "I want you, and I will give you $20 a day to stay here. You must stay right here."

At McKenzie's side in the main wagon was the sullen Hume, a reluctant traveler, but from McKenzie's prudential point of view, a necessary confederate, to be implicated by deed in every step of the operation. McKenzie also brought along a deputy federal marshal, his best insurance policy against active resistance. Bob Chipps came too. It promised to be a long evening, with some five miles of boggy tundra ahead to reach Anvil Creek, then visits to claims strung out along the winding creek for another six miles or so. Discovery was the first stop. Ordering the boys to stay put, McKenzie and the marshal walked a few hundred feet to the office and presented the judge's orders. Without incident, possession of the mine was surrendered—but not before, unknown to McKenzie, a crew in the back room quietly opened a vault and spirited away a substantial amount of gold dust. McKenzie had one of his men stay behind to secure the site while the wagons lumbered onward. It was midnight by the time he arrived at Number Ten Above Discovery. Originally the claim of Jo Hahn Tornanses, this was the property that Louis Melsing of Council City had been jailed for trying to jump the year before. Now McKenzie aimed to take the claim—only he was up against its purchaser, Charles Lane, who had a crew of men working it, one shift after another, twenty-four hours a day. On McKenzie's unexpected nocturnal arrival, Lane's lieutenant, Gabe Price, the manager of the site, was asleep, but McKenzie roused him from his bed and showed him the court orders. Price could do nothing but relent. Relieved of his duty, he saddled up his horse and prepared to depart. McKenzie, though, wasn't ready to leave. Number Ten's late-shift workers were seated at a table, busy eating their supper. The boss grabbed a plate and helped himself to the grub, a plate for the marshal too. After a long day of work, he was hungry. Besides, it was his property now—he had the papers to prove it.

Chapter 12

THE LAWYERS RESIST

I T WAS PAST THREE O'CLOCK IN THE MORNING BY THE TIME McKENZIE got back to the Golden Gate Hotel. Sleep in the white nights of the summer could be difficult for any newcomer to Nome, but he managed to desist from his labors for at least a few hours. Even before his return to the hotel, word of a takeover of the Anvil Creek mines had spread throughout the town. Everyone now knew the targets. Besides Discovery and Number Ten Above, these were Number Two Above, held by the Swedish missionary P. H. Anderson; Number Two Below, held by Charles Lane; and Number One on Nakkeli Gulch, a tributary of Anvil Creek named for a Lapp, a claim also now held by Lane. In the excitement and uncertainty of this moment, soldiers were summoned to ride out to the creek and take stock of the situation. Calm was restored only when it was explained that the mines had been taken by a receiver appointed on the official orders of the new judge. "The assignee is Alex. McKenzie, late of North Dakota, formerly of New York," the *Nome Gold Digger* informed its readers. "The gentleman is possessed of excellent executive ability . . . which fit him admirably for the responsible position to which Judge Noyes has appointed him." It was a statement of innocence and hope, shaded by ignorance. The newspaper had not stopped to consider, for one thing, just how unorthodox McKenzie's abrupt appointment was.

Had the new receiver seen this story, along with the *Gold Digger*'s account of the "sweet peace" settling upon Nome, now that "everybody" had reached "a proper understanding of the situation," he might well have guffawed. McKenzie understood that he was in the first phase of what promised to be a difficult campaign. None of his bids for wealth and power in his career had been easily won. Resistance was sure to arrive—and so it did, on the morning after his raid. It came in the form of a gaggle of lawyers making urgent calls on Judge Arthur Noyes in his suite at the Golden Gate. On behalf of their clients, the holders of the claims over which the judge had made McKenzie receiver, the attorneys had many questions. On what basis was a receiver being appointed for these properties? Why hadn't their clients been consulted on these orders or at the least been notified by the court on their signing? Why had the receiver been authorized, directed even, to work the claims? Why had the receiver's bond been set at such a low amount?

The attorneys represented the first wall of resistance to McKenzie's scheme and comprised, in their own right, a formidable group. The lawyers of Gilded Age America were a varied lot, their contrasting types reflected in the Nome bar. Some, like Oliver Hubbard, were out for themselves, with no particular loyalty, as Hubbard would demonstrate, to their clients. They were in Alaska to get rich, quickly. But others, like, for the most part, the lawyers who now knocked on Noyes's door, were of a higher caliber. They worked for clients with deep pockets and expected, of course, to be well compensated for their work. Some made their own personal investments in mining claims. But they were devoted to their clients, and on behalf of their clients they welcomed, relished even, a good fight. Alaska, in their minds, was ground on which to prove their mettle—a test of strength such as might not be faced in the more genteel mainland. In this sense, McKenzie's raid, sanctioned by the new judge, was akin to a call to arms. All of them immediately grasped that they were at the start of the adventure of their legal careers, although they likely didn't suspect that they might have to risk their lives for the mission.

Their ranks included two men familiar with Alaska—experience that gave them an understanding of the warlike methods McKenzie brought to the contest. Kenneth M. Jackson, a Texan, better than six

feet tall, had a background in Texas Democratic politics and arrived
in Alaska as Grover Cleveland's appointee as US commissioner in
Wrangell, on the southern tip of the territory. He heard of the original
discoveries on Anvil Creek, the story went, while presiding over a trial
concerning illicit sales of whiskey. "He immediately fined the defendant $100—the price of a ticket to Nome—sent his resignation to the
Department of Injustice, as they call it up in Alaska, and left for the
North." Jackson, who liked to go by "Judge," arrived in Cape Nome
early in the summer of 1899, possibly the first lawyer to set foot in
the district. The jumping mania was in full swing, and he developed a
practice, his retainer paid in gold dust, among the Scandinavians who
found their claims repeatedly pounced on. His client in the battle with
McKenzie was the missionary P. H. Anderson of Number Two Above
Discovery. Also well acquainted with Alaska was the second of these
attorneys to go by "Judge": Charles Sumner Johnson, the Nebraskan
appointed to the bench by McKinley, who had made a stop in Nome
to hear cases in August 1899. Now he was in private practice in Nome,
and his client in this struggle was the Pioneer Mining Company, the
holding for Discovery and other properties of Jafet Lindeberg, Erik
Lindblom, and John Brynteson. Pioneer, presided over by Lindeberg,
had become one of the wealthiest and most powerful corporate interests in Nome and was determined to counter any threat to its claims
from any quarter.

In addition to Jackson and Johnson, the lawyers included a pair
of newcomers to Alaska who possessed the finest legal brains of the
quartet. Samuel Knight, thirty-seven years old, was raised in the San
Francisco area and went east for college at Yale and law school at Columbia; on graduation he stayed in New York to join one of America's premier law firms, Evarts, Choate & Beaman, whose most famous
partner was Joseph Hodges Choate, known for his role in helping to
break up the ring of Boss Tweed, chief of the Democratic machine
that ran Tammany Hall. Knight had returned to California for health
reasons and worked his way up to the position of district attorney for
the Northern District of California. He arrived in Nome the day before

McKenzie landed and might have seemed ill-suited for the Alaska assignment, but he proved tenacious in his duties, so much so that the McKenzie camp came to detest him and tried at one point to have him locked up on spurious charges. Knight was the chief attorney for Wild Goose Mining & Trading, the holding company for Charles Lane's Alaska mining operations.

Of all the attorneys to confront the McKenzie combine, though, the most formidable was William H. Metson, the chief attorney for Pioneer Mining, who seemed to regard the seizure of Discovery as a personal affront. Metson arrived in Nome just before Knight and took an office above the El Dorado saloon. Thirty-six years old and a graduate of the Hastings Law School in San Francisco, Metson grew up in Virginia City, Nevada, a mining town created following the discovery of the Comstock silver lode. He had an encyclopedic knowledge of mining law, and his round, rimless spectacles suggested bookishness. But that look was undermined by a handlebar mustache with a hint of danger. He was aggressive and fearless, no stranger to a pistol. "I had been raised on the frontier, where we were taught never to entrench on anybody's rights and at the same time allow no man to entrench on ours," he once explained. Perhaps because of his upbringing, he possessed an instinctive understanding of men like McKenzie, and as he was to prove on several occasions, he was not in the least intimidated by them. He couldn't help but feel a certain admiration for the boss's daring, although that sentiment did not dampen his fighting spirit. The boss, in turn, paid him a grudging respect, one frontiersman to another.

KNIGHT WAS THE FIRST TO CALL ON NOYES AT THE GOLDEN GATE ON THE day after the raid. Noyes, possibly hungover, was irritated by the intrusion and even more annoyed when Metson showed up with ex-judge Johnson. All these attorneys, so far as he was concerned, were in cahoots, a combined force sure to make his life unhappy. In a sense he was right, because the attorneys grasped from the start that their strength lay in unity. It was Noyes's nature, in any case, to feel oppressed by circumstances, even those of his own making. In his mind, the orders appointing the receivers were not subject to challenge. The point was to have the lawsuits heard—then the attorneys could have their say. His plan, he now told them, was to depart Nome for Saint Michael, the official seat of the second division, and formally open his main court there. Until his return to Nome, where he would keep a branch court, the lawyers would have to wait.

But the lawyers persisted, asking the questions about his hasty departure that any decent attorney would pose. Knight requested a hearing before the judge, that day, on a motion for the court to set aside the order appointing the receiver. Too soon, Noyes said. Not in the least, Knight retorted, saying he planned to serve notice on the opposing counsel at Hubbard, Beeman & Hume for a court hearing at three in the afternoon. Knight had found, on this very first encounter with Noyes, the judge's weak spot: his desire to avoid, if at all possible, confrontation or really any form of unpleasantness. Noyes relented. They would convene at three.

THE HEARING UNEVENTFULLY HELD, NOYES SAID HE WOULD RENDER HIS decision on the defense motion to set aside the receiver's appointment on his return from Saint Michael. Until then, he ruled, the orders stayed in place. McKenzie didn't attend the proceeding. He had his own plans, which focused on Discovery. His men intended to confiscate everything at the site, not only the scales Pioneer Mining used to weigh gold dust and the company's business ledgers but also the personal property of the men hired to work the mine, down to their tents, clothing, and food. The operation was underway even while the attorneys were arguing the motion before Noyes in town. On learning of the seizure, an outraged Metson stomped over to the Golden Gate and demanded that Noyes, at a bare minimum, allow Pioneer's men to stay in their tents and keep their personal effects. The judge wilted and so directed.

And then Noyes thought better of it. Or, more likely, McKenzie, on learning of Noyes's on-the-spot concession, modest as it was, insisted it be taken back. Appeasement was in the style of the judge, not of the boss. Especially at the outset of a campaign, McKenzie believed in meeting resistance with an even greater display of force. The day after the hearing, Noyes readied a new set of orders on Discovery, clarifying his original directions to the receiver. On hearing that the judge planned to make the new orders even stricter than the original ones, Metson once again sped to the Golden Gate and tried to reason with him, this time meeting with a stiffer reception. "Your people are preventing the receiver from working the Discovery claim," the judge told him. "I am going to tie your people up all around. I am going to make an order which will take everything away from them." So Metson later testified—an account that Noyes, in his own testimony, did not challenge.

Metson was furious. He had the impression that someone was blackening his name with the judge. In their testy conversation, just concluded, Noyes had referred to McKenzie as an "old friend" and "a man of integrity, a man who had been used to handling large properties" (a reference to McKenzie's experience as a receiver for Northern Pacific). The judge also had advised Metson to see McKenzie about the Discovery receivership—a suggestion that baffled Metson since, as he told Noyes, he had "no business with Mr. McKenzie." But as he was making his way down the staircase leading out of the hotel, he came across McKenzie by chance. The sight of the large man at the bottom of the well might have given anyone pause, but Metson plunged right in: Have you been talking against me with the judge? McKenzie parried the question with one of his own: Are you interfering with my takeover of Discovery? Metson angrily denied the accusation that he was, in effect, defying the will of the court. He straightened out the matter in a telephone call to the mine from Pioneer's office in town on a dedicated line connecting the two points. Cooperate fully with the receiver, he told the mine's foreman, with McKenzie listening on. The confrontation ended peacefully, entirely on McKenzie's terms. Metson's blood was up, but he stayed his temper.

The judge's "Order Enlarging the Powers of Receiver," issued on July 25, one day after the hearing, directed McKenzie to "take possession of all sluice boxes, pumps, excavations, machinery, pipe, plant, boarding houses, tents, buildings, safes, scales, and all personal property fixed and movable, gold, gold dust, and precious metals, money boxes or coin, and all personal property upon said claim." In short, whatever McKenzie's boys had not already snatched at Discovery, the court ordered them to take. And so they did. It was a comprehensive defeat for Metson and the client he was battling to protect. McKenzie stood triumphant, with Discovery as a first stark example of his reign and its tenor. As for Noyes, his immediate business accomplished, he departed with relief for the more tranquil setting of Saint Michael, not to return to Nome until the following week. Ever attentive to his press clippings, he must have felt pleased by an editorial in the *Nome Daily News* on the eve of his departure, calling him "a broad-minded, cultured man, a product of the boundless west" with the good sense to bring with him to Alaska "a corps of competent and courteous officials."

Chapter 13

"CLEAN MONEY"

IN ADVISING PIONEER'S FOREMAN AT DISCOVERY TO COOPERATE WITH McKenzie, Metson was bowing to the tactical necessity of the moment, but it was really for his client, Pioneer Mining, to determine how to deal with the assault on the property. The same held for Charles Lane, with three of his claims captured by the receiver, and for P. H. Anderson. After all, they were the owners; the lawyers operated at their direction. But a clear course of action was hard to see. The question, difficult to answer in the first days of the conflict, was exactly what they were up against. Why was the new judge coming down so hard on them? And why did Noyes seem to be deferring to McKenzie? The court's orders appointing the boss as receiver made no mention of his other position, as president of the Alaska Gold Mining Company, with interests in the properties now assigned to him. Nor were the Hubbard law firm and plaintiffs like Robert Chipps understood at this time to be part of a larger campaign, of which the lawsuits were just an opening salvo.

At bottom, the question for the owners was whether they had a chance of a favorable outcome in the legal proceeding in which they now found themselves immersed or whether the court was simply fixed against them. If the latter, one option was, literally, a counterattack—an attempt to recapture their properties by force of arms. P. H. Anderson, a Christian missionary and educator, was not the man to organize this sort of operation. But Pioneer Mining and Charles Lane's Wild Goose, especially if they joined hands, as was in their interest, almost certainly could come at McKenzie with more than he could handle. Both companies had teams of hired hands at their call, the men the boss had just unceremoniously booted out of their camps, and while not trained militia, these men all knew how to handle guns. McKenzie was unfamiliar with the Anvil Creek terrain and had only just started to put together crews to work his receiverships. Their loyalty could not be assured; in the event of an attack, there was a decent chance that they would simply take flight at the first sight of a muzzle. All the elements of battle seemed to favor the forces backing the original claimants.

All the elements, that is, except one. The owners could not be sure that the US Army would take their side. The 7th Infantry now had a barracks in town, its base camp for Companies A and K three miles east of town by the Nome River. McKenzie, if overrun, might demand an intervention by the troops, which his compliant judge would probably approve. Was the 7th Infantry likely to resist a plea by a federal court? Were the owners prepared to take on the army? McKenzie had calculated well in formulating his play—he understood that he could use the protection of the court as a shield to block resistance, whatever form it took. That was his trump card.

As the boss assessed the opposition, he was apt to dismiss as a threat not only P. H. Anderson but also the Discovery owners. McKenzie shared the widespread prejudice that Scandinavian newcomers to America were more or less peasants, meek by disposition and unable to think and act for themselves. His Nome raiding party included no Scandinavians, except for the court clerk, whom neither he nor Noyes had asked for. He tended to lump all people from this region of northern Europe together as Swedes, "Give me a barnyard of Swedes and I'll drive them like sheep," the boss was once heard to say. But in the battle he now waged, this attitude would cost him, for "the Swedes" were not so easily driven. In particular, Pioneer's president, Jafet Lindeberg, the acknowledged leader of the trio who claimed Discovery, was a formidable presence. At the age of twenty-six, three years after leaving his native Norway to join the reindeer expedition to Alaska, he cut a figure that would have astonished family and friends back home, who knew him as a plain lumberman. Jafet was now far from the somewhat naive figure who first walked the settlement that became known as Nome. He was usually seen not in muddy miner's boots but in polished leather shoes, a tailored business suit, a white-collared shirt and a tie. He operated out of Pioneer's office in town, not out in the tundra with his workers. Flush with success, he was stockier, and he was sometimes seen in the gambling parlors. One witness reported he had lost $12,000 at the roulette wheel in a single night—a sum worth nearly $400,000 in 2020 dollars. Discovery had made him rich, but he wanted to be richer. He was building a mini empire of his own in Alaska, showing that he too possessed predatory instincts characteristic of the Gilded Age. He was a shareholder in the Nome Mining and Development Company, the company that, in the previous year, had posted notices warning miners that anyone working the beach without a permit would be prosecuted for trespass and larceny. He also was starting to develop a reputation outside Alaska. On a trip to the Great Lakes area after the mining season of 1899, fellow Scandinavians greeted him with awe for his achievement in Cape Nome. Far better than McKenzie appreciated, Lindeberg understood the business arena as a theater of political and legal combat, and this understanding showed, too, in his choice of the bulldog Metson as Pioneer Mining's lead attorney. If Lindeberg lost this fight, it would not be for a lack of aggression on his part. He would not hesitate to evict McKenzie from Discovery by armed force if he thought he could get away with it.

It was unusual for the boss to underestimate any foe, and he did not make that mistake with Charles Lane. The two had already clashed once in Washington in the battle over the Hansbrough amendment, when Lane took his objections directly to the leader of the opposition in the Senate. McKenzie had lost that round. Although he did not know Lane personally, he had an ingrained respect for any adversary of Lane's stamp, a self-made man of political influence and substantial wealth. The tribute, though, was not returned, for while Lane could appreciate a tough, frontier-bred man with quick wits and proven survival skills, he had a typical miner's disdain for those who operated through maneuvers like a stacking of the legal deck. He had never used lawsuits as a business tactic to win a prize. For the likes of McKenzie, he had nothing but contempt.

McKenzie's surprise raid on Anvil Creek put Lane's entire Alaska mining foray at dire risk. Wild Goose Mining & Trading, his holding for his Seward Peninsula claims, was nothing like McKenzie's flimsily constructed and murkily backed Alaska Gold Mining Company. Its success did not depend on shares distributed "where they will do the most good." Wild Goose had true shareholders actively financing the company's activities in return for real stock certificates. Lane had his own money in the stock, the initial subscription equaling $1 million, joined by investor friends in San Francisco and Baltimore. If McKenzie succeeded with his plans, Wild Goose shareholders stood to lose their capital—including the $300,000 already paid to acquire dozens of claims in the Cape Nome district originally held by Lapps and others. With his eldest son, Tom, operating as his right-hand man, Lane was laying track for a five-mile railroad linking the town of Nome by the Snake River sand spit with the Anvil Creek area for the transport of passengers, lumber, coal, and other freight. That alone was a $60,000 project. He had bought a freight steamer, the *Irrawady*, for his exclusive use in ferrying supplies and employees from San Francisco to Nome, and a passenger steamer, the *Oregon*, for general use in bringing people to Nome. And he was in the early stages of building a plant, at a cost of $150,000, for pumping water from the Snake River to a height of seven hundred feet up Anvil Mountain. The machinery was on order from Chicago, along with four miles of eighteen-inch pipe from San Francisco. Once completed, he had promised, the plant would make plentiful water available to all claims holders in high mining ground along Anvil, Dexter, and other creeks in the district, not just to his own properties. To serve lower-ground claims, he planned to install a system of six or seven pumps placed on barges. But how could he proceed faced by a court seemingly in the grasp of a political boss and apparently bent on confiscating his prime mining assets?

Yet Lane had something important on McKenzie that the boss could never take from him—a base of support among the plain miners in Alaska—and that came to matter as the fight between them heated up. Lane was not, like McKenzie and so many of the country's rich businessmen, a McKinley Republican. He subscribed to populism, the creed of his father, a Jacksonian Democrat. His allegiance was with his friend William Jennings Bryan, and notwithstanding his reverence for gold, he even supported "free silver," a plank of the populists, so despised by the hard-money men who dominated the Republican Party. "Lucky Lane," these miners largely believed, was one of the few men of wealth and power who in their experience did not seem bent on muscling out the little guy. Lane, notably, had no designs on the beach—unlike McKenzie or Lindeberg. "The money he has made has been clean money," a Nome contemporary wrote admiringly. "It was not filched from one class of people to enrich another class. It was drawn from the bosom of Mother Earth."

With his stature, his resources, and the breadth of his experience in the mining business, Lane was the natural leader of the claims holders targeted by the Noyes court. While not an especially patient man, he felt that under the circumstances of McKenzie's raid, with so much unknown, there was no need for hasty action. Time should be allowed for matters to play out in court; the option of retaking the mines by force remained a live one—but before attempting such a maneuver, his side would need to consult the army and cultivate its support. In the meantime, Lane decided, McKenzie could have a go at working the mines in receivership on Anvil Creek. There was an old miner's wisdom in this seemingly passive attitude. The boss was a master at manipulating the political system and the courts, but he did not know the first thing about mining. It was a lot more complicated than it looked. As valuable as the Anvil Creek claims were, they required, as

Lane well knew, a reliable supply of water for sluicing the mounds and mounds of gravel and dirt from which gold could be extracted. In the absence of a pumping plant, a generous amount of rain would suffice. But sadly for the boss, no rain fell, as a parched Cape Nome slipped into drought conditions, the tundra flowers withering. Not even Big Alex could control the weather.

Chapter 14

THE BATTLE OF THE BEACH

MORE PROOF OF McKENZIE'S MINING INEXPERIENCE CAME WITH THE first effort at working the beach with the equipment he had spent so much time and money acquiring and having shipped from the mainland. "Captain" Mike McCormack, in charge of the project, had the machinery taken to a section of Cape Nome beach initially claimed by a speculator and now transferred to the Alaska Gold Mining Company in return for stock. But McCormack's engineers could not get the machinery, a system of pumps meant to force the slurry of ocean water and sands through sluices, to work. Ordinary miners, more efficiently capturing the tiny gold flakes with primitive rockers, had a good laugh at the expense of the McKenzie team. McCormack pondered on a better spot for the equipment, if it could be used at all.

This stumble, though, did not diminish the boss's appetite for the beach. He must have known this was a sensitive issue—how the effort the year before by beachfront claims holders to use the army to round up "trespassers" had backfired and stoked stiff resistance. Still, he had no patience for anyone "squatting" on what he regarded as company turf. "I want you to go up and clear that beach off—those beachcombers off the property," he ordered a man from whom he had acquired a claim in exchange for stock. Senator Carter's relation, Jimmie Galen, assisted in the strongman efforts, but Alaska Gold stockholder E. M. Walters refused to participate. "I felt," he later said, "that the beach was open to everybody to a certain extent. I thought there was enough men doing dirty work without my starting in on it."

As the "dirty work" continued, it became an organized team effort, the team in this instance made up of the boss, Galen, McKenzie's young family friend District Attorney Wood, and a fourth man, Reuben Stevens. Stevens had been a member of the party that arrived in Nome on the *Senator*, and his role in the scheme was not immediately clear to the others in the group. The mystery would soon be dispelled. Before Noyes left for Saint Michael, McKenzie had him appoint Stevens as US commissioner for the Nome district, a kind of justice of the peace position that would give Stevens the authority to rule on a variety of legal matters, typically routine, such as charges of petty crime and disputes over wills and trusts. Though hardly routine, one of those matters, McKenzie and Stevens determined, was the status of the beach as a mining ground. Such an important question probably belonged to the district court or even to Congress, which had debated the beach question, without resolution, in its consideration of the Alaska code. But such points of jurisdiction were of no concern to the boss. It was time for new rules.

Unlike Noyes, Stevens slipped into Nome without fanfare. Nobody knew who he was, at first, and that was just as he liked it. He moved with his family into a house on Steadman Avenue, just up from Front Street, using the front room for his court, living in the back room, and billing—in fact, as later came to light, overbilling by a considerable amount—his new employer, the US government, for all expenses, personal and private. James Wickersham, who came to know Stevens in Alaska, thought of him as "so crooked that his blood only circulates once a year," an expression used in mining camps to describe unsavory types.

Stevens, though, was no mere grifter. He was clever and cunning and had patience for the long game, the qualities that had drawn McKenzie to him years before and made him such a valuable resource in Alaska. Stevens had come west with his family at an early age, studied law in Illinois, set up a practice in the Dakotas, served for a few years as editor of the *Bismarck Tribune*, and performed a stint in Washington, DC, as an assistant attorney in the Department of Justice, working on Indian affairs. He also had been elected to the legislature in Bismarck in North Dakota's early days as a state. An episode from that time offered a telling illustration of Stevens's wiles. At the behest of a dubious private company from outside the state that aimed to operate a lottery in North Dakota, the McKenzie team undertook to get the legislature to approve a bill authorizing one. The governor, opposed to the initiative, hired the Pinkerton Detective Agency to look into talk that the McKenzie camp was promising cash to lawmakers in exchange for their votes. A Pinkerton man went undercover and confirmed that this was being done by a "boodle gang," "boodle" being slang for money or goods acquired illicitly or put to illicit use, like bribery. Stevens, whom the detective encountered "drinking very hard" at a bar frequented by political types, was identified as an integral part of this crew. McKenzie's lieutenant had not only the guile to arrange bribes to grease the lottery bill, the agent found, but also the brass to demand cash for his own vote as an elected member of the assembly. As both distributor and recipient of boodle, he was "the worst boodler of them all," the detective told the governor.

Such was the man McKenzie had recruited to come to Alaska on behalf of the Nome scheme. The installation of Stevens as commissioner completed the circuit. To set matters in motion, Jimmie Galen would identify a "trespasser" working on a portion of beach targeted by Alaska Gold and swear out a complaint for arrest. Next, District Attorney Wood, also part of this operation, would have the "violator" taken into custody and brought before Stevens for disposition of the case. Precisely this happened to civil and mining engineer J. C. Barton, hailing from the Dakotas, who was arrested on July 29 while enjoying his Sunday dinner in a Nome restaurant. He was taken to see Commissioner Stevens, who told him he had no chance of winning his case but that Wood would dismiss the arrest warrant so long as

Barton wrote a note promising to desist from taking gold from Alaska Gold's property. Stevens added a sweetener: "You had better see Aleck McKenzie in regard to this; he might make some arrangements with you by which you can work it." The next day, Barton sought out the boss and produced a letter, signed by US Senator R. F. Pettigrew of South Dakota, vouching for Barton's skills as an engineer. "If I had known who it was, I would never have bothered you," McKenzie told him, "but it is too late now; we have started these arrests against these people to keep them off the beach, as we have bought that property, and are going to have it." He offered Barton instead the consolation of work on one of his receiverships.

The crackdown, though, was only a prelude to the main event: a full-scale assault by the Stevens court would follow on July 31. Miner Frank Sieger was brought before Stevens, arrested on a complaint of beach trespassing. But instead of dismissing the complaint, as he had done for Barton, Stevens invoked the Sieger prosecution as the basis for a sweeping ruling applying to all beach miners. He decreed that the beach above the ordinary high-tide line was not a commons, on which staking was prohibited, but the same as any other piece of mining ground. Noyes, still away from Nome in Saint Michael, probably would have been incapable of this ruling, because it displayed careful preparation and thought, even a mastery of the complicated issue at hand. Stevens had done his homework, immersing himself in the legislative debate in Congress, applicable government regulations and case law, and the federal criminal code. The crux of his decision concerned the sixty-foot-wide strip above the mean high-tide mark, the strip that the beach miners had always maintained was a reserved public space, in accordance with US law governing seacoasts. Wrong, the new commissioner ruled—this law did not apply to Alaskan mineral lands. What was thought to be public land in fact was private.

Following this reasoning, Stevens found that Sieger, the defendant before his court, would have to stand trial on charges brought by the prosecution of violating a legitimate claim. Under the federal criminal code, the defendant could be deemed a thief, "with intent to commit a felony," subject to a prison sentence of not less than one year or more than five, a fine of not more than $1,000, or both. This was extraordinarily harsh punishment, much more severe than any contemplated for "trespassers" in the past.

And who possessed the claim that miner Sieger could be sent to the penitentiary for violating? Stevens identified the property as the Ophier Beach Claim, held by S. R. Calvin and George W. Beardsley. He neglected to mention that Calvin was actively helping McKenzie to manage the Anvil Creek claims worked by McKenzie as receiver— he had accompanied McKenzie on the nighttime wagon ride to seize those mines—and that both Calvin and Beardsley had sold beach claims to the Alaska Gold Mining Company in return for shares. These connections showed that McKenzie was the true power behind Stevens's ruling—although the hand of the boss remained hidden for the time being.

All shareholders in Alaska Gold stood to gain from the ruling, since the company's beach claims, deemed valid and enforceable with the commons wiped out of legal existence, were immediately worth more. And that was true even for claims not being actively worked. In an offering of shares to the public by the company, after all, Wall Street would value Alaska Gold on the basis of not only how much gold already had been extracted from its various properties but also how much gold potentially could be taken. Beach sands yet to be mined were of established worth, akin to the proven but untapped reserves of a petroleum company. Such was the power of a court, as McKenzie shrewdly understood, to enrich private interest.

"BEACH LAND NOT FREE," THE *NOME GOLD DIGGER* DECLARED IN a front-page headline, its story printing Stevens's decision in full. As could be expected, the ruling shocked and infuriated the beach miners. At this point in the season, a good number of the fortune seekers, not knowing the first thing about mining and finding the work and the crowded and unsanitary conditions of Nome not to their liking, had left Alaska on a steamer headed back to the outside. Still, thousands of miners, encamped in their tents, were avidly working a fertile stretch of beach running from the town some thirty miles west to Cape Rodney. In some spots, very fine-grained gold could be found in deposits in a band as wide as one hundred feet. Those willing to put in the hours stood to make a lot of money.

The miners sensed that a fix was in—a decision like this could not come from nowhere. And the ruling, if enforced, was devastating: Stevens's action, as the *Nome Daily News* noted, "meant the practical closing down" of the beach as a commons from Nome to Cape Rodney, since virtually all of that terrain had been staked and recorded as private claims. On the day after the ruling, the word went out for a mass meeting by the sand spit on the west side of the Snake to decide on a response. Some five hundred "diggers" showed up. Someone had to start. H. T. Jones, known around Nome as "Deep Creek," climbed into a boat stranded on the sands and stood in the bow, the assemblage gathered around him, reporters for the papers there too. The main thing was that the miners had to stand together, Jones began; their strength lay in their numbers. Resistance by the lone individual was useless, and violence was not an answer. The miners, he urged, needed to form an organization to protect themselves against "grasping corporations," to prevent the "poor laboring man from being arrested by the military and dragged to court as a common felon." Alaska was part of America, he noted; the miners enjoyed the same rights as all Americans, and to act on these rights was not "anarchistic in any respect." This was a careful phrasing, perhaps intended especially for the reporters: the anarchist movement, largely imported from Europe, its most militant members advocating violence against capitalists, had gained many followers in America. The business class was intent on smearing labor "upstarts" as anarchist bomb makers, in the mold of the anarchists convicted for their involvement in the infamous incident at Haymarket Square in Chicago in 1886, when a bomb tossed at police trying to break up a labor demonstration killed seven officers and several others. Nor, Jones took equal care to say, did the miners have any intention of raising the "red flag"—the popularly understood symbol of an uprising of the working class, that banner displayed by the revolutionaries of the Paris Commune in 1871.

It was a speech steeped not in gunpowder anarchism or "nothing to lose but your chains" communism but in the reigning populist sentiments of America's Democratic Party. Probably Jones had given an address like this before, as he was active in Democratic circles back in the state of Washington. His remarks went over well—collective action and a new organization it was to be, then, with Jones unanimously elected as chairman and a committee tasked with crafting a resolution, for submission to the assemblage, setting forth the reason for the formation of the group and its objectives. The meeting broke up with an agreement to reconvene in the evening.

Feelings were raw over Stevens's ruling. Some miners must have been tempted to wreck the expensive machinery the corporations were hauling in to work the beach sands. A sledgehammer could do a lot of damage with a few powerful swings. But no destruction of property was reported. A few hours after the gathering on the spit, the miners filed into the Theatre Comique in town and took their seats on the wooden benches. A draft resolution, starting with a statement of grievances, was read out loud:

> Whereas, There are more than five thousand American citizens mining on the beach in this district, who have come here from a distance of 3,000 to 5,000 miles to earn an honest livelihood at honest toil, and believing that the beach was and is open and free to all, and believing and knowing that the said beach is . . . held in trust by the federal government for all the people of this territory, and is not subject to entry or patent, and
>
> Whereas, We are law-abiding citizens of the United States, and are conscious of violating no law, nor do we desire or intend to do so . . . and now, in mass meeting assembled, assert and claim the right as American citizens to explore and mine the said lands without the interference of any man or corporation, and

Whereas, The strong arm of the criminal law has been and is being evoked and used against us, and many of us have been summarily arrested as common criminals and deprived of our rights as Americans.

This, then, was the complaint. As for the miners' response, the speaker continued,

Resolved, That we unqualifiedly condemn the action of the men and corporations in using and enforcing the criminal law to oppress and deprive us of our liberty and rights as Americans. . . .

Resolved, That it is the sense of this meeting that the miners of Nome here and now organize for the purpose of protecting our rights, as we believe them to be, and preserving them in the courts, and we here and now pledge ourselves one with the other to the mutual assistance necessary to secure and protect those rights.

The resolution passed unanimously. The miners had spoken as one and done so eloquently, clearly marking themselves not as dangerous subversives but as loyal Americans. In fact, they were not all US citizens; Canadians, for example, easily could reach Nome on steamers out of Vancouver. Yet Nome was an overwhelmingly American place, the town now alive with patriotic tunes played on the fife and drum. "Come up and enlist boys," a military recruiter bellowed from his spot in front of the Horseshoe saloon. "Let's show Uncle Sam and the people outside that the people of Nome are all right." Some five hundred men stepped up in a single day, proof that Nome's miners were as eager to fight for their country as for their right to take gold from the beach.

Of course, many miners could not help but feel dejected as corporate claims holders, backed by law enforcement authorities, swooped down upon them in the wake of Stevens's ruling. "Well, here we are tied up on the golden beaches of Alaska," Will McDaniel wrote to his family back in San Jose, California, on the day after the gathering at the Comique. Will and his brother Ed had been prospecting in Nome since their arrival in mid-June, surviving on fried rice, biscuits with syrup, and coffee. "We had papers served on us this morning prohibiting us from working, moving our plant or sluice boxes," he now explained. "Everything on the beach is a great mix-up. There have been a lot of arrests made. . . . It's a shame and outrage that the thing has gone as it has."

THE NEWS RAN THE FULL TEXT OF THE RESOLUTION APPROVED BY THE miners, the story bearing the headline "Condemning Men and Corporations for Invoking the Arm of the Criminal Law." Possibly McKenzie was surprised by the depth of resistance to Stevens's ruling and generally by the tenor of feeling among the miners. Since arriving in Nome, he had stayed away from the tent city and from the saloons and gambling parlors and other spots frequented by prospectors. He typically breakfasted alone, at the Golden Gate, a short walk from the office suite he took on Steadman. He reserved his social time, in moments to spare, for a tiny few, invited to partake of the port he kept at the office. Stevens and the boss, maybe over a glass or two of the wine, perhaps with the company of Wood, now armed with a legal mandate to prosecute "beachcombers,"' may have had a chuckle over the miners' earnest determination to secure their rights "in the courts," as the resolution declared. The commissioner's ruling indeed was subject to appeal by the miners—to Judge Arthur Noyes.

Chapter 15

"WE SLEEP WITH OUR REVOLVERS"

ON AUGUST 2, TWO DAYS AFTER STEVENS MADE HIS RULING ON THE
beach, Noyes, now returned from Saint Michael, sat for opening arguments in the matter of the lawsuit by Chipps alleging
that Jafet Lindeberg, Erik Lindblom, and John Brynteson held an invalid claim to the Discovery property on Anvil Creek. His makeshift
court—a small room in the middle of a cramped suite of offices in a
building at the corner of Steadman and First Avenues—overflowed
with attorneys as well as reporters for the newspapers, the crowd spilling over into the clerk's quarters. Metson, on behalf of Lindeberg and
the other two Pioneer partners, begged Noyes to "vacate"—wipe out
altogether—the judge's original orders appointing McKenzie to take
charge of Discovery. There was no need for a receiver, he said, and
moreover, as the gold was as safe in the ground as out of it, if the defendants were not to be allowed to work the property while the lawsuit
was heard, nobody else should be able to either, including any receiver.
Wilson Hume, representing Chipps, responded that a receiver was a
necessary protection for his client. And more than that, Hume said,
"Every penny that has come out of that claim is as much ours as theirs
until this contest is decided." Whether intentionally or just clumsily,
Chipps's legal team misrepresented the facts in asserting that all three
of the Pioneer partners were aliens at the time the claim was staked.
That was only true of Lindeberg.

The arguments heard, Noyes made no immediate ruling on Metson's
motion to vacate—nor did he make a decision following the arguments

on the other four Anvil claims in receivership. When might he rule? No one could say. The delay suited the boss, since it meant he could continue to work the Anvil properties without interruption. Even with the continuing shortfall of rain, his crews still were extracting daily quantities of gold from the Anvil mines, the sacks first brought to the safe kept at the Discovery site and then taken to McKenzie's office in town and deposited by him, the sole keyholder, into boxes he rented at the nearby Alaska Banking & Safe Deposit Co. The pokes were piling up there, the gold to be kept in McKenzie's custody, according to the order making him receiver, until the litigation was resolved. A shareholder in Alaska Gold asked Oliver Hubbard what was to become of this treasure. Not to worry, the attorney said, "it will be turned in to the company for the benefit of the company"—once the jumpers won their cases. And would the jumpers win their cases? It was "a cinch," Hubbard replied.

With the Anvil Creek gold accumulating and the beach in his grasp, McKenzie might have found reason to pause. But that was not his nature. With no more than three months left to the mining season, he intended to make the most of the remaining time to enlarge his holdings. With this goal in mind, the Hubbard firm held a meeting for the clients—the jumpers—it had agreed to represent in litigation in return for an interest in their claims. The lawyers explained that they had signed their interest in the claims over to the corporation known as the Alaska Gold Mining Company in return for a promise of shares, and they encouraged their clients to do the same. The company was well capitalized, Hubbard said, and the man at the top, Mr. McKenzie, was wealthy and influential with a good record in business.

Many of the jumpers found this offer tempting. Chipps, after all, had deeded his Discovery claim to Alaska Gold and was a director in the company. Did that not show proof of the enterprise's good standing? Among those considering the proposition was Kirke Requa. It had been a year since she had filed claims on Number Eight on Dexter Creek and Number Four Below Discovery on Anvil Creek—and nearly a year since the Hubbard firm had agreed to represent her. Yet nothing had happened since then. She had been unable to attend the client meeting called by the firm, but now Hubbard explained the situation in a private conversation. Shares in Alaska Gold, he told her, represented her best chance of seeing money on her claims. With other jumpers already in, the company had amassed some two hundred claims either already in litigation or headed for the courts. He boasted, too, of the company's substantial claims on beachfront property, with machinery for working the sands. Requa asked who was behind the company—behind McKenzie as president—and Hubbard, she later testified, answered, "Many rich and influential men," including Senators Carter and Hansbrough. Requa didn't say yes right away; she did some due diligence and found that the mining equipment was there on a four-mile stretch of beach, just as Hubbard said. And so she took the deal they worked out for her two claims, a pledge of stock shares along with a promise of $2,000 in cash. "I had confidence in the whole thing." Soon afterward, Hubbard introduced her to McKenzie during a chance encounter in the offices of the law firm. "This is the little lady that walked seven hundred miles" across Alaska, Hubbard told the boss. "Yes? I expected to see a woman three times her size," McKenzie replied—and, ignoring his new shareholder, turned his attention to another matter.

With Requa's claims signed over to Alaska Gold, though she had yet to receive her promised money, "her" properties went into receivership, by order of the court, with McKenzie as the receiver. Only now she was no longer, in the eyes of many of her fellow miners, the plucky "little lady" with an amazing story to tell. The word was out: the receiver and the judge were working in combination somehow, and to anyone who had had any contact with these two, it seemed obvious that the receiver was the dominant member of the pair. Many now cursed McKenzie's name, and any jumper who had gone in with him became an object of derision, treated like "a villain," as Requa found to her dismay. Since its best claims were frozen in receivership, Lane's Wild Goose Mining & Trading announced a suspension of all its mining operations in the district for the rest of the season and laid off more than thirty workers.

Lane's vision for the development of Cape Nome remained intact and was partially completed, with the Wild Goose Railroad now open for business, ferrying freight and also passengers, for $1 each way, between the depot on the sand spit in town and Anvil Creek. Lane also had his team actively exploring for gold deeper in the Alaskan interior—out of the reach, he could hope, of the receiver. But his pressing need was to deal with the legal assault on his holdings—and recover the gold actively being extracted from his Anvil properties and deposited in McKenzie's boxes at the bank. So far as Lane was concerned, that was stolen property. Could anyone feel sure that the receiver was not spiriting some of the gold out of Alaska? While Lane stayed his hand on an effort to recapture his property by force, he was not afraid to show his feelings to the boss's face. When they crossed paths one day outside the post office, Lane gave McKenzie a tongue-lashing. The incident might have escalated into a physical altercation—and perhaps gunplay—had not friends of each man intervened.

The threat of arrest and prosecution simply for taking a rocker to some promising-looking spot on the beach, the dry conditions crimping the haul from tundra claims, the ever expanding reach of the receiver—these conditions stoked a growing sense of frustration in the tent city along the shoreline and in the streets of town. The great majority of the thousands who had come to Alaska from distant points on the American mainland simply wanted to put their energies to productive use. Yet the possibilities for plunder in Nome had also attracted a criminal element, and as the mining season progressed, this element flourished and became a more active threat to the community. "Men up here are getting in such desperate straits, they have begun to rob and murder," the miner Edwin Sherzer wrote to his fiancée Clara in Saint Louis, now five weeks after his arrival in Nome in late June. "A man was found the other night all beat to pieces, even his hands and arms which he had held up to protect himself with. We sleep with our revolvers right where we can lay our hands on them."

A revolver, though, was no protection against the inventive thief who rigged together a series of sticks, fishing pole–like, at the end of which he attached a capsule of chloroform. The contraption could be poked through a slit in a tent, the capsule dangled over the face of the dozing occupant and overturned, the knockout drug administered with barely a sound made by the intruder. A miner and his partner were taken for $41.50; luckily for a fellow robbed of $38, he had just sent $1,000 back home to his wife in Platteville, Wisconsin. The thief prowled Front Street, too, lifting a few hundred dollars and a gold watch from a married couple and two men sleeping on the floor of a restaurant. Two doors down, the grocer F. H. Howard had a few dollars removed from his clothes.

The remains of a murdered man, his skull crushed in, were found on a gold-rich patch of beach. At a theater in town, Daisy Staws, a "lady of ill repute," took a hammer to the head of a fellow with whom she was having a dispute. He recovered and lay in wait for her, gun drawn, by a cigar store, only to be moved along by a passing soldier. One rustler relieved a drunk of a jug of whiskey and a watch; another tried to his cut his way through the canvas roof of a store, only to flee on detection. A restaurant by the beach was burglarized.

CAPE NOME'S CRIME WAVE DID NOT ESCAPE THE ATTENTION OF FEDERAL authorities, who bore the primary responsibility for keeping order in Alaska in the absence of a state government. The Nome region had "more murderers, cut-throats, thieves, confidence men, gamblers, prostitutes and bad characters than any camp I ever saw or heard of, and I have been on the frontier continuously for over thirty years," wrote US Marshal C. L. Vawter to McKinley's attorney general, John W. Griggs, in a letter dated August 7. Vawter, from Montana, was his own man. He had arrived in Nome separately from the McKenzie-Noyes party aboard the *Senator*, and although aware of the McKenzie ring, he stood apart from it. In a separate note to Griggs, C. A. S. Frost, a young attorney recently arrived in Nome as a special examiner for the Department of Justice, passed on a list of the more prominent criminals active in the area: "Fred Welsh, alias 'Big Fred,' general crook and clever confidence man . . . ; Doc. West, all-around crook and clever pickpocket . . . ; Boston Page, pimp and all-around crook; Nick Burkhardt, New York thief and confidence man, has been ordered out of a great many cities of the United States . . . ; Bill Doherty, general tough, killed a man in Boise, Idaho." And those were just a few of the names. "Compared with Nome today, Butte, Montana, which is famous as the wickedest city in the United States, is a righteous and law-abiding community," Frost reported.

Vawter, as the head marshal for Alaska's second federal division, asked Washington for permission to hire six more deputies, to add to the several already under his supervision. The townspeople, anxious to protect life and property and not of a mind to wait for help to arrive, met among themselves and organized the Nome Vigilantes, the idea being that hanging a well-known bandit or two would send an instructive message to the rest. Mining camps in Montana and California, old-timers noted, had taken similar steps to stamp out crime. If nothing was done, citizens reasoned, Nome was at risk of being hijacked by a cabal of gangsters. The same thing had happened in Skagway during the Yukon gold rush, that town held in the grip of the notorious crime boss Soapy Smith, a former Texas cowboy. A city engineer belonging to a vigilante group finally put an end to Smith with a bullet fired in a confrontation on a wharf. "The way of transgressors is hard," the pastor, citing Proverbs, declared at the gangster's funeral.

McKenzie was at least as concerned as anyone else about the protection of property from the varmints. After all, there was no more attractive target in Nome to a thief than his sacks of gold at Alaska Banking & Safe Deposit. Anxious about rumors of plots to raid the bank, McKenzie paid a visit to its general manager, Cabell Whitehead. The lone security guard Whitehead kept on watch was not enough, he said—a detail of soldiers was needed. McKenzie took the manager over to the Golden Gate to confer with Noyes. After some discussion, the judge and Whitehead together walked over to the army barracks for a talk with the officer in charge, Captain Charles D. French of the 7th Infantry. Informing the captain of the receiver's "large amount of gold dust on deposit" at the bank and the "uneasiness felt as to its safety," Noyes asked for the army's help. Starting the next day, a rotating pair of soldiers stood sentry at the bank at all hours. The receiver—the greatest "transgressor" of all in Nome, in not just a few minds—could now sleep more peacefully.

Chapter 16

THE TAKING OF TOPKUK

IN HIS LETTERS TO ELVA FIRST MENTIONING THE NOME PROPOSITION, when it was no more than a gleam in his eye, McKenzie seemed, if anything, to underappreciate the potential scale of this scheme. As Congress eventually allotted the domain of the second division of the federal court of Alaska, Cape Nome was just a small portion of this realm, extending as it did to all of the Seward Peninsula—about 180 miles long and 130 miles wide. And for as long as Noyes had jurisdiction over this expanse, McKenzie's protection ran to its full breadth, to any spot where there was gold. A gilded empire lay within his grasp, and with his usual aggressiveness, he now seized on reports that a spectacular bounty was being harvested from a place known as Topkuk, on the mouth of Daniels Creek, about sixty miles east of Nome on the Bering coast. The miners actively working this ground had heard about the receiver in Cape Nome—and thought themselves safely out of his reach. They were wrong.

For the many months of the year in which the Seward Peninsula was covered with snow and ice, the ground frozen solid, it was just about impossible to mine gold. Just about—but not entirely. Daniels Creek, at the spot where it emptied into the Bering, was an exception. In the middle of January 1900, four explorers found gold there on the surface, eighty cents' worth to a pan. The men organized the Black Chief Mining Company to develop the claim and spent $6,000 on mining equipment—only to have the ground stampeded after word of the find reached Nome and was published in the newspapers in March.

As everyone could then see, this was remarkably rich ground: the beach sands commons below the Black Chief claim could easily yield a lone miner $300 in gold in a day's work. Word rippled through the throng that three beach miners had taken an amazing $10,000 worth over three days. By the first week of July, $600,000 in gold was taken out of a strip no more than one thousand feet long. The paystreak, three to four feet wide, was just one foot below barren sand, the gold lying on top of clay. Nothing in the coastal area around Nome could equal this treasure—in fact, no better marine deposits had been found anywhere in the world. Inevitably, near the end of July, the military cleared the beach, and a jumper filed a lawsuit contesting the Black Chief enterprise's claim.

There matters stood until McKenzie, after his arrival in Nome, heard about Topkuk. Possibly Noyes tipped him off—the Black Chief camp had approached the judge about the lawsuit in Saint Michael. The question for McKenzie was a logistical one—with his hands busy extracting gold from "his" properties, as receiver, in the Anvil Creek area, how could he also exploit Topkuk? That problem was readily solved. On August 13, Noyes appointed as a receiver for Topkuk a friend of McKenzie's from the Dakotas with mining experience in the Yukon. By now, Noyes was well aware of criticism by miners of his appointment of McKenzie as receiver, but in response, he dug in his heels. "I will not only appoint McKenzie to every claim he wants to be receiver of," he was heard saying in McKenzie's office in Nome, while the boss himself was not present, "but I will also appoint anyone he shall recommend, that is, if he does not want it himself."

The designated receiver for Topkuk, William B. Cameron, immediately proceeded to the site with a barge loaded with boxes marked "Alexander McKenzie, Nome, by way of Seattle." The boxes contained mining equipment—the failing pumping machinery that McKenzie had purchased back on the mainland to work the Cape Nome beachfront for the Alaska Gold Mining Company. The machinery also might fail to work at Topkuk, but by a neat bit of financial chicanery, McKenzie arranged for Alaska Gold to be paid back for its initial purchase of the equipment, no matter how well the pumps functioned. The directors of the company—the boss, Oliver Hubbard, Robert Chipps, and Mike McCormack—met in McKenzie's office and agreed to sell the equipment to a sham company associated with the Topkuk receivership, the money for the sale to come from the gold the receivership would be extracting. With Topkuk a proven find, the proposition was without risk for Alaska Gold.

McKenzie knew in advance of the impending order for a receiver at Topkuk, for he arranged to load his mining equipment on the barge for transport two days before the order was made. Cameron also brought along several dozen wage hands to work the Black Chief claim, a pair of cooks, and two horses. It was a full-scale appropriation of the property. The foreman at the site was Captain McCormack, who before arriving joked to a friend in Nome that "Cameron has all the responsibility" to work the Topkuk site and "I have all the money." Of course, McCormack was there for the boss. Topkuk's gold went into sacks brought to Nome for deposit into McKenzie's boxes at Alaska Banking & Safe Deposit. Much like the nighttime raid on Anvil Creek, this was a well-coordinated military-style operation.

McKenzie may not have known it, and if he had, he might not have cared, but one of the Black Chief partners he was taking on had political connections in Washington. This was Sam C. Dunham, a veteran of mining camps in California, Nevada, Colorado, and Utah. Dunham, formerly private secretary to US Senator Daniel Voorhees, a Democrat from Indiana, had arrived in Alaska in the summer of 1897 on a mission for the federal Labor Department to appraise conditions for workers in the gold fields of the region. He filed his first report in 1898, and in the following year he was present in Cape Nome on discovery of the gold in the beach sands. In the struggle between the plain miners seeking to keep their commons and the corporate interests and speculators aiming to capture the ground for private stakeholding, Dunham's sympathies lay entirely with the miners. He was a published poet, his verse admired by California's Jack London, soon to be famous for tales like *The Call of the Wild*, drawn from London's experiences during the Klondike gold rush. Dunham wrote lyrically on the Nome beach drama in a report for the *Bulletin of the Department of Labor* filed in March 1900 from Saint Michael and printed in the July edition. "Ragged and half starved . . . they had been cast on the beach at Nome like driftwood," he said of the miners. "But here, in this barren, forbidding waste, their dreams were coming true; for there was scarcely a man . . . who could not return home with gold enough to enable him to spend a restful winter among his friends." In his report, Dunham anticipated the arrival in Alaska of a type like McKenzie, writing of "procurers" using their political clout in Washington to win advantage in the chase for gold. And now he found his own claim under assault. Dunham was not intimidated by McKenzie, McCormack, or Cameron, and in time he would attest to their machinations in court testimony and in affidavits inserted into the *Congressional Record* in Washington, DC. But for now, powerless to expel the team that had taken charge of Black Chief's claim, he rendered his grievance in verse:

> *We have a sub-receiver here, who's working out our mine*
> *In a systematic manner which makes our hearts re-pine.*
> *He brought a damned expensive plant, shipped in his boss's name,*
> *And planted it against our "kick" upon our richest claim.*
>
> *He brought a gang of bosom friends, helped up here from below,*
> *And wouldn't give a single job to any one we know,*
> *And when he took the riffles out and weighted his shining swag,*
> *He wouldn't let us see the scales or even heft the bag.*

Dunham was not alone in complaining about the invasion of Topkuk by the McKenzie forces. After the initial clearance of the beach by the military, a small mining camp had cropped up there, with several dozen independent miners living in tents and profitably at work. Though not parties to any litigation, these men too were rudely halted in their labor by Cameron and McCormack, and their frustration spilled over into talk of reprisal. A former sheriff of California's

Alameda County, prospecting in the region, stayed at the camp for some days and heard angry words openly expressed. "The sentiment," he later recalled, was there was "a clique"—a ring—"that came there for the purpose of getting hold of mining properties through the influence of the Court. . . . They told me that this man McKenzie and the judge up there, Judge Noyes . . . they were the foremost operators." As for what might be done about the situation, there were mutterings, the ex-sheriff said, about lynching the judge.

Still, McKenzie could feel emboldened by the swift capture of the Topkuk prize, surrendered with no meaningful resistance despite the grumbling. His methods were working to make him Boss of Alaska, just as they had earlier worked to make him Boss of the Dakotas. The question was where to expand his reign next. Why not invade, say, the Kougarok district, eighty or so miles from Nome in the heart of the Seward Peninsula? The Kougarok was a range of serrated mountains, cut by streams running through valleys thousands of feet below the peaks. Ice formations, some made of frozen mud, rose from the streams up to a height of one hundred feet along the walls of the valleys, thick blankets of moss keeping the ice from thawing even as air temperatures warmed. Despite these challenges, miners based in Cape Nome rushed the Kougarok and found gold in the streams there in the summer of 1900. Lane's Wild Goose Mining & Trading had been in the forefront of the exploration and was now planning for a long-term presence in the area. Perhaps Lane thought that the Kougarok lay beyond McKenzie's reach. But the boss undoubtedly knew that Wild Goose had "secured many valuable claims" in the Kougarok, for the Gold Digger reported this intelligence. To read of the latest strikes from the comfort of his quarters in Nome, to have a word with a judge pledged to follow his recommendations, to dispatch his teams to the targeted site—that, for McKenzie, was the mining business: a sure thing.

Chapter 17

"THE MCKENZIE EVIL"

A S THE MINERS AT TOPKUK VENTED OVER BEING CUT OUT OF A RIGGED game, so did the disheartened fortune seekers in Nome. In mid-August, Edwin Sherzer wrote to Clara that "all the claims are tied up in lawsuits and the place is simply a land of milk and honey for the lawyers and officials. Corrupt is no name for a government official, and the military officers simply boss things to suit themselves. A little petty officer refused to let people catch fish in the Nome River, allowing one man the privilege. If that is not tyranny, I don't know what it is." His bile still not spent, he completed his outburst: "Liberty is a name unknown and I wonder what our country is coming to."

Into this fray stepped a newspaper to take up the cause of miners feeling oppressed by the McKenzie band and to give a sustained public voice to their outrage, beyond the grumblings in the tent camps and the bitter letters sent to sweethearts back home. Here was a voice that might even catch the attention of authorities on the mainland, as Nome's newspapers could be sent by steamer to Seattle and San Francisco. The publication was not the *Nome Gold Digger*, which mostly focused on the activity in the fields, and most certainly not the town's oldest newspaper, the *Nome Daily News*. The *News*, in the hands of manager H. G. Steel and editor J. F. A. Strong, was a Republican vessel, supportive of McKinley, in general sympathy with the business class, and wary of populism. It had greeted McKenzie's arrival in Alaska with the goodwill due any Republican mogul, and even as his abusive methods became evident to anyone with a clear eye, the

News refused to credit the idea that the boss and his henchmen had set up an organized ring to take possession of the gold riches.

The voice for the miners came from a new entrant to the press pack, the *Nome Daily Chronicle*. The *Chronicle*, twenty-five cents a copy, could not be considered impartial. It was launched with a "loan" from "the Swedes'" Pioneer Mining Company—never repaid, apparently, and perhaps always intended as a gift. In his embrace of the printing press as a tool to nourish a climate of opinion favorable to his interest, Jafet Lindeberg yet again showed his keen grasp of how to get things done in his adopted country. He refrained from the use of force against McKenzie, but he could deploy ink as a weapon. The editor of the *Chronicle*, working out of offices to the rear of town on Third Avenue, was Fred A. Healy, also a special correspondent for the *San Francisco Call*, one of California's leading newspapers. Healy wrote his commentaries with verve, in the high-dudgeon voice of a Mark Twain and with the populist sensibility of a William Jennings Bryan. His screeds anticipated the better-known castigation of the McKenzie ring, years later, by his Nome compatriot Rex Beach, a young law school dropout who had arrived in Cape Nome as a prospector but whose imagination and pen were stirred by the figure of the boss. For added punch, Healy printed the verses of the poet miner Sam Dunham with their barbs directed at McKenzie. So the boss became an improbable muse—a villain to those drawn to writing about him, one with a seductive magnetism.

In a series of masthead editorials, Healy took "the miner against the schemer" as his theme. On August 16, in a first salvo, he warned his readers not to be fooled by the initial strike against "the Swedes" at Anvil Creek: "The fact that the first play was made against the foreigners is merely an incident, serving to show the craft with which the entire affair has been managed, and to divert the attention of the public away from the overwhelming scope of the whole idea." This was only the beginning, he stressed: "There are others marked out for slaughter, and they will be made to feel the point of the knife before many days have passed." Healy stopped short at naming McKenzie as the chief culprit, with the Alaska Gold Mining Company as the hidden beneficiary of these machinations. Perhaps he still lacked the hard information to do so. Yet surely the *Chronicle*'s readers knew exactly the fellows he had in mind with his jibe at the "wise men from the East" coming ashore in Nome, "following the light of the star that glittered in the North." He exhorted the miners to take a unified stand against this chicanery, just as urged by "Deep Creek" Jones in the call for beach miners to join hands to resist the encroachment of "grasping corporations" on their rightful commons. Except Healy, more candid than Jones, made no pretense that the miners were all Americans: "it behooves the men of the Nome district to stand together and to remember that there is neither 'border, nor breed, nor birth,' when a great calamity is threatening all." The essential division, he stressed, was not between foreigner and American but between prey and predator, lamb and wolf.

THIS PAIRING OF OPPOSITES WAS AS OLD AS THE BIBLE AND, FOR THAT matter, could be said to define the central antagonism of the Gilded Age. Yet the wrath of Jehovah did not strike McKenzie down. Instead, the skies took a turn in his favor. The rains fell, making easier the task of separating gold nuggets and dust from dirt and gravel, and the boss's collections improved. By the middle of August, he had amassed from "his" Anvil Creek holdings alone gold worth more than $100,000— some $3 million in 2020 dollars. Here was a cache that surely would impress Wall Street in a public offering of shares in Alaska Gold. The trove exceeded in value by four times the total amount of his bond, $25,000, for the five Anvil claims in receivership; yet Noyes disregarded pleas by the defense for an increase in the bond.

The weather smiled on the boss—and so, less surprisingly, did the Noyes court, as the judge, after waiting day after day to issue his ruling on the defense motions to revoke the orders appointing McKenzie receiver, finally supplied his answer: denied. The receiverships would stay in place for as long as it took to dispense with the litigation, he said. Observers who had first assumed, as the *News* said, that Chipps had "not a ghost of a show" of wresting control of the Discovery prize, now recalibrated his odds of success for the better. The *News* noted a "hue and cry" in the mining camps at the prospect of seemingly permanent receiverships in the region, which the paper tried to subdue with a rare public statement by "Receiver McKenzie." In a concession on his part to the demands of public opinion, printed on the front page under the headline "NO TURNING BACK," the boss spoke directly to concerns about his integrity: "I will conduct the work on the claims on business principles, and there will be no rake-off in any way. A receiver can administer a property honestly and economically." He added that he was hiring the best men he could find to work the properties and planned no cut in wages.

The miners weren't buying it, and now their resistance to "King Alex" took an unusual but understandable form: a work stoppage. The miners kept their treasure underground for the time being, ceasing to excavate it so long as the threat of "legal" confiscation remained. "They discussed it this way," a visitor to the Seward Peninsula at the time said, in wonderment, of the miners: "That it was a queer procedure to think for a moment that the gold in a claim was in jeopardy, and they concluded that it was safer in the gravel bank than it would be in the hands of anybody."

With less gold—less money—circulating in the local economy, the region plunged into a depression. Prices for many goods fell by half, a Nome restaurant now offering a plate of ham and eggs, with coffee and toast, for a quarter, with fresh oranges and apples sold on the street for fifty cents to a dozen. Rent for office space dropped at an even greater rate, and steamer services cut their fares to as low as $15 for steerage back to Seattle.

At the same time, with Noyes displaying his willingness to consider lawsuits initiated by jumpers, there was a rapid acceleration of such filings in his court, always accompanied by requests for a receivership. Some of these cases were connected to the McKenzie ring, but some were not—the plaintiffs were acting on their own, trying to take advantage of the accommodating legal climate, as they saw it. In these dismal circumstances, "the only man to be seen mushing over the tundra is the official carrying the court's injunction to some rich claim that will be looked after by a receiver," Healy wrote in the *Chronicle*.

The paper, after its initial hesitation, named McKenzie as the author of this ruin. In "THE McKENZIE EVIL," as the *Chronicle* titled its editorial, Healy said that "property grabbing" on the peninsula and the mass of litigation and receiverships were "the result of a deep laid scheme on the part of the Alaska Gold Mining Company . . . to cabbage everything in the entire territory; and this same corporation is not particular to the means it employs to acquire property. McKenzie is president of this company and is the controlling influence to which practically all of this evil may be traced."

"McKENZIE IS PRESIDENT"—THAT BIT OF INFORMATION PROBABLY CAME to the *Chronicle* through its financial backer, Pioneer Mining. The company's voice also could be heard in the newspaper's plea that "it is to the interest of both merchants and mining men" to discourage litigation and to "see that the country, from which they must get their living, is freed from the bonds that the law is weaving about it." This was an effective public campaign as a means of countering the support for McKenzie from the *News*; yet newspaper editorials on their own were not going to break the grip of the receiver. With Noyes plainly in the grip of the boss, there was, apart from the last resort of physical force, only one real option available to the defendants in the Anvil lawsuits: appeal to a higher court. The higher court, in this instance, was the Ninth Circuit Court of Appeals, based in San Francisco, which held jurisdiction over the courts in Alaska and was just one rung below the US Supreme Court in Washington.

An appeal, though, was a tricky matter. For one thing, Noyes made clear to the team of defense lawyers—namely, Metson, Johnson, Knight, and Jackson—that he did not consider his orders appealable. And here, in principle, Noyes had a point. An appeal of a trial judge's order for a receivership indeed was unusual—typically in civil litigation, the appeals process commenced after the judgement of the court on the underlying case, not while the lawsuit was still being tried. The defense camp would be asking San Francisco to step directly into litigation that had only just begun—to slap down, in his first important set of cases, a judge just appointed by the president and confirmed by the Senate, with the express mission of bringing civil order to unruly Alaska. It was a lot to ask.

Nevertheless, in defiance of Noyes, the defense side opted for appeal to the Ninth Circuit—in practical terms, to write its briefs and ship them by steamer to San Francisco, a voyage likely to take two weeks. Through an informant, a clerk in the Noyes's court privy to requests that the defense side was making for legal papers, McKenzie learned of the maneuver. And now, probably for the first time since his landing in Nome, he felt a tremor of concern. As unlikely as it seemed, what if San Francisco went against him? Here was a threat of high magnitude. The imperative, as he saw it, was to get word to his connected friends on the inside—to alert Senator Carter, especially, to the peril. He held a war council among his lieutenants. There was no need for panic; "he would take care of the fight at this end of the line, down at San Francisco," he told his confederates. But someone had to get to Carter. Hume could not be spared, as he was arguing the Anvil cases before Noyes, Hubbard also needed to be in Nome, and the firm's third partner, Edwin Beeman, refused to go, an indication, perhaps, of a lack of faith in the boss. McKenzie settled on Jimmie Galen for the mission. Hume dictated a letter addressed to Galen's brother-in-law, describing the situation in Alaska and stressing the urgent need for the appeal of the defense camp to be countered in San Francisco, by Carter personally if possible. McKenzie instructed Galen to proceed directly to Portland to show the letter to John A. Hall, a US district attorney and former law partner of Hume, and from Portland to try to reach Carter.

McKENZIE WAS BECOMING ANXIOUS—AND SO WAS NOYES. "I HAVE BEEN intending to write you for some time," the judge began a letter to

Attorney General Griggs in Washington, dated August 20. The third paragraph made clear what circumstance had prompted Noyes to write. The defense appeal was well on its way to San Francisco, he knew, likely to reach the Ninth Circuit by the end of the month, and Griggs needed a heads-up. Noyes kept his explanation brief. "I have made it a rule to appoint a receiver" on request from litigants, he said, and in so doing to order the receiver to continue the work on claims in dispute "inasmuch as this whole camp is depending upon the output of the mines. . . . That I should have met the serious opposition and harsh criticism of some is of course to be expected. . . . I think I can truly say that up to date I have been guided by what in my conscience I believe to be the best thing to do." As to the particular nature of the opposition and criticism, Noyes did not elaborate. All of Washington, though, received a clue in a story filed from Nome in mid-August and published several weeks later in the *Evening Times*, a Democratic newspaper in the capital. The report identified McKenzie and Hubbard as the backers of the effort earlier in the year to get Congress to pass legislation to revoke "alien" claims in Alaska's gold fields. Doubling as president of the Alaska Gold Mining Company and as a court-appointed receiver, McKenzie had seized hold of "the richest" claims in all of western Alaska, the paper informed its readers, and he had also targeted the golden beach sands of which Americans had heard so much.

The *Evening Times* story was a first sign that the "Alaska Scandal," as it would soon be called, had the makings of a national political firestorm. The scandal was about to wreak havoc in quite a few lives from Washington to Nome—from the friends of McKenzie in the Senate and the occupant of the Executive Mansion to Judge Noyes and most of all the boss himself. For a judge in San Francisco, on being informed of the strange goings-on in the most remote outpost of his court's jurisdiction, was determined to do something about it.

1. "Three Swedes," the founders of the rich Discovery claim on Anvil Creek. Jafet Lindeberg, a native of Norway, center, flanked by two natives of Sweden: John Brynteson, right, and Erik Lindblom, left. *Courtesy of Carrie M. McLain Memorial Museum.*

2. Pioneer Mining, the company of the "Three Swedes," operated this and other lucrative Cape Nome gold mines—and through its lawyers waged fierce battle against McKenzie's bid to capture these properties. *Courtesy of Carrie M. McLain Memorial Museum.*

3. Beach miners. Many miners made use of homemade "rockers"—cradle-like wooden boxes with screens to separate the gold flakes from beach sands. The beach was a commons; any miner could pick any spot to work. *Courtesy of Carrie M. McLain Memorial Museum.*

4. Natives at sea. Alaska's native peoples helped prospectors arriving from outside the territory to find gold in the streams. But the natives generally were kept from sharing in the riches, and many succumbed to diseases brought in by the outsiders. *Courtesy of Carrie M. McLain Memorial Museum.*

5. Alexander McKenzie. The frontier sheriff rose to become "Boss of the Dakotas" and tried to fix Alaska's courts to put Cape Nome's gold in his hands. Jailed by the Ninth Circuit Court of Appeals in San Francisco for his misconduct, he begged his powerful friends to rescue him. *Courtesy of State Historical Society of North Dakota (image no. 00169a).*

6. Judge Arthur H. Noyes was McKenzie's tool for the Alaska gold conspiracy. A jangle of nerves, he admitted to a superior that emotional strains invariably drove him to the bottle. *Courtesy of Wikimedia Commons.*

7. James J. Hill. The railroad baron was McKenzie's most valuable friend and political ally. Of McKenzie, "you can place absolute reliance upon what he says or does," Hill told Mark Hanna, President William McKinley's top political operative. *Courtesy of Wikimedia Commons.*

8. Thomas Henry Carter. The Montana senator huddled behind closed doors with McKenzie and maneuvered to advance the Alaska scheme in the Senate, even as he publicly denied he had anything to do with the matter. *Courtesy of Wikimedia Commons.*

9. William Morris Stewart. The Nevada senator insisted on a public airing of the Nome conspiracy. Told that the plot was a "private" issue, he shot back, "Is it not a matter of public business that a whole country is tied up and robbed?" *Courtesy of Wikimedia Commons.*

10. Judge William W. Morrow. From his seat on the Ninth Circuit Court of Appeals in San Francisco, the McKinley-appointed judge thwarted McKenzie's Alaska caper. "We say the law is supreme," he declared. *Courtesy of the Ninth Circuit Archives.*

11. President William McKinley. He told friends that "in all his long political career he had never before been subjected to such tremendous pressure from influential men as he had been to pardon McKenzie." *Courtesy of Wikimedia Commons.*

12. Front Street, Nome. Saloons, dance halls, and gambling parlors lined the town's main thoroughfare. A visitor called the scene wilder than anything "in the worst days" of Montmartre in Paris or State Street in Chicago. *Courtesy of Carrie M. McLain Memorial Museum.*

13. Tent City. Thousands of Nome's miners camped directly on the Bering seashore—unprepared for the rigors of the Alaska outdoors and for McKenzie's effort to wrest the "golden sands" away from them. *Courtesy of Carrie M. McLain Memorial Museum.*

14. Seattle docks. From the "Gateway to Alaska," as Seattle was called, cramped steamers ferried gold rushers directly to Nome on a weeks-long journey through waters strewn with icebergs. *Courtesy of Carrie M. McLain Memorial Museum.*

Part Four

DEFIANCE

"Arrest me? Bah! I can't be arrested."

Alexander McKenzie, September 1900, Nome, Alaska,
quoted in Rex Beach, "The Looting of Alaska"

Chapter 18

"THE LAW IS SUPREME"

ICTURE A THICK BUNDLE OF IMPORTANT LEGAL PAPERS, CAREFULLY typed and assembled, carbon copies made. The bundle is walked through the crowded streets of downtown Nome, past the saloons and restaurants and dance halls and down to the shore, rowed out on a skiff for a mile or so, and transferred to a steamer. The bundle embarks on a long voyage, southward on the Bering, through the narrow straits of the Aleutian island chain, past Vancouver, Seattle, and Portland on the Pacific, ultimately arriving in San Francisco Harbor, in the company of seabirds. The steamer docks, and the bundle is transported down the pier and over to the nearby US Appraisers Building at Sansome between Washington and Jackson. The bundle, finally, is taken to Room 44½ and, after a knock on the door, is deposited there, in the Office of the Clerk, United States Circuit Court of Appeals for the Ninth Circuit.

So the appeals brief of the defense camp in the Anvil cases at Nome arrived in the last week of August 1900 at the headquarters of the Ninth Circuit. The panel now had to field this unexpected matter—a challenge that proved a defining moment for its reputation. Its history and traditions offered little guidance, as there was not much to go on. The prevailing system of regional "circuit" appeals courts—the last stop before a case got to the Supreme Court in Washington—was the product of legislation enacted by Congress in 1891. In its short life, the Ninth Circuit had not distinguished itself with its jurisprudence. The first judge to serve on the panel, Joseph McKenna, was a former

Republican congressman, better known for tending to his political pals than to his cases. There were whispers that he owed his appointment to the Southern Pacific Railroad. But so far as McKenna's career ambitions were concerned, this strategy of cultivating a network of influential supporters could be said to have paid off. When a former colleague from Congress, William McKinley, was elected president, he announced his intention, in February 1897, to nominate McKenna to head the Justice Department as attorney general. McKenna did the loyal Republican thing—which was to delay his retirement from the Ninth Circuit until after McKinley's inauguration. That way, the selection of his replacement on the panel fell not to a Democrat, outgoing chief executive Grover Cleveland, but to a fellow Republican.

At the recommendation of his new attorney general, McKinley tapped another former Republican congressman to fill the open slot on the Ninth Circuit. The choice was William W. Morrow, a friend of McKenna's, then serving as the federal district court judge for the Northern District of California. Morrow took his seat on the panel in the spring of 1897, moving into his office at Room 46 of the Appraisers Building, two doors down from the clerk, one door down from the US Marshals. And that's where the package from Alaska found him. The Ninth Circuit panel in 1900 consisted of three judges altogether, and only one, Morrow, was permanently based at the headquarters in San Francisco. The second operated out of Portland and the third from Los Angeles. In the fall, the court would be in session, the three judges hearing cases together in San Francisco, but in August, Morrow was alone. It fell to him, then, to consider how to handle the appeal from the defense camp in Nome.

Based on his political affiliations and patrons, McKenzie might have viewed Judge Morrow as a soft touch, "reliable" in the way that the boss felt judges, with proper deference to their sponsors, ought to be reliable. How else could the system work? But Morrow, though still in the Republican fold and sensitive to political currents, was not McKenna. His life and his makeup suggested a streak of independence and a determination to act on his convictions—in other words, the possibility, in McKenzie's terms, of proving unreliable.

MORROW WAS BORN IN FARM COUNTRY IN INDIANA, NEAR THE TOWN OF Milton, in 1843, his father a Scots-Irish immigrant from Ireland, his mother a native of North Carolina. The death of his father, when William was nine, left the family with barely the means to get by. The Morrows moved to Illinois, and William worked farm jobs during the growing season, attending school in the fallow winter months. An education in books was of interest to him—he managed to gain private instruction in Latin and modern foreign languages, mathematics and engineering. He served a teenage apprenticeship in the mechanical trades, his career path seemingly set. His choice in the matter, in any case, was his own; for his mother, in 1856, left him, not yet fourteen, in Illinois and returned to North Carolina. War between North and South was brewing, and she was a partisan for the slave South—a slaveholder herself, by inheritance.

The seed of his independence of mind, the trait that took sturdy root as he matured, perhaps lay in his choice to align himself on the opposite side of the political spectrum from his mother. This could not have been easy for him or for her—she may well have seen him as going against her, and by extension, his southern heritage. But her son came of age at the very time that Abraham Lincoln, operating out of the Illinois capital of Springfield, captivated hearts as a voice on behalf of stopping the spread of slavery to territories like Kansas and Nebraska. William developed a passion for Lincoln and this cause. He was fifteen when Lincoln, in 1858, crisscrossed Illinois in the series of debates with Stephen Douglas in their contest for a US Senate seat. He was seventeen, in 1860, when Lincoln was elected president, the first-ever Republican president of America. By then William was living north of San Francisco in Santa Rosa, having headed west to California the previous year. But Lincoln was always his shining star. The Republican Party, for Morrow, was foremost the party of Lincoln, its principles, at their best, the eternal principles of his hero.

He might have headed back to Illinois to enlist, at the outbreak of war at Fort Sumter in the spring of 1861, when he was just shy of eighteen, but he stayed in California and the following year joined a party of explorers in search of gold in Idaho. Somehow, after weeks of wandering through treacherous wilderness, the original destination nowhere in sight, the prospectors ended up in Oregon, east of the Cascades. And there, blind luck with them, they struck gold at a place that came to be called Whiskey Gulch. A few months later Morrow was safely back in Santa Rosa with gold dust in his sack. He was not rich, but he was at the least ahead of his starting place, and he had had an adventure. The experience taught him the hazards and vagaries of prospecting from the point of view of the ordinary miner—of value when the Alaska matter came to him decades later.

With the mechanical trades proving not to his liking, the thought of college tugged at him. He headed east, all the way across the country, with a plan to enroll in some program of study, but the war, now in its third year, swept him up. He joined the National Rifles, a company of the District of Columbia Militia, and participated in Union army operations in and around Washington. As the tide turned against the South, his concern grew for the welfare of his mother in North Carolina, in the heart of the conflict zone. He managed to obtain a special pass, signed by Lincoln and sent to officials in the Confederate government, authorizing her passage through military lines to join her son in Washington, but the pass never reached her, and she died before he could see her again. Ten years after the end of the war, he visited her grave in North Carolina. One of her former slaves introduced himself: "Why, I used to belong to you." His mother had willed him her slaves.

Morrow studied the law and set his sights on politics, as had Lincoln. Happily for his ambitions, California, to which he returned to make his career, was a hospitable state for Republicans, twice voting for Lincoln, twice after for the former Union commander Ulysses S. Grant, and in 1876, narrowly, for another figure of Morrow's admiration, Rutherford B. Hayes, the former Ohio governor and an attorney who, before the war, had advocated for the end of slavery and defended runaway slaves in court. On the strength of a stint as an assistant US district attorney, Morrow had a credible political platform as a man of law and order. But while the party's door was open to him, he was not an immediate success—nominated by the GOP, in 1879, for a state senate seat representing a San Francisco district, he lost the general election. Three years later, a Democrat beat him in a bid for the US Congress. Finally, in 1884, San Francisco sent to him to Washington to serve in the US House, the first of three consecutive terms in Congress, his time on Capitol Hill overlapping with that of both McKinley and McKenna, fellow members of the House Republican caucus.

Morrow lacked the customary skills of a successful politician—he was not a backslapper or story swapper; his rhetoric tended to be colorless, lacking the earthy wit and humor that figures like Lincoln used to such great effect. He believed in persuasion by logic and frowned on appeals to emotion. But these very same qualities suggested he might make a good judge. On retiring from Congress in 1891, he competed with McKenna for the prize of a seat on the newly constituted Ninth Circuit Court of Appeals. Losing that bid, on Benjamin Harrison's selection of McKenna, he accepted the judgeship of the Northern District of California and bided his time. And when his chance came to move up, on McKenna's return to Washington as McKinley's attorney general, he was the choice, not only of McKenna but also of the San Francisco Bar Association, unanimously, to occupy the circuit seat. Morrow "has no entangling alliances with any of the great interests of the Coast," one advocate of his nomination, a former Nevada judge in law practice in California, told McKinley. San Francisco attorney Barclay Henley, a Democrat and former member of Congress, praised Morrow for "perfect impartiality, cool judgment, wide learning."

His position won, Morrow ascended in San Francisco's estimation and occupied a position as a kind of civic wise man in robes. Unlike Lincoln, a skeptic of organized religion, Morrow joined a personal belief in the sacred truth of Christianity with the conviction that the American republic and its constitution represented prizes of "Christian civilization," hard won by "the Anglo-Saxon race" and in need of vigilant protection. "You know, we expect all our young men," he said in a speech on patriotism, "to be familiar with the Ten Commandments. And while we honor these Commandments, and many of us have been required to commit them to memory, as the fundamental law of mankind," he continued, "we ought to be able to name with equal fluency and intelligence the essential principles of the Constitution of the United States. We ought to be able to enumerate these as we do the Ten Commandments or the Lord's Prayer or the Litany of the church to which we belong." On another occasion, at a banquet, in response to a toast to the judiciary, he struck a note that harkened to Lincoln's Gettysburg Address: "It is written by the finger of the Almighty God on the everlasting tablets of the Universe that no nation or state can endure or prosper into whose life justice does not enter and enter to stay." Lincoln's speeches, it seemed, were inscribed in his memory.

Morrow could be faulted for sanctimony and, on the ripe question of Chinese immigration to America, for a distinctly unchristian hypocrisy. Heathen Chinese were pouring into the country from across the Pacific, especially large numbers settling in California, and Morrow joined in crude calls for banning their entry to the nation. "The Asiatic tramp forces his way through the western gate of the continent contrary to the spirit and purpose of our laws," he said during his time in Congress. But so far as "Anglo-Saxon" California was concerned, Morrow stood out for an unusual dedication to bringing order to a place that not long before had been a lawless frontier. "He is a man of large stature, superb, sinewy frame, and robust health. He is scrupulously neat in dress, methodical in his plans and habits, simple in his tastes, and stainless in his private life," an admirer wrote in a profile. "He is a plain, prudent, earnest, resolute man, a fine type of American character—*sans peur et sans reproche.*"

AND NOW THE APPEAL FROM THE DEFENSE CAMP IN THE NOME CASES LAY on his desk. For the court's consideration, specifically, was a request by the defense side for "writs of supersedeas"—for explicit orders from the Ninth Circuit overriding, as in superseding, the orders of the Noyes district court in halting the work of the defendants on the five Anvil claims while at the same time appointing a receiver to work the claims and take custody of the gold. The Noyes directives deserved to be overturned, the defense argued, because they were terribly unfair to the owners of the Anvil properties and had no basis in legal precedent.

Alaska, a place he had never visited, must have felt daunting to Morrow. He might have, at this point, turned to his two colleagues on the appeals panel, both with more experience. William B. Gilbert, a Republican, was the senior judge on the court, appointed by Harrison in 1892. Erskine M. Ross, a Democrat, was appointed by Grover Cleveland in 1895, two years before Morrow arrived on the Ninth Circuit. The problem was time. Gilbert was in Portland, Ross in Los Angeles. Receiver McKenzie, meanwhile, had already extracted a substantial amount of gold from these properties, according to the defense. Moreover Nome would become unreachable once the weather turned and the Bering froze over. If the court agreed that the Noyes orders deserved to be overridden, the defense said, McKenzie needed to be stopped immediately. So Morrow felt he had to act alone. His colleagues, he knew, had confidence in him. Gilbert, in a letter to McKinley, had encouraged Morrow's appointment to the circuit judgeship, saying the selection would be "gratifying" to both him and Ross.

The defense side had one important advantage over the McKenzie camp. Two of the lawyers in Nome, Pioneer Mining's attorney, William Metson, and Wild Goose's attorney, Samuel Knight, were well known to Morrow as longtime, respected practitioners in San Francisco. In addition, the Nome lawyers managed to make contact with one of their friends in San Francisco, attorney E. S. Pillsbury, who now appeared before Morrow on behalf of the defendant P. H. Anderson. Morrow had a high regard for Pillsbury, one of San Francisco's most prominent lawyers. No attorney for McKenzie or the plaintiff parties came before Morrow at this time. Probably the boss, whom Morrow must have known by reputation, did not figure on the Ninth Circuit's acting so quickly on the appeal. In any event, he was outmaneuvered, for once, his promise to his Nome teammates to "take care of the fight" in San Francisco unfulfilled. Jimmie Galen had proceeded, as instructed, to Portland, with the letter to Carter in hand, but Hume's former law partner, District Attorney Hall, was away from the city. So Carter, at this crucial moment, had no idea that the McKenzie ring desperately needed his help.

Morrow granted the defense appeal and on the most sweeping terms possible: he cast the Anvil receiverships as illegitimate from their inception. Under his new orders, Noyes was to halt the receiverships, and McKenzie was to stop work on the claims and return to the defendants all the gold he had extracted from the mines and deposited in the bank. These countermanding directives came in the form of five identical writs, one for each of the Anvil claims for which McKenzie was receiver, each writ issued under the official signature of the clerk of the Ninth Circuit, F. D. Monckton. The writs applied in full force to Noyes and McKenzie along with Chipps and all the other plaintiffs, stating, in language crafted by Morrow, that they must "entirely surcease and refrain as being superseded" and containing a special set of instructions for the boss: "that you, the said Alexander McKenzie, do forthwith return unto said defendant the possession of any and all property of which you took possession . . . as you will answer the contrary at your peril."

MORROW'S FAITH IN THE FACTS IN ITSELF WAS ENOUGH REASON FOR HIS action: for out-of-the-ordinary circumstances, an out-of-the ordinary ruling—not the usual refusal to allow, at the outset of a lawsuit, an appeal of a trial judge's order—was appropriate. But the warning directed at McKenzie—you defy these orders "at your peril"—hinted at a deeper reason for writs of this stringency. Morrow evidently feared defiance and was saying he would have none of it: return the gold or else. In Morrow's framing, the question at issue, larger than this single case, was whether the rule of law could be effectively established in a distant frontier land like Alaska, where defiance was the norm. He intended to set an example. Years later, in a lecture on the Cape Nome affair given at the School of Jurisprudence at the University of California, Berkeley, he began with a line from a Rudyard Kipling poem, "The

Rhyme of the Three Sealers," a tale of seal poachers in the Bering Sea: "There is never a law of God or man runs north of Fifty-Three." A defiant poacher, unsheathed knife in hand, utters the line as a dare. Morrow concluded this address to an assemblage of future law practitioners with his reply to the pirate, spoken for everyone in attendance and phrased in his typically lofty manner: "we say the law is supreme."

Chapter 19

"BREAKERS LIKE RACE HORSES"

O N AUGUST 29, CLERK MONCKTON OF THE NINTH CIRCUIT PUT HIS signature on the last of the writs crafted by Judge Morrow. The writs left San Francisco aboard the steamship *Ohio*, bound for Nome. The McKenzie team had been caught flat-footed. At the moment, the only attorney the ring had at its disposal was thirty-two-year-old Milton S. Gunn of the Helena, Montana, law firm at which Senator Carter once had been a name partner. And Gunn had little to go on other than the letter carried by Galen, addressed to Carter, describing the state of play in Alaska. His efforts to learn more gained him a reply from Washington, not from Carter but from Minnesota's Cushman Davis, the lead senator on behalf of the Noyes nomination: "I have seen our people here and they are all right and everything here will be all right." Perhaps everything would be "all right" on the Washington end, whatever that meant exactly, but the live question was how to deal with the Ninth Circuit's ruling. Gunn demanded an immediate hearing before the panel in order to contest Morrow's authority to issue the orders overriding the Noyes court. In response to this plea, the Ninth Circuit agreed to hold an oral argument at a branch courtroom in Seattle.

Galen and Gunn sped to Seattle to prepare for the hearing. Uppermost in Gunn's mind, it seemed, was stressing to the Ninth Circuit the personal connection of Montana's Carter to the parties challenging the writs. Even Monckton received this treatment: on meeting with the clerk, in Seattle, Gunn pointedly introduced Galen as the senator's brother-in-law. But if the idea was somehow to steamroll the Ninth Circuit, maybe catching the defendants in the Anvil cases off guard, it failed. The defense camp quickly arranged for capable representation of its interest at the Seattle hearing, in the person of John Beard Allen, a former US senator from the state of Washington with a law practice in Seattle. Allen, a Republican and also a former US attorney, was a much more experienced figure than Gunn, thirty-three years his junior. Probably he already knew a good deal about the situation in Nome from letters from his son George, a participant in the Alaska gold rush.

On September 12, Gunn and Allen appeared in Seattle before the Ninth Circuit's William Gilbert, up from Portland, and Morrow, up from San Francisco. The panel's third judge, Erskine Ross, based in Los Angeles, was not there. Gunn argued that the Ninth Circuit lacked the jurisdiction to grant the defendants an appeal from the orders of the Noyes court appointing a receivership for the Anvil claims and therefore lacked the authority to issue writs of supersedeas. The writs, he said, should be set aside. Morrow, in defending his authority to allow the appeals and grant the writs, cited legislation expressly giving circuit court of appeals judges this power in cases like these. Gunn, speechless, had to admit that he had never heard of this legislation. He was trying his best, but his best was not nearly good enough. He told Gilbert and Morrow to expect the filing of a written brief on behalf of his argument, for the full panel to consider. The hearing concluded with the writs intact and with no good reason for anyone to think that the Ninth Circuit, on further reflection, would set them aside. Gunn could only deliver to his overseers the disappointing news that not just one but two judges now stood behind the writs. And that was the end of the young attorney's involvement in the affair.

As the lawyers and judges jousted in Seattle, the *Ohio* bore down on Nome. The town did not know of the surprise awaiting it. The storm season was underway. The winds began to howl and the seas to roll as September began, a heavy rain coming down almost without stop. "The breakers come in like race horses and look like mountains," Will McDaniel, the miner who had camped with his brother, Ed, close to the beach, wrote in a letter to his family back in San Jose. In these conditions, he reported, "we are shut in the tent like mice in a trap." Their stovepipe fell off in the gale, filling the tent with acrid smoke and forcing them to dash outdoors. There was a lull, a spectacular sunset, a sure feeling among some old-timers in Nome that the worst was over, but two days later, Will was writing the family that the rough weather was back, now "increased in fury."

By September 10, the weather was calm enough to permit the brothers a three-mile walk along the beach. They gaped at the destruction: mining pumps and engines buried deep in the sands; metal pipes twisted into knots; a three-masted sailing ship, the *Sequoia*, run aground and wrecked; a second vessel, the *Katherine Sudden*, broken in half, on the bar off the Snake River; numerous barges and small craft smashed into kindling. The dead bodies of a pair of drowned seamen, the swollen corpses mutilated by the raging ocean waters, had washed ashore. Still there was worse to come. The winds gathered again on the night of Tuesday, September 11, and reached hurricane velocity at seventy-five miles per hour. By Wednesday noon, floodwaters surged through downtown, lifting entire buildings from their foundations and shattering them into pieces, as townspeople tried to tie down the structures with ropes. A bank of the Snake collapsed, dispatching three cottages out into the Bering, while others bobbed in the river like corks, precariously secured to the soaked land by lines. A throng of a thousand or so gathered to watch the valiant effort of a mammoth barge, the *Skookum*, to withstand the tremendous pressures of the waters until it broke up with a colossal crash, its contents of lumber and liquor set upon by looters.

It was the severest set of September storms in the memory of any white settler. The tempest raged far along the coast, sparing not even the mighty. At Topkuk, the sea came for the mining equipment sent there by McKenzie and swallowed the machinery up in one gulp. From the sanctuary of his room at the Golden Gate, the hotel at a remove from the worst of the flooding, the boss could know nothing yet of this misfortune—or of the greater calamity in store for him. For the *Ohio* had arrived off the coast of Nome.

Chapter 20

"THE RING IS BROKEN"

WHEN THE STEAMER FIRST CAME INTO SIGHT ON THE EVENING OF Thursday, September 13, the seas still were too rough for anyone to row out to the *Ohio* from shore. On Friday morning, Charles Lane offered the job for cash to anyone brave or foolish enough to try—and found a taker. The fellow managed to reach the steamer in his skiff and return to shore without capsizing. In his hand were the documents everyone was so eager to see.

The word immediately spread—from storm-battered tent camps by the beach to the shops and saloons in town, to the offices of the Nome papers, the *News*, the *Gold Digger*, and the *Chronicle*. "The Ring Is Broken," the *Chronicle* declared in a celebratory headline for an edition of this day; "its leader has been deposed and deprived of his power." A small number of people were disappointed, the *Gold Digger* reported—those who still viewed the McKenzie receiverships as a just response to "the foreigners'" unfair seizures of the best Anvil properties in the first phase of the gold rush. But "the great majority," the paper found, "feel inclined to cry out, with the waiting souls in the Bible: 'How long, O Lord, how long?'"

The word filtered out to the miners at Anvil and Dexter Creeks and Snow Gulch—and beyond Cape Nome to the encampment at Topkuk. The poet Sam Dunham received the news with glee. Four weeks earlier, McKenzie's ring had shoved him along with his comrades out of their claim. Now they could be twice thankful—to nature, for destroying the boss's mining equipment in the storm, and to

171

San Francisco, for these writs ordering McKenzie to release his grip on
Anvil and seemingly spelling the end of his reign everywhere on the
Seward Peninsula. As was his custom, Dunham composed a poem for
the occasion, addressed to "the Swedes" of Anvil Creek, "from their
fellow-sufferers at Topkuk":

> We learned today that you've received a message from the Sound
> Which loosed the legal ligatures with which your Claims were
>   bound.
> We send our warmest greetings, and hope that you will get
> The dust the Boss Receiver is a-hanging onto yet.
>
> We had our little laughs last year, and chuckled at your woes
> Caused by the festive jumpers and the mournful old Sour Doughs
> But we've ceased to smile and laid our laughs upon the upper
>   shelves,
> For we have learned to our regret just how it is our-selves . . .
>
> Last week the foam-crowned Sea King came and Served his
>   unbought writ,
> And Aleck's high-priced plant now lies deep down be-neath the
>   spit . . .
>
> We join with you in praise today and raise a joyful shout
> In honor of the righteous laws that knocked the jumpers out.
> Let's celebrate in dry champagne the powers that wield the rod—
> You thank the U.S. Circuit Court while we give thanks to God.

But had the ring been broken? McKenzie, too, heard the word on
the street that morning, that the writs had arrived and San Francisco
was demanding his return of the gold. Just as anticipated by Morrow,
the boss's instinct was to resist, no matter the peril he was told he
would answer for. "We'll save every ounce of it. I'll get it now," he
declared at a gathering at Hubbard, Beeman & Hume attended by

District Attorney Wood among others. This was a brave decision, because a mob had started to form outside Alaska Banking & Safe Deposit at the corner of Front Street and Steadman Avenue, a short walk from the law firm's offices. The throng consisted largely of miners, the same miners kicked off the beach by the McKenzie combine, and at the sight of the boss, his large frame unmistakable on the street, their anger boiled over. "Give up the gold or face the rope," some in the crowd yelled. A young man pulled a gun on him. McKenzie plowed forward, keeping his own gun in his pocket, and no shot was fired. Stones pelted him as he pushed his way into the bank, the heavy doors locked behind him. The miners smashed the bank's glass windows to try to gain entrance to the building. Bank employees gamely resisted with chairs and stools. The melee ended only with the arrival of reserve troops from the 7th Infantry.

Inside the bank, McKenzie reconsidered his plan to retrieve the gold. His boxes now contained dust worth about $200,000. In aiming to "save" the gold, "every ounce of it," he meant to keep it out of the defendants' hands. Unless he could do that, his ultimate scheme, to use proven gold finds to float shares of the Alaska Gold Mining Company, would collapse. But with the mob calling for his neck, the gold, he prudently decided, was for now best left in the vault. When he exited the bank, US Marshal Vawter approached him outside the front door and formally served him with copies of the writs. He had just come within an inch of his life and yet hardly seemed shaken. "I am not prepared to say what course I shall pursue," he coolly told a reporter for the News. "When the writs are interpreted, I shall confirm instructions." Edwin Beeman, speaking for the Hubbard law firm and for the plaintiffs it represented in the Anvil cases, similarly told the paper, "We have not determined upon our policy. Perhaps we may question the legality of the writs. . . . No money nor property will be transferred to the defendants until the district court here interprets the orders which have been received from San Francisco."

And how would the district court "interpret" orders that required no great effort to decipher? Judge Noyes had yet to show up at his

chambers that morning. Marshal Vawter found him at the Golden
Gate Hotel. It was eleven o'clock, but Noyes was still in his nightgown,
having just awakened. Vawter entered the bedroom and handed him
a copy of the writ for the Discovery claim. The judge shuffled to the
anteroom, sat down, and began to read. It shouldn't have taken him
more than a few minutes to get through the document, but the marshal departed before Noyes had offered any response. Noyes, it might
be imagined, was rubbing his sleepy eyes in disbelief. As irritated as he
had been by the defense appeal to the Ninth Circuit, he apparently
had not considered that San Francisco might go against him. Denial
was a state of being for him, a protective quilt he could snuggle under.
In Nome high society, such as it was, Mr. and Mrs. Noyes were treated
with esteem. Three weeks earlier, shortly after he had denied the Anvil defense the right of appeal to the Ninth Circuit, the judge and his
wife were the guests of honor at a formal-dress ball held at the Golden
Gate for 150 attendees, at which the dancing continued until three
o'clock in the morning. Mrs. Noyes was known for her "delightful"
Saturday teas, as the Gold Digger called them: "the guests, the Russian
tea, dispensed in frail and dainty porcelain, all suggest a London or
New York drawing-room rather than the popular idea of Nome." But
suddenly the cold blade of reality had pierced this make-believe world.
The appellate court had repudiated and humiliated him. Everyone in
town would see that.

He kept to his rooms at the hotel. Perhaps he was concerned for
his safety should he venture outdoors. Unlike McKenzie, Noyes lacked
physical courage. Perhaps he was drinking to try to relieve his stress.
Although never seen imbibing at the saloons, he sometimes drank in
his chambers, a habit openly talked about in town. But the attorneys
for the Anvil defendants were hardly willing to leave him undisturbed.
Samuel Knight for Wild Goose showed up at the Golden Gate with
a request for an immediate order enforcing the writs. He found Noyes
still in bed, though conscious. "I can do nothing," the judge told him.
"My hands are tied. . . . You gentlemen have got to fight this thing
out among yourselves. . . . I shall make no order; it is not my duty to

do so; it is not within my province or right to do so." Others heard Noyes bemoan the failure of the McKenzie camp to take care of the "San Francisco end." Judge Morrow, he said, simply had no say in the matter. Perhaps in this stubborn attitude he was channeling Oliver Hubbard, now heard to say, in starker terms, "What do we care for Morrow anyway? What does he amount to? Noyes is the Czar up here. He is the one who will look out for us."

The defense attorneys also pestered McKenzie, demanding "all" the gold on deposit at Alaska Banking. They delivered their demand to him in writing, that afternoon, but he ignored it, claiming to be a mere "layman," unable to interpret formal legal directives on his own. Crafty as ever, the boss already had thought to add a layer of insulation to his receivership in the form of a pair of attorneys, pulled from the Nome bar, to advise him, as receiver, on his legal position. Neither was part of his Alaska Gold scheme.

The first, Dudley Dubose, was a former district judge for the territory of Montana and the son and namesake of a Confederate brigadier general. The second, Thomas J. Geary, was a former congressman from California, a Democrat best known for an early 1890s law, named after him, requiring all Chinese laborers in the United States to register with the federal government or face arrest, imprisonment, and deportation. Whether out of professional opinion or a desire to tell the client what he wanted to hear, both attorneys now advised McKenzie that the writs out of San Francisco were invalid. They were "void," Geary maintained, because the orders of Judge Noyes to appoint McKenzie as receiver were not "appealable"—Judge Morrow had "no jurisdiction" over the matter, and neither did the Ninth Circuit as a whole. San Francisco, of course, did not see the matter that way, and Geary and Dubose would both come to suffer for tendering such dubious advice to the boss at this time. But in the moment, they supplied McKenzie with an excuse for not complying with writs that he was determined to fight regardless.

Stymied in the attempt to remove the gold from the bank, McKenzie stalled for time to figure out how to handle the situation.

He needed intelligence on the enemy camp—what it was thinking, its next move—and, unsurprisingly, he already had a pipeline in place. His conduit was young C. A. S. Frost, the Justice Department special examiner who had arrived in Nome nearly two months earlier. Through the sort of psychological pressure that often worked for him with malleable subjects and probably through financial inducements, by late August McKenzie had made Frost part of his team as an informant. "He is putty in my hands," McKenzie boasted to Marshal Vawter. For the purpose of funneling timely information to McKenzie, Frost hired and put on the US government payroll a trio of detectives tasked with tracking the movements of the defendants and their attorneys in the Anvil cases. Frost also was useful to McKenzie in a second way, through his official responsibility, for the Justice Department, to advise the US marshals. Now he went to one of the deputy marshals and said that he had learned, from one of his detectives, that the Anvil defendants were planning a raid on Alaska Banking that night—an organized assault, not a mob uprising—to take back their gold. "It must be prevented," Frost said in a tone of alarm. His anxiety was warranted, considering the mounting frustration of the Wild Goose and Pioneer Mining camps over the refusal, so far, of Noyes, McKenzie, and the plaintiffs to honor the writs. In response to this stated concern, the military guard on the bank was strengthened.

As the day wound down, Vawter returned to the Golden Gate. Noyes was still in his rooms, just as the marshal had left him in the late morning. The judge was in a grumpy mood and no further along in his thinking. Drunk or sober, he was incapable of being "the Czar" of Cape Nome. "I told him I was there to support the Court, and asked him if there was anything could be done in relation to that writ," Vawter later said. "He answered that McKenzie could do as he pleased."

Chapter 21

"STAND ASIDE!"

HE BANK WAS LEFT UNMOLESTED THAT NIGHT. FIRST THING IN THE morning on Saturday, September 15, one day after the arrival of the writs, Kenneth Jackson, attorney for P. H. Anderson, climbed on his horse and rode three miles east out of town to the base camp of the US Army's 7th Infantry by the Nome River. Trouble was brewing, he reported to Major J. T. Van Orsdale, the commanding officer in charge of keeping order in the Cape Nome district. With McKenzie refusing to comply with the orders from San Francisco, a "vigilance committee" was being organized to take possession, by force if necessary, of his Anvil Creek receiverships, Jackson said. And if this "committee" swung into action, "there was no knowing where it would end," the attorney added. "Bloodshed" loomed.

Van Orsdale already had his hands full trying to keep roving bands of looters from scooping up the valuable contents of ships run aground by the September storms. He had a squad of men out making arrests. But this news, he understood, demanded immediate attention. He rode into Nome to confer with his second-in-command, Captain Charles French, in charge of the 7th Infantry's barracks behind Front Street. French confirmed the imminent danger, and the major and his captain went to find Noyes to urge him to give clear instructions on the enforcement of the writs. It was eleven o'clock in the morning, and for the second day in a row, Noyes had yet to leave his rooms at the Golden Gate. Told by Van Orsdale that this was a "serious state of affairs, likely to result in rioting and bloodshed," he was as ineffective as ever. The matter, he said once again, was "out of his hands"; he "did not know what Mr. McKenzie was going to do." Noyes had renounced his authority for any decision making.

The officers called on the boss at his office on Steadman Avenue. In "the interest of peace and good order," Van Orsdale asked, what was he planning to do about the writs? McKenzie said he still wasn't sure. He needed more time to consult with his lawyers and would call on the major in the barracks later that day. Shortly after one o'clock in the afternoon McKenzie arrived there. He had to proceed "very cautiously," he now said, since he was at personal financial liability for the care of the Anvil properties and the gold dust in the bank. He could see his way, he said, to giving up the Anvil properties to the defendants but not to handing over the gold—not until the Ninth Circuit had a chance to hear from the plaintiffs "the other side of the matter."

McKenzie was stalling, but at that point, he couldn't have known, as no one in Nome knew at this time, that the Ninth Circuit already had heard "the other side of the matter " in oral arguments in Seattle, three days earlier, and had kept the writs in place. With Noyes seemingly incapacitated, the army and the US marshals were in a quandary. Hearing that McKenzie would yield the Anvil properties helped, but did he really mean it? And what about the gold in the bank? Should McKenzie's custody be protected, as he demanded and as the district judge appeared to endorse? Or, in fulfillment of the orders of a higher court, should the marshals go with the 7th Infantry to the bank, demand that the manager surrender the key to McKenzie's boxes, and attend to the orderly return of the dust to the defendants?

The answers weren't obvious to them. Sensing their indecision, attorneys for the rival parties jammed into the barracks, turning the quarters into a kind of makeshift courtroom. Dubose and Geary, on behalf of McKenzie, and Jackson, Metson, and Knight, on behalf of their defense clients, vied for the ear of the "judges"—first Major Van Orsdale and then Marshal Vawter, who had arrived in the midst of an argument growing more heated by the minute. Jackson asked Geary flat out whether he was advising McKenzie to disobey a writ of the circuit court, and Geary replied that, even though he viewed the writs as void, he had not given that advice. Metson put the same question to Dubose and got the opposite answer: "I certainly do advise my client to disobey the writ." As for the military, Dubose continued, addressing Major Van Orsdale, the 7th Infantry had no right to assist in the enforcement of invalid writs. This was an astonishing position for any attorney to take, going beyond giving professional advice to a client to encouraging active resistance to a court order. Just as McKenzie was putting himself in legal jeopardy by resisting the writs, so was Dubose.

Also present at the barracks was the Justice Department's C. A. S. Frost. In allegiance to his secret benefactor, McKenzie, he told Vawter that the writs out of San Francisco were not only "void" but likely to be declared so by the US Supreme Court. The marshal, Frost said, must "swear in a large posse comitatus"—a body of able-bodied armed men, drawn from the townspeople—"to prevent the delivery of the gold dust to the Lane crowd or the Pioneer people." Vawter replied that protection of the gold was a job for the army, not a citizens' posse. "To hell with the military," Frost shot back, "you can't trust them." Vawter wisely ignored Frost. He understood that the marshals could be held at fault by the Ninth Circuit for resisting the writs.

The day's *Nome Daily News* informed its readers that "Judge Noyes is still too sick to exercise his judicial functions," but the judge, whatever exactly was ailing him, rallied. At four thirty in the afternoon, with the argument over the writs still unresolved, a letter arrived for Van Orsdale at the barracks:

My Dear Major:

After you called with Captain French this morning I saw the original papers on file from the Circuit Court of Appeals, and I find that it is necessary for an order to be entered by this court, which will be entered of course as soon as the same can be prepared, and such further steps will be taken as will be a full and complete compliance with the order of the Circuit Court of Appeals. My anxiety in this matter is to do everything in my

power, and have all those whom I can in anywise control fully
comply with the order of the court above, which of course will
be done. In the meantime it is necessary that matters should
rest in status quo, and peace and order should be preserved,
and I therefore request that you render such assistance to the
marshal as may be necessary to maintain that peace and quiet.
Assuring you of my desire to cooperate in every effort
that is needful in order to preserve life and property, I
am, very sincerely yours, Arthur H. Noyes, Judge.

A similar note arrived for Vawter. It certainly sounded like good
news for the defendants, with Noyes abandoning his initial position
of allowing McKenzie to "do as he pleased" about the writs. But would
Noyes follow through? Where was the order requiring the boss to return the gold and yield the Anvil properties to the defendants? His
letter promised action; yet he still seemed to be dawdling.

Jafet Lindeberg's patience was spent. Forty-three days had passed
since that evening in late July when McKenzie, accompanied by Bob
Chipps, an order signed by Noyes in hand, had showed up at Discovery and evicted Pioneer's crew from the site. He had sought relief in
the courts, and now the Ninth Circuit had spoken clearly, with its
directive for the boss to return Discovery to the Pioneer Mining Company immediately. Yet McKenzie had not done so. It was time, Lindeberg determined, to act forcefully on his own. His attorney, Metson,
agreed. As the arguments continued at the barracks, Pioneer quietly
dispatched a team of armed men out to Discovery. On arriving at the
site, they gave the surprised work crew ten minutes to evacuate the
property. The workers hesitated to comply. A Pioneer man fired a gun
in the air, and that did it—a full-scale retreat by McKenzie's hands
from the mine followed. They had no stomach for a fight.

The failure of the crew at Discovery to offer resistance in this first
instance of confrontation was telling. It appeared that none of the men

hired by McKenzie to work the properties he held in receivership bore him any deep loyalty, all the more so because he was regularly behind in the wages due to them. Several McKenzie hands visited the offices of the *Chronicle* and, according to the paper, "apologized for their employment and stated that they were merely trying to get together a few dollars and would desert the cause of the ring on the first sign of trouble."

Word of the recapture of Discovery quickly reached the boss, still at the barracks, and he turned on Metson with fury. Pioneer Mining's lawyer feigned ignorance of the raid (although he had known of Lindeberg's plan, he did not know it had been carried out until McKenzie told him so). McKenzie said that a large amount of gold in the sluice boxes at the site had better be accounted for. Metson retorted that Pioneer's people always were careful, especially with gold. McKenzie replied that if they took that gold, "it was just like stealing it." That set Metson off. "I answered that there were some people who came from his country who were trying to steal that whole area up there," as he later recalled this incident, "and if there was stealing going on, he was doing it." And that did it for McKenzie:

Wait till I get you outside.

Now, let's understand it. Does that mean that the first time we get outside it is a case of "turn her loose?"

You cut loose right now.

Both men went for their guns. Metson had a small-caliber handgun and figured he had to blast McKenzie point-blank in the head to have a chance of coming out of the shoot-out alive. But the soldiers grabbed them both before either could get off a round. "Of course, it was all in the day's work," Melton felt. "I went to Nome with some standing, and I figured I might just as well come out in a box as show the white feather."

As Metson and McKenzie came out of the barracks, a small fellow rushed at them with a gun but was blocked and disarmed by McKenzie without incident. The assailant was a miner, as it turned out, who was probably coming to make good on the mob's threat of the day before to bring McKenzie to a rough justice. The boss asked Metson to come to his office. Metson said anywhere was good for him to finish the fight. McKenzie, though, had already cooled down. He had in mind a new tactic. Sit down, he told the lawyer as they entered the office, before locking the door behind them. Metson refused—he'd rather handle any "gun play" on his feet, he said. There's no need to fight, McKenzie insisted. He proposed instead a "bribe," as Metson called it, and was willing, by the lawyer's account, to go as high as $1 million to get Metson to stand down. It was an enormous sum, one McKenzie likely didn't have on him in Nome. Still, the gesture expressed his measure of Metson as a formidable antagonist, a leader of the forces pitted against him. The discussion was interrupted by a banging on the door. It was Charles Lane, accompanied by a team of his men, anxious to extract Metson from McKenzie's clutches.

Once Metson had been liberated, there was a dash for the bank: Lane was done waiting for his gold. McKenzie, still unwilling to give it up, joined the race. Bank manager Whitehead, loyal to the boss, pointed a shotgun at Lane. The Lane men trained their weapons at McKenzie. At this affront, the boss flared with indignation: "I am an American citizen. I have committed no crime and I am going out of here. Stand aside!" Hands above his head, he walked out unscathed, the tense silence broken by the sound of a gun accidentally dropped on the floor by one of Lane's hands. Lane, though, had his path to the vault blocked by Captain French, who arrived at the scene with reinforcements. Metson explained that Lane had come to enforce San Francisco's writs, but French felt bound to enforce Noyes's written instructions to preserve "peace and order" in Nome. "It looks as tho' you would have to enforce them by arms," he replied to the lawyer. Outgunned, Lane and his men retreated. The gold, for the moment, remained in the vault.

Chapter 22

"THE SUPREME COURT
WILL KNOCK THEM OUT"

WHILE THE GOLD IN THE BANK STAYED OUT OF THE REACH OF THE defendants in the Anvil cases, they now took back, in addition to Discovery, the four other claims McKenzie had seized for receivership back in July at the start of his campaign. And, in more unhappy news for the boss, Hume resigned his position as deputy US attorney and quit the ring. The lawyer was seeking, no doubt, to save his own skin. McKenzie always had seen Hume as a weak link, and now he had to be concerned about betrayal: Hume, after all, knew all the details of the Alaska Gold scheme.

"McKenzie is ruined and he knows it!" So the *Nome Daily Chronicle* exclaimed in a front-page story asserting that the boss, as the head of a "desperate gang," could be held in contempt for defying the Ninth Circuit and was unlikely to hold on to his "boodle" in the bank. That was an accurate assessment of the legal jeopardy faced by McKenzie but an altogether wrongheaded assessment of his state of mind. He didn't consider himself ruined; nor was he desperate. Nome, he certainly understood, was a mortally dangerous place for him at the present time. Since the arrival of the *Ohio* with news of the writs, he had faced four plausible threats on his life: from the mob calling for his hanging, from Metson in a shoot-out, from the enraged miner at the barracks, and from Lane's men at the bank. There may have been a bounty on his head. In these circumstances, he might easily have abandoned his venture—handed the keys to his safe deposit boxes over to the marshal, caught the next steamer to the outside, dissolved the Alaska Gold Mining Company, and lived for the next get-rich opportunity that was sure to come along. The Ninth Circuit, surely, would have no further interest in him.

But flight probably never crossed McKenzie's mind. In his view, the game was going against him, but it was by no means over. Judge Noyes, Commissioner Stevens, and D. A. Wood were still in his camp, and C. A. S. Frost, giving up his position as a special examiner for the Justice Department, replaced Hume as Wood's deputy. Had he been able to dash off a letter to Elva, he probably would have mustered his usual hardiness, saying no more than "I am in a tight spot but have plenty of friends, and I will come out alright." This was his instinctive mentality. Perhaps some part of him thought the fates could not catch him; they never had and never would. "Aren't you afraid," a man now asked him, that "the 'Frisco courts will take some drastic action against you?" The boss greeted this question with laughter and a query of his own: "What can they do?" Well, "they might arrest you," the fellow suggested. It'll never happen, McKenzie shot back.

Sunday passed without Noyes fulfilling his promise of the previous day to issue orders enforcing San Francisco's writs. On Monday morning, at last emerging from his rooms at the Golden Gate, he opened court. Presented with a motion by the defense to make good on the writs, he balked. In fact, he seemed to be rethinking his vow. Confronted in private about his backpedaling by Marshal Vawter, he responded, "In the first place I have got a right to interpret those writs. . . . In any event the Supreme Court will knock them out when it gets there."

Just like McKenzie and the boss's attorneys, Noyes was now risking a contempt-of-court citation from the Ninth Circuit for his defiant behavior. Still, the notion of the US Supreme Court galloping to the rescue to save the day for the McKenzie ring could not be completely dismissed. After all, the action of any circuit court of appeals was subject to review by the nation's highest court. In 1900, the Supreme

Court consisted of six justices appointed by Republican presidents, three by Democratic presidents. Perhaps it would be receptive to a complaint lodged by a Republican kingpin backed by Republican senators like Carter, Hansbrough, and Cushman Kellogg Davis and a business magnate like James Hill. The Court, led by long-serving chief justice Melville Weston Fuller, an appointee of Grover Cleveland, a Democrat, was generally accommodating to the barons of the Gilded Age and their accumulated piles of wealth. In 1895, the Fuller court had struck down as unconstitutional a tax enacted by Congress on stock dividends, interest income, and other forms of wealth. The McKenzie camp spread the gospel in Cape Nome, so that it became, in some quarters, an article of faith, that the Ninth Circuit's writs were unlikely to stay in place for long. Major Van Orsdale considered transferring the gold in McKenzie's safe deposit boxes to the barracks so that the dust could be safely guarded until the Supreme Court rendered a decisive judgment on the validity of the writs. He did not seem to consider that such a ruling could be months away or that the court might choose simply not to get involved. But he could hardly be blamed for not being a legal expert; the army was trying to fill a vacuum left by a sulky district court.

For the defense camp, the state of affairs was infuriating. McKenzie was not going to hand over the gold to them willingly, and neither the judge nor the military nor the marshal in Nome was going to make him do it. Only one course of action remained: to get word to San Francisco of McKenzie's defiance and the unwillingness of Noyes to enforce the writs. Surely the Ninth Circuit would be interested to know that its orders were being flouted. The problem, as ever in Alaska, was one of time and distance. October was nearing. What if the Bering froze over before the Ninth Circuit could sort this out, leaving the antagonism to fester for the winter months when Nome was sealed off to the outside?

A CLIMATE OF MUTUAL DISTRUST AND SUSPICION, SCENTED WITH GUNPOWder, settled on Nome. Men from the allied Pioneer and Wild Goose camps, shotguns and Winchesters at the ready, watched the bank, guarded by a 7th Infantry detachment, from the upstairs windows of a building across the street. Any attempt by McKenzie to leave the bank with a sack or two of gold would meet with a hail of bullets from that quarter. A detective retained by Frost to gather intelligence for McKenzie bored a hole through a wall of Metson's office to listen in from an adjoining room on the conversations within the defense camp. Kenneth Jackson's office got the same treatment. Frost also had his detectives watch Lane and Samuel Knight. The boss considered that, like Frost, the detectives belonged to him, and he shared their reports with bank manager Whitehead. But McKenzie's antagonists also used detectives: men hired by Metson drilled a hole in the ceiling of Noyes's chambers and listened from above. Metson also had the pleasure of reading and editing the reports of a detective hired by Frost to keep watch on him—unbeknownst to Frost, the detective was already on Metson's payroll.

The result was a testy stalemate—everyone knew what everyone else was doing and thinking, but there was no action-forcing event. On being questioned in the Noyes court about his plans, McKenzie stated, "I have discontinued operations on all the claims under my management. . . . I am not in a position to state what course of conduct I shall pursue in regard to the quantities of gold dust which I have in my possession." Asked by the Gold Digger about a rumor that he planned to build a second railroad line from Cape Nome to Council City, Lane boiled over with frustration. "I have done nothing but talk to lawyers all summer," he said. "I am tired of it and am not going to spend any more money here. If things had been different I could have made a living here and have invested money, but at present I am like the captain when he ran his steamboat ashore. They asked him what he was doing and he said, 'I've quit.' It's just the same with me—I've quit."

As in August, when it became widely known in Cape Nome that the embattled defense had run for help to San Francisco, the word was out on this second try. But as October arrived and the days passed without a response, the chances grew that the Bering would freeze over with the dispute at an impasse. The sparring spilled over into a town meeting called by the chamber of commerce to elect three delegates to represent the business interests of Cape Nome in Washington. Lane got word that McKenzie planned to pack the gathering with followers pledged to vote for a slate favorable to the boss. Some were probably jumpers like Kirke Requa, with a vested interest in McKenzie's success. Lane made sure that his own, much larger number of supporters showed up. The meeting, called for the evening of Monday, October 8, began in a room over the Hobbs saloon but moved to the larger hall at the Columbia Theater to accommodate all those wanting to take part. McKenzie stayed away but not Lane, who took the stage. "I come among you as a miner," he said to boisterous cheers. "I hope you will choose [delegates] who will represent the miners. I don't believe we need receivers or lawyers. I made the suggestion some time ago that I was willing to go in with the miners and raise a subscription for this object: if we find a man coming here to practice law we will try to persuade him that it is a bad country for that business, we will give him a pick and shovel and sixty days provisions, and if he is found practicing law after that—hang him." Laughter trailed his words. Next to speak was Lafe Pence, a former member of Congress, elected as a candidate of the Populist Party to represent Colorado in the House. Pence sang Lane's praises as a friend of the working man. There would have been jobs for six hundred, he said, if the legal snarls had not kept Lane from building a pumping plant, as Lane intended at the start of the mining season. "As long as this regime lasts,' he said, 'while receivers can take possession clandestinely in the night, capitalists won't make money." Use this vote, he urged the throng, to send a message directly to McKenzie and the boss's confederates: "Let us elect our delegates now," cried Pence. "There is one little office on Steadman Avenue where they are waiting now to hear the result of their emissaries' work." The McKenzie ticket, which included H. G. Steel, manager of the *Nome Daily News*, went down to defeat. The meeting voted for a pro-Lane slate headed by his attorney Samuel

Knight. The gathering also approved by voice vote a resolution introduced by Pence that took sharp aim at McKenzie's methods since arriving in Nome—and by extension at Noyes for endorsing them— and called on the delegates to bring these abuses to the attention of the US Congress.

Noyes ignored this popular repudiation of his court. On October 10, two days after the meeting at the theater, with Pioneer actively back at work on the Discovery claim, he approved, at the urging of Chipps, an order barring the company from taking any of the gold dust out of the jurisdiction of his court. On October 12, with the Justice Department in Washington now aware of the protracted battle over the writs, through a report sent by the distressed US Marshal Vawter, Noyes typed out a rambling letter to Attorney General Griggs seeking to explain his conduct. "I have had considerable trouble and many efforts have been made to bring the court into disrepute," he began. Taking note of the writs issued by San Francisco, he called them "all out of proportion" to his own orders for the appointment of a receiver and added, "You can imagine that I was placed in a very embarrassing position." Still, he assured Griggs, he felt sure that the writs would be dismissed and his own rulings sustained, as his conduct "will bear the most severe and strictest scrutiny" and the "conduct of the Receiver also has been most exemplary."

In his letter to Griggs nearly two months earlier, Noyes had mentioned that his court had met with "harsh criticism." Now he identified his prime tormentor:

C.D. Lane, who is the President of the Wild Goose Mining Company . . . is here and has been here for a couple of months past or thereabouts, and has in every way attempted to bring the court into disrepute. He is a man of means, as you know, loud mouthed and blatant and has many followers as you can understand such a man would have. . . . Lane is as you know a Democrat or Bryanite and contributed as I am informed $50.00 to the Bryan campaign four years ago and is doubtless doing something this time. He has sought to make it a political issue and his henchmen have sought to make political capital out of Alaskan affairs or at least so far as that pertaining to the civil government here.

Noyes signed off with a fawning reminder of where his own loyalty resided:

Trusting that President McKinley may be reelected by a majority superior to what he received four years ago and believing that he will be, I am My Dear Sir,

> Very Respectfully and Obediently Yours
> Arthur H. Noyes

Although Noyes pointed the finger at Lane as the source of efforts to bring the district court "into disrepute," the judge didn't offer Griggs any examples. Perhaps he had in mind an allegation later made public in an affidavit filed by a Nome man charging that the Lane camp had paid him, P. F. Reese, $750 to swear out a claim that Noyes had accepted a bribe in return for favorable treatment in court. Possibly this allegation was true; it was certainly the case that Lane and his attorneys saw themselves at war with the Noyes-McKenzie combine and perhaps they did resort to foul means in their prosecution of the conflict—not because they were Democrats opposed to a Republican-appointed judge, as Noyes framed the issue for Griggs, but because they so badly wanted to win back Wild Goose's mining properties and its gold. For the same reason, the Pioneer side might have fought dirty: a detective accused Metson of a ruse in which Judge Noyes would be given marked $20 gold pieces as a bribe for the appointment of a commissioner; the judge and Mrs. Noyes would then be shadowed to obtain, on the use of these pieces, proof of Noyes's dishonesty. Even so, such conduct was not a justification for the favoritism Noyes showed to the boss. His letter to the attorney general, with its frantic plucking of the chord of partisan fellowship, was the best he could muster under the circumstances. Even as he was writing this missive, fresh trouble was drawing near. A steamer was bearing down on Nome, maneuvering around floating chunks of ice, and on board the *Oregon* was a pair of deputy US marshals dispatched to Nome out of San Francisco. Word had reached the Ninth Circuit that its writs had not been enforced—and the judges on the panel were furious about it.

Chapter 23

"THE GAME IS ALL UP"

T HE NINTH CIRCUIT RECEIVED NOTICE OF THE DEFIANCE OF THE WRITS on Monday, October 1 in the form of affidavits sworn by the defense camp in Nome, brought before the panel by attorneys from San Francisco engaged by the defense. Judge Morrow, on his own back in late August when the Nome matter first was brought to the court's attention, this time had company: with the court at the start of its fall session, both of his colleagues, Judges Gilbert and Ross, were in the city to hear cases with him. Gilbert was familiar with the issue from the oral arguments presented on the writs at the Seattle proceeding he presided over with Morrow in September. The newcomer was Ross, the sole Democratic appointee to the court.

Gilbert and Ross often were at odds on questions before the court. Their differences reflected, in part, a personal divide. Both were natives of Virginia, and both had settled on the Pacific Coast after the Civil War, but there the similarities ended. Ross, born in 1845 and raised on a slave plantation, was a true son of the antebellum South. He enrolled at the Virginia Military Institute at the age of fifteen and fought in the war under Stonewall Jackson at Cedar Run in 1862. Gilbert, born two years after Ross, grew up in a Unionist family that left Virginia for Ohio as tensions mounted, and he attended college at Williams in Massachusetts, the school and the state a hotbed of abolitionism. But in this instance, the troubles "north of Fifty-Three" proved an occasion for the two of them, along with Morrow, to come together—to close ranks in the face of the blunt challenge to their authority by the targets of the writs. And with Alaska soon to be sealed off by ice, the judges acted at once through the office of the US Marshals Service for the Northern District of California, with which the Ninth Circuit shared quarters at the Appraisers Building. Marshal John H. Shine was told to have his men proceed immediately to Nome "to attach the person of the said Alexander McKenzie, and produce him before the United States Circuit Court of Appeals for the Ninth Circuit at the City and County of San Francisco, State of California, to answer to his refusal to obey the said writ of supersedeas." In other words, Judges Morrow, Gilbert, and Ross ordered McKenzie's capture and arrest.

The judges also wanted answers from McKenzie's attorney, Dudley Dubose, cited in the defense affidavits for actively urging the army to disobey the writs. In their view, this conduct amounted, if true, to contempt of court. They did not order Dubose's arrest and detention, however, instead instructing Marshal Shine to have his men hand the attorney a summons to appear before the Ninth Circuit to show why he should not be punished for contempt. As for the gold in the bank at Nome, under armed guard, the judges directed Shine to restore it to the defendants. Exactly how this was to be accomplished they left to the marshal.

Morrow and his colleagues might have gone further than these measures. As they now learned from the defense affidavits, Noyes had been heard muttering that the Ninth Circuit had no business intervening in the Nome litigation. The judge was as disparaging of the writs as McKenzie—arguably a worse offense, since the boss, as receiver, was a creature of the Noyes court. Still, as angry as the judges were with Noyes, they let him be, ordering neither his arrest nor his summons. Perhaps they felt that hauling the judge in would be too disruptive to the district court. Perhaps, too, they felt that, as a political matter, taking down a receiver appointed by a district court was one thing, going after a judge appointed by the president and confirmed by the Senate quite another. Noyes would have to be dealt with at another time.

The fastest way to get to Alaska from San Francisco at this time of year was by rail to Seattle, then by steamer to Nome. Freshly signed orders in hand, Marshal Shine's two deputies boarded a train that evening. It was still Monday; they were due to arrive in Seattle on Wednesday morning. The last steamer of the season bound for Alaska was scheduled to leave on Thursday. They made their connection with one day to spare.

Had the boss a taste for poetic justice, he might have appreciated that his nemesis, Charles Lane, was an owner of the vessel that conveyed the men coming to take him into custody. Marshal Shine's men disembarked from the *Oregon* and made landfall in Nome at about seven o'clock in the morning of October 15. A blanket of snow on the beach greeted them. The town was just waking up, and their target, the marshals quickly learned, was eating his breakfast at the Golden Gate. How best to approach him? They feared, expected even, armed resistance from the McKenzie camp. And they were just two. There was plenty of strength in numbers in the military, but the 7th Infantry and, for that matter, Marshal C. L. Vawter and his men had yet to show a willingness to take a stand against McKenzie. So the marshals turned for assistance to a figure whose determination to capture McKenzie could not be questioned. Encountering Metson on Steadman Avenue, around the corner from the Golden Gate, they told the attorney of their mission and asked if he might be willing to approach McKenzie while they waited just outside the hotel. Metson agreed to do it. Despite—or perhaps because of—having nearly "turned it loose" with McKenzie two weeks earlier, he believed he had McKenzie's respect.

The boss, seated alone, was almost done with breakfast when Metson arrived and took a chair at the table. The attorney delivered the tidings politely, with no wish to inflame: marshals had arrived from San Francisco with a "writ of attachment" for his arrest; if "a suggestion" might be permitted, he might find it best, after the meal, to accept an escort to the office of his lawyer, Mr. Geary. The boss offered no resistance. Once he had finished his breakfast, he walked out of the hotel with Metson and was introduced to the pair of marshals.

"Marshals from 'Frisco, after McKenzie!" The bulletin raced through town, gossip and rumor close behind. Robert Chipps dashed to the home of Kirke Requa, his fellow shareholder in the Alaska Gold Mining Company. "The game is all up; McKenzie has thrown us all down," he breathlessly declared. He was considering selling his claim in Discovery to Pioneer Mining he said—in other words, to revoke the sale of the claim he had already signed over to Alaska Gold. Alarmed by the perplexing turn of events, Requa went off in search of her attorney, Oliver Hubbard, for an explanation, but she couldn't find him. Seeing a mass of people spilling out of an office in town, she discovered that the center of attention was McKenzie, holed up in a back room, visitors lining up to see him. The stampede was on: all those with business of one sort or another with McKenzie had a sudden interest in having a word with him. These folks included jumpers, like Requa, who had deeded their claims to Alaska Gold in return for a promise of stock shares and, in her case, a promise of $2,000 in cash, not a cent of which she had been paid. Hubbard had brokered her deal and most of the others, but it was McKenzie's company. She took her place in line.

Inside the office, McKenzie was conferring with Geary and Dubose, while the marshals kept a wary eye on him. The boss still sounded determined to hang on to the gold, even though both his attorneys now advised him to surrender it as ordered by San Francisco. Asked by the marshals for the keys to his safe deposit boxes, he replied that he didn't have them on him—they were with District Attorney Wood. Somehow McKenzie had slipped the keys to Wood, beneath the notice of the marshals. When Wood was summoned and the keys demanded, he refused to hand them over, declaring nonsensically, "I don't know whether I have them or not." On the way out the door, he muttered, "I will see you later." To refuse to hand over the keys was to invite the wrath of the Ninth Circuit, but Wood had faith in McKenzie and believed, even now, that the boss's political connections ultimately made him invincible. "As soon as Alexander McKenzie got on the outside," Wood now told a skeptical Hume, the "fix" would be applied to the judges on the San Francisco panel.

In a side conversation, Geary told Metson that McKenzie preferred to leave Alaska, not under arrest and escorted by the marshals, but "at large," making his own arrangements. But as for returning the gold to the defendants, the boss wasn't going to yield it voluntarily, Geary relayed. As Metson later testified, "Mr. Geary told me that Mr. McKenzie would not give up the gold dust without a fight, and that if I persisted in getting the dust that there would be bloodshed; there would be four or five or six men killed, and I might get killed myself, and that if I did not get killed I would be responsible for those who did get killed."

Perhaps, Geary suggested to Metson, there was a peaceful alternative: "the gold dust would go out at the same time as the United States marshals, and we would all go out together to protect it." No deal, Metson responded. If McKenzie wanted a fight, he would have one. His conversation with Geary over, Metson told the marshals of McKenzie's belligerent attitude and asked for permission to go and get his Gatling gun. The Gatling, invented during the Civil War by physician Richard Jordan Gatling and adopted by the US Army, was a hand-driven machine gun, the multiple barrels rotated by a crank. Permission granted, Metson went off to retrieve his weapon.

As battle loomed, the boss dealt with the visitors lined up to see him. To her surprise, he granted an audience to Mrs. Requa. It was their second encounter, the first since Hubbard's introduction of her as the "little lady" who walked hundreds of miles across Alaska:

I have come to you, Mr. McKenzie, to ask you what is the matter with everything here. . . . I believe you are president of this company Mr. Hubbard got us all into. Now you are going out and where is all this [promised] money and stock?

Well, Madam, I don't know you, I never heard of you and I never promised you anything.

Well, Mr. Hubbard knows about me. . . . [Y]ou are going out and I want to know before you go out what this means.

Hubbard was sent for. McKenzie put it to him: had anything been promised to Mrs. Requa? Looking in Mrs. Requa's eyes, Hubbard said no, nothing at all. She stormed out.

The marshals left McKenzie in the office—he was hardly a flight risk, considering that a mob was ready to pummel him with stones, or worse, should he venture out onto the streets by himself—and walked over to the bank. It was time to get the gold out of the boxes, keys or no keys, with crowbars if necessary. Manager Whitehead, anxious to protect his property, asked them to wait while he hunted down Wood. But the district attorney still refused to relinquish the keys. The "sons of bitches" knew where to find him if they wanted to see him, he told Whitehead. "Let them proceed with their damned burglaries."

Gatling gun strapped to his chest, Metson sent for sledgehammers and chisels. What happened next became a matter of legend. By Metson's theatrical account, proudly conveyed to a San Francisco newspaper months later, the job was done by "the men from the Pioneer Mining Company" with "the whole town of Nome turned out to see" as the hinges were knocked off the boxes, splinters flying. By the marshals' account, accepted by the Ninth Circuit and probably closest to the truth, they did the demolition work themselves. Yet a third version, least likely of all, had the task painstakingly performed, without damage, by a locksmith. As for the violence threatened by the boss, there was none. It was a bluff—or maybe men he expected to put up a fight failed to appear. The military gave no resistance: shown the order of the Ninth Circuit instructing the marshals to remove the gold from the bank, Captain French of the 7th Infantry stood down.

Judge Noyes absented himself from the drama. Visited by the marshals, he told them grumpily that if they had a warrant to bring him to San Francisco, which they did not, it was fine with him. He dashed off an ardent letter to Senator Hansbrough in Washington, vouching for McKenzie's "economical" stewardship of the Anvil mines. As for his own conduct, "I never did a dishonorable thing in my life," he insisted. "The golden opinions of my fellow-men are treasures far too rich to be swapped for golden dust." He concluded the missive with an allusion to Metson's weapon: "nothing short of a Gatling gun or an order from the Government" would get him off the bench.

NEWS OF THE LIBERATED GOLD MET WITH CELEBRATORY GUNFIRE AS THE crews working the mines along Anvil Creek discharged their weapons into the air. The pokes were removed from the vault, and the marshals fetched the boss, the treasure now set before his doleful eyes. Then began the weighing and the counting, the defense attorneys crowded around, all eyes on the scale as the dust was measured and the amounts compared against the logbook in which McKenzie had recorded how much gold he had deposited from each of the Anvil properties under his receivership. He was short—short on the amount taken from the Wild Goose properties, short on the amount taken from Pioneer Mining, short on the gold taken from P. H. Anderson's Number Two Above Discovery. Where was the missing gold? The boss took exception to the question hanging in the air and pulled aside Pioneer attorney Johnson. "When you know me better, Judge Johnson," he said, "you will know I am no nickel thief. I have my own notions and ideas of business, and carry them out on my own plans. That dust will be accounted for." The deficit, though, was not a matter of nickels; it amounted to $40,000, more than $1 million in 2020 dollars. McKenzie said he could produce "receipts"—meaning that his expenditures in working the mines could account for the shortage. He indeed did have expenditures, such as the wages he paid hired hands (and was notoriously behind on). But did his spending account fully for a deficit of this size? Had he made off with some of the Anvil dust? The matter could not be settled there and then. For now, the marshals toted the dust to the Alaska Commercial Co., around the corner, and there the attorneys took custody, depositing the gold in accounts held by the defendants. The Ninth Circuit's will had been done.

Ninety days after he set foot in Nome, McKenzie completed his visit to these parts with an evening aboard the *Valencia* in the company of his captors before the steamer set sail in the morning. "Exit Mephistopheles," the *Nome Daily Chronicle* crowed in an "extra" dedicated to McKenzie's comeuppance. "In the vernacular of the street he is a 'dead one,' and the probability is that Nome will never again be offended by his presence. . . . He is stripped of his power, decayed in his glory and sunk in his worth. He has been exposed to the people, clothed in all the infamy of his iniquitous practices, and they now know him for the schemer that he is."

Yet, even as the *Valencia* steamed south with its unhappy cargo, his rogue spirit remained behind. Noyes was still judge of Alaska's second division, Wood was still district attorney, and Reuben Stevens was still a US commissioner. As for Dubose, McKenzie's hapless Nome attorney, he was mulling whether to resist the summons from the Ninth Circuit to appear before the panel and explain why he should not be held in contempt. He told Metson he was "sorry that he had misconstrued the first writ," yet offered to pay an associate of Metson $1,000 "if you can find a law that will relieve me of going to San Francisco." Told there was no such law, he said he supposed he would have to go—but didn't sound especially resolute about it.

The gold dust from the five Anvil properties put into receivership had been recovered—except for the $40,000 shortfall. But the vault at Alaska Banking & Safe Deposit still contained dust taken from other properties worked by the McKenzie combine, like the one at Topkuk. And Stevens's ruling evicting miners from the beach remained on the books. With their grip still on the mechanisms of law enforcement on the peninsula, and infuriated by San Francisco's incursion onto their turf, as they saw the matter, McKenzie's confederates sought to settle scores, namely against the Wild Goose and Pioneer camps. A friend tipped off Metson that he was about to be arrested on a bribery rap for trying to entrap Noyes. Pointing to a skiff on the beach, the friend advised him to slip away—the skiff could get him to a tug, and the tug could meet up with a steamer at sea, bound for the outside. Metson spurned the suggestion: "I had done nothing I was ashamed of, I certainly had not committed contempt," he later said. "If I went out . . . it would be before the townspeople or else I would not go." Instead, he called on Noyes in chambers and told the judge that if the idea was to put him in jail, there better be a good reason for it. Noyes retreated, and Metson took his leave of Nome in plain sight. Charles Lane's lawyer, Sam Knight, though, chose to flee on hearing that he too had been marked for arrest for trying to entrap Noyes in a corrupt act. Witnesses reported seeing a man they thought was Knight, disguised in women's clothes, slinking out of town. Once safe in San Francisco, Knight owned up to scurrying out of Nome on the sly, but apparently feeling his masculine honor to be at stake, he insisted he had not donned feminine attire.

His Topkuk property still tied up in litigation, Sam Dunham took passage on a steamer and, while aboard, penned "Homeward Bound," his last poem of the season:

> There's a smooth absconding lawyer,
> Wearing diamonds like a sport,
> Who spends all his lucid moments
> Praising Nome's imported Court.
> He has beefsteaks in his stateroom,
> Purloined by the pantryman,
> While his clients in the steerage
> Eat cold corn-beef from a can.

The Ninth Circuit showed good instincts in sensing something badly amiss in Nome. But from its distant perch, the court still had no more than a dim idea of the shady turn taken by the great Alaska gold rush of 1900. In particular, the extent of the scheme—its reach into high places in Washington—was not known. There was a larger story here, as the *Chronicle* insisted in its editorials—a story that begged the question of what kind of country America was to be at the dawn of a new century. Were political bosses still to rule, with judges and senators as their instruments? In that kind of society, where was the opportunity for the little person? How could the "money power," the clout of the titans of business that supported men like McKenzie, be countered? The Nome story was a knotted one, hard to untangle. But it could be untangled, and so it would be, to the nation's rapt attention.

Part Five

EXPOSURE

"It is quite evident that a most wicked conspiracy was formed to loot the Nome Country through judicial proceedings."

—*Letter from H. G. Orton, Missouri Republican*
friend of William McKinley,
to Attorney General Philander C. Knox, September 1901

Chapter 24

"NOW ALASKA HAS A SCANDAL"

ESCORTED BY THE MARSHALS, McKENZIE, NATTILY ATTIRED IN A SILK-lined overcoat and black derby, arrived in San Francisco early in the evening of Monday, November 5. There to greet him on the wharf was the press. "The accused receiver towered high above the officers, his big frame and broad shoulders making him appear like a veritable giant," the *San Francisco Call* told its readers. "The newspapers have been having their inning," McKenzie remarked to reporters, "and I propose to have mine before long." The marshals brought the boss not to jail but to the Palace Hotel at New Montgomery and Market Streets. A European-style luxury establishment, the Palace could be considered a substantial upgrade over McKenzie's previous lodgings at the rickety Golden Gate of Nome. It featured a grand court for the entrance of horse carriages, redwood-paneled hydraulic elevators, and a fireplace in every room.

On the following day, the first Tuesday of the month, Americans went to the polls to elect a president. McKinley beat Bryan in their rematch, taking 292 votes to 155 for the Democrat in the electoral college and receiving nearly 1 million more votes than his challenger in the popular tally. The Republicans also retained sizable majorities in both houses of Congress. McKenzie, ordered to appear before the Ninth Circuit on the morning of the day after the election, could consider these results a relief. The Democrats, who surely would have investigated, with relish, a Republican boss suspected of a corrupt plot to seize control of Alaska's gold fields, stayed out of power on both ends of Pennsylvania Avenue.

Still, the grievances that gave life to Bryan's two tries at the presidency and more broadly to the populist movement remained deeply felt. Bryan won 45 percent of the popular vote, including in states like Montana, Colorado, and Nevada (the "Silver State"), with sizable mining constituencies. He lost California but won handily in the Sierra Nevada county of El Dorado, site of the discoveries that ignited the gold rush of the Forty-Niners. And unfortunately for McKenzie, it was San Francisco, not Washington, that had him by the collar. He was now on the home turf of his tormentors in Alaska—Charles Lane and lawyers William Metson and Samuel Knight. And perhaps no city was more eager to break with the seamiest features of the Gilded Age. McKenzie's timing could not have been worse. He walked onto the stage as a ready-made villain and as a symbol, too, of old-style methods that reformers in California were determined to eradicate, in their state and indeed everywhere in the land.

A HALF CENTURY BEFORE THE IMPROBABLE APPEARANCE OF A TENT CITY ON the Alaskan tundra, there was the marvel of San Francisco, its unplanned birth likewise a testament to the American appetite for conquest, adventure, and riches. The discovery in 1848 of gold at Sutter's Mill, in the western foothills of the Sierra Nevada mountains, gave San Francisco its character. Few prospectors made profitable strikes in the Sierra Nevada. The "real fortunes," as a chronicler noted, were made in the city, "above all, by those speculating in land and engaging in fraud on an epic scale." In time, a demand for cleaner government took root. The *San Francisco Call*, destined to be the most biting critic of McKenzie, voiced this demand. Founded in 1856, by the mid-1880s the *Call* had twice the circulation of any other city daily. A favorite of the working classes, it was a Republican newspaper but, as such, a tribune for eradicating "bossism" from the party, a platform for what was sometimes called the party's "progressive wing." The proprietor in 1900 was John D. Spreckels, a wealthy financier who pledged allegiance to "the honest, the respectable and the loyal Republicans of San Francisco, backed by the decent Republicans of the entire State." A figure like Judge Morrow of the Ninth Circuit, a pillar of civic life, was exactly the sort of person he had in mind. The mission statement of his newspaper reflected this righteous creed: "The *Call* is a FEAR-LESS newspaper; it will expose any man or set of men whom it finds doing wrong, no matter how powerful he or they may be."

With McKenzie in its midst, the *Call* served up a sensational account, "tales that savor of the middle ages," of the battle over the Anvil Creek properties, accurate in the essentials if not all the details. "The course of the litigation reads like a romance," the paper wrote. "It includes bodies of armed men seeking by force what the law would not give them. It includes threats of bloodshed, of forcible disposses-sion and of wholesale murder, and it ends with the breaking open of a safe deposit box and of big boxes of nuggets and carting them away in the full sight of a whole town of people, who cheered as they looked on." The prime source for the story was Metson, who had reached San Francisco from Nome a day earlier than the boss. The paper printed an enormous photograph of the lawyer, resplendent in handlebar mous-tache, over the caption, "ONE OF THE ATTORNEYS WHO HAS BEEN FIGHT-ING FOR THE MINERS AT NOME."

As for McKenzie, his "inning" was just beginning. The Supreme Court, he had told his ring members back in Alaska, would come to the rescue and put the Ninth Circuit in its place. He meant it. Wheels were in motion even as the *Valencia* sped him to San Francisco. The Saint Paul law firm of McKenzie ally Minnesota senator Cushman Kel-logg Davis petitioned the Supreme Court to review the actions of the Ninth Circuit taken against McKenzie culminating in his arrest. The Court responded with an order for Morrow and his colleagues to sub-mit a brief showing why such a review should not be undertaken.

McKenzie had won, at the least, a postponement of his trial, show-ing himself worthy of his reputation for "big political pull," the *Call* reported to its readers. As "a matter of courtesy" to the Supreme Court, the paper explained, the Ninth Circuit released him from his velvet confinement at the Palace and set him free to leave the city on bail of $5,000. McKenzie promptly left San Francisco for Saint Paul, planning to go on to Washington. "I have had plenty of trouble," he wrote Elva at Hamilton Terrace in New York. "Dear Wife, do not worrie. It will come out all OK in the end." Elva was well aware of the "trouble," as she was amassing a growing pile of press clippings on the "Queer Tales," as one headline called them, emerging from Alaska involving her husband. She pasted a number of the cuttings into a school notebook the couple's young son, Sandy, the middle child, had once used for rudimentary exercises in penmanship and arithmetic. McKenzie, though, had one less friend to count on as he headed east to try to salvage his affairs: Senator Davis, who had led the charge on the Noyes nomination and petitioned the Supreme Court through his law firm, was dead of kidney disease at the age of sixty-two.

DIRECTED BY THE SUPREME COURT TO ACCOUNT FOR ITS CONDUCT IN THE McKenzie case, the Ninth Circuit might have paused to wait for the outcome in Washington. That would have been the prudent thing to do, taking into account the political weight of McKenzie and his friends. Instead, while Judge Morrow and his colleagues on the panel postponed consideration of the contempt charges against the boss, they decided at the same time to launch a full-scale investigation into the Nome affair, aimed at getting to the bottom of this murky matter that San Francisco was reading about in the papers. The judges wanted to get beyond the relatively narrow question of whether anyone had committed contempt of their court and answer the root question of whether there was, in fact, a conspiracy to loot the gold fields of Alaska and, if so, how it came to be. This was a question, arguably, best taken up by Washington—whether by the Congress or the McKinley Justice Department, both with wide-ranging jurisdiction over Alaska. Nevertheless, the Ninth Circuit decided to plunge forward on its own, perhaps out of an understandable lack of faith in Washington's dedication to sorting out the matter. The panel's decision had far-reaching consequences, and actors in Washington with their political hides at risk were worried with good reason.

The hook for the investigation was Dudley Dubose, McKenzie's bumbling attorney in Nome. Dubose had made himself fair game by not responding to the summons to come before the court to answer charges of advising disobedience to the court's writs. Unless he had somehow snuck out of Alaska, undetected, he presumably was wintering in Nome. But he could be tried in absentia. The proceedings "in the matter of the alleged contempt of Dudley Dubose" began on November 8, just two days after McKenzie's landing in San Francisco. The Ninth Circuit's judges excused themselves from presiding over this lengthy fact-finding exercise, choosing instead to delegate that task to E. H. Heacock, a former state senator and a Republican, nearly seventy years old and in his ninth year as US commissioner for the Northern District of California. If Heacock, operating out of Room 87 of the Appraisers Building, had questions on how to proceed, he easily enough could check with Ninth Circuit judge Morrow, stationed in Room 46 and keeping close tabs on the probe. McKenzie and Noyes would not be required to appear, for the time being, but other witnesses could be called, by subpoena if necessary, to give testimony under oath, subject to cross-examination.

At two o'clock in the afternoon on November 8, opposing counsel filed into Heacock's chambers. Dubose's former colleague from Nome, Thomas Geary, undertook his defense. In one sense, Geary was a curious choice, in that he also was under suspicion by the Ninth Circuit, though not facing any charges, for his role in advising McKenzie on the writs. Then again, Geary had an intimate acquaintance with the sequence of events under investigation and was in a good position to pounce on weaknesses in the prosecution. He also was well familiar with San Francisco, having moved there with his family from Boston at the age of nine in 1863. He attended college in the city, at St. Ignatius, developed a law practice in Santa Rosa to the north, and served as district attorney of Sonoma County before getting elected to

Congress in 1890. Affable on the surface, he had a pugnacious streak, once planting his fist in the face of a legislator who dared criticize his signature legislation cracking down on Chinese immigration. As became clear when the Heacock proceedings got underway, he viewed his main role as protecting his "shadow" client, McKenzie, the real target of the investigation.

Pitted against Geary was the formidable figure of Evans Searle Pillsbury, founder of the San Francisco law firm of Pillsbury, Madison & Sutro, his roster of blue-chip clients including Wells Fargo and Standard Oil of California. Pillsbury was performing the job without charge, as amicus curiae, or "friend of the court," his presence a sign of the great weight that the judges attached to the matter. His mission was to expose the Nome scheme in every particular, and he approached the task not only as a friend of the court but also as a committed party in his own right. After all, back in August he had appeared before Morrow on behalf of one of the Anvil defendants, P. H. Anderson. He was as dedicated to McKenzie's just desserts as was Morrow. A former district attorney, he shared with the judge a righteous streak. "My lot has been thrown with the people and state of California," he wrote in his diary in 1864, after migrating west from his native home in Maine. "I have used my influence to make the American people what they should be—honest, loyal and devoted to the maintenance of the Constitution and laws."

Pillsbury elicited tales of wild Alaska from Metson, who told of strapping on the Gatling gun to prepare for combat against the McKenzie ring. As Pillsbury strove to unearth the role, not of Dubose but of McKenzie, in the affair, Geary objected repeatedly, complaining that McKenzie was not the target of the proceeding. Heacock promised to take the objection up with Morrow, but little sympathy could be expected from that quarter, and Pillsbury, who had little patience for Geary, ignored him.

Any hope the McKenzie camp had of keeping the story bottled up ended with Pillsbury's calling Robert Chipps to testify. No one had dreamed with greater fervor of possessing the golden treasure of Anvil

Creek, but now Chipps was a new man altogether, his main interest in fending off a contempt charge and potential jail time for his own defiance of the Ninth Circuit's writs. Four days after McKenzie's arrest in Nome, he had cut a deal with Jafet Lindeberg formally abandoning any claim to Discovery. Now, prompted by Pillsbury, Chipps told of the plotters' first meetings at Everett House in New York, the setup of the Alaska Gold Mining Company, and McKenzie's boast of having the pull to get a judge appointed to the key court in Alaska. Chipps tried to parry some of the questions, but Pillsbury insisted on answers.

Pillsbury also forced Chipps to admit to meeting Noyes at a hotel in Washington on introduction from McKenzie—the eyebrow-raising encounter between a future plaintiff in litigation and the future judge who would preside over it. Guiding the witness to the Alaska portion of the tale, Pillsbury had Chipps tell of the nighttime wagon ride to seize Discovery and other Anvil properties and of McKenzie, working through Commissioner Stevens, arranging for the eviction of the beach miners. Chipps also testified to the conscription of Jimmie Galen, Senator Carter's brother-in-law, to try to thwart the defense appeal to San Francisco. How, Pillsbury wondered, did Chipps know so much about McKenzie's operations in Nome? "I met him every day," Chipps replied. His testimony made for several hundred pages of typed transcript. The impression was unmistakable, of McKenzie as a fixer extraordinaire, a greedy eye trained on Alaska's gold. In pushing for this probe Morrow could scarcely have imagined the depth of intrigue, implicating senior elected officials of his party and casting a shadow on a McKinley judicial appointment.

THE WASHINGTON PRESS CORPS COULD NOT POSSIBLY LEAVE SUCH A JUICY political story to their brethren in San Francisco. "Now Alaska Has a Scandal," the *Washington Sentinel*, a Democratic newspaper, proclaimed on its front page on November 17, the day after Chipps finished his testimony. "If half the charges which are now bandied about are true, there will be enough disclosures and scandals to shake the government at Washington to its foundation," the paper declared. "Indeed, the charges involve United States Senators who are very close to the Government," the *Sentinel* said, "and some go so far as to allege that the name of Mark Hanna will be dragged into the affair before the investigation is through." Should McKinley yield to the "enormous pull" of McKenzie and fail to remove Noyes as judge, Congress was likely to launch impeachment proceedings against Noyes, the paper warned.

While there were many Republicans in McKinley's Washington on the side of the boss, there were others intent on investigating the Alaska affair, even at the risk of embarrassment to the president and the party. The Republicans had their mavericks, unwilling to go along to get along, and these ranks included a junior congressman, Abraham Lincoln Brick, forty years old, the son of a farmer, a former prosecuting attorney for St. Joseph and La Porte Counties in Indiana, elected to the House in 1898 and to a second term in 1900. Colleagues found in him, as one remarked, "a keen sense of integrity"—not the sort of thing said of everyone in his chosen line of work. Brick was following, with mounting indignation, the testimony in San Francisco. In the second week of December, a visitor from Alaska showed up in his office. It was one of the pro-Lane delegates elected at the town meeting in Nome, back in October, to represent the district's interests in Washington. The delegate told Brick of the depravations of the McKenzie ring, confirming firsthand the revelations in San Francisco. The next day, December 13, Brick introduced a resolution calling for the appointment of five members of the House to investigate the Alaska scandal and report back to Congress.

In response, Senator Carter countered with a resolution for the Senate Judiciary Committee to conduct a probe. Only in Carter's framing of this investigation, one purpose would be, as stated in the resolution, to examine the "innuendo and insinuation" fanned by charges "through the press" of a possibly nonexistent "conspiracy" to defraud gold miners in Alaska. McKenzie possibly had a hand in this stratagem; the boss was now in town, encamped at the National Hotel on Pennsylvania Avenue, as the Supreme Court weighed whether to review the Ninth Circuit's case against him.

Probably, though, Carter was bluffing, as he had enemies in the Senate, and any probe, no matter how it began, could go badly for him. Sensing, perhaps, his vulnerability, a political opponent in Montana publicly accused him, in an interview with a Helena newspaper, of a variety of crooked deeds, including participation in McKenzie's illicit Alaska scheme. In an "Open Letter" to his accuser, published in pamphlet form, Carter indignantly denied the charges. Regarding the "alleged Alaska scandal," he said he had "never heard" of the Alaska Gold Mining Company until a San Francisco newspaper brought public attention to the venture. Nor, he added, did he think that any of his Senate colleagues were involved in such a scheme, including, he took pains to say, the late Senator Davis.

The Open Letter sounded like another show of bravura by Carter. As any diligent student of the scandal could see, his denial was at odds with the sworn testimony already on the record in the Heacock proceeding, which traced his involvement in the Alaska scheme back to the first meetings at the Everett House in New York at the start of the year. He had no explanation for his brother-in-law's role as a member of McKenzie's team in Nome—or for the note addressed to him on the legal predicament faced by the McKenzie camp, carried out of Alaska by Jimmie Galen four months earlier. He could confidently assert that he held no shares in Alaska Gold because he undoubtedly knew that McKenzie took care not to record the names of any friends in politics to whom shares had been promised. The stock book deposited by Chipps at J. Kennedy Tod & Co. on Wall Street posed no threat to him.

With the press picking up on Brick's quest for a House investigation of the Alaska matter, the president asked the congressman over to the Executive Mansion—in all likelihood to mollify him. On the appointed day, shortly before Christmas, Brick arrived in the company of Alaska's territorial governor, John G. Brady, a McKinley appointee. Brady could speak directly to conditions in the territory. The two

guests were of like mind on the Alaska scandal and the need for ac-
countability, and they spoke frankly to the president, Brady especially.
To begin with, the governor said, Noyes was McKenzie's tool; there
was no other way to see it. Moreover, the situation in Cape Nome was
so bad, with popular dissatisfaction with Noyes so intense, that the
judge was at an appreciable risk of being violently attacked. It might be
best, he advised McKinley, to transfer Noyes to some other position.

The meeting over, neither the congressman nor the governor would
tell the press what the president said, "but it is understood," one paper
noted, "that he listened with much interest and said that the case had
now reached a stage where a prompt and full investigation was necessary, both for the reputation of the men involved and for the honor of
the judiciary." No doubt, McKinley did listen with "much interest" to
his visitors, but the president had not signed on to an investigation.
The top Republican in the House, Speaker David Henderson of Iowa,
refused to bring the Brick resolution to the floor for a vote, and that
was the end of it. A disappointed Brick suspected Henderson of acting
at McKinley's urging.

As for the Supreme Court, the reputation of McKenzie was such
that many of those in Washington following the matter expected the
justices to intervene on his behalf and force the Ninth Circuit to desist
in the contempt charges against him. So it was "a surprise," as the *Seattle Post-Intelligencer* reported on its front page, when the Court, on the
day before Christmas, announced its denial of McKenzie's petition to
review his case. No explanation was given. San Francisco was now free
to proceed directly against McKenzie and punish him as it thought fit.
Amid the cascade of bad headlines, McKenzie advised Elva to take the
family to Bermuda, and for once he sounded a note of self-pity. "They
are trying to besmirch my character," he said of his enemies, "and they
are resorting to all kinds of dirty work." The star of a drama in which
he wanted no part, he had no choice but to make his way back west to
California.

Chapter 25

"HIGH-HANDED
AND GROSSLY ILLEGAL"

THEIR PATH CLEARED BY THE SUPREME COURT, JUDGE MORROW AND his colleagues on the Ninth Circuit let the New Year pass and then, on January 7, 1901, ordered McKenzie to appear in court in a week's time to show why he should not be punished for contempt. The boss, though, made no such appearance, sending Geary, as counsel, to stand in for him on January 14. Two days letter, the defendant, still not facing the judges and reserving "all objections . . . to the jurisdiction of this Court," submitted "under protest," as he took pains to say, a sworn written statement attesting to his innocence. In this declaration, he conceded almost nothing. He said that he had been "regularly appointed receiver" by Judge Noyes and was qualified for the job. He acknowledged not complying, immediately, with the Ninth Circuit's writs demanding return of the gold extracted from the Anvil claims. "That said," the statement continued, "defendant is not learned in the law, and desired to be made acquainted with his rights and duties in the premises . . . by his counsel." He concluded with a sliver of an admission of personal responsibility for his conduct, sounding a note that approached contrition but fell short of the mark: "it was never the intention of this defendant to exhibit or be guilty of any contempt of this Honorable Court or to disobey any of its lawful orders or writs."

Such was McKenzie's spare answer to the contempt charge. On January 28, nearly two weeks after he swore to this statement, the Ninth Circuit tried his case in court, Judge Gilbert presiding. Geary appeared for McKenzie; the prosecution was a team of three lawyers, acting as friends of the court, including Wild Goose's Samuel Knight. "We admit the fact that the demand was made upon us to turn over this gold dust, and we declined to do it," Geary said. Nevertheless, he continued, McKenzie was acting on advice of counsel that the writs were "void paper." This was familiar ground. But the defense had a surprise for the court. Geary acknowledged that, even now, McKenzie had not returned all the gold dust to the Anvil defendants. Dust from the claims he had worked as receiver was deposited at the Seattle assay office of the US Mint in an account he controlled. He had sent it there from Nome, some $12,000 to $13,000 worth. And why, the prosecution asked, was McKenzie still holding on to this gold? The boss regarded at least some of this stash as his due for "personal services" rendered as receiver, the defense explained. In other words, he felt he was owed a commission.

The trial lasted one day. On the following day, his proceeding also concluded, E. H. Heacock signed off on and sent to the judges of the Ninth Circuit two bound volumes, 987 pages' worth, of testimony and related materials collected in his probe. It was a mountain of damning evidence. The judges chose to rule first on the charge against McKenzie, Dudley Dubose always being considered a peripheral figure in the scandal. On February 11, Erskine Ross, with Morrow and Gilbert beside him, read aloud the opinion and verdict of the court. The boss was seated in a chair before them, Geary at his side, the press in the rear with notebooks in hand. A "shocking record" had been presented to this court, Ross declared. The evidence was "to the effect, and we so find the fact to be, that the respondent McKenzie at all times had it within his power to comply with the writs . . . that he contumaciously refused to restore the gold, gold dust, and other personal property to the defendants, as required by those writs, and has continued such refusal ever since." Ross might have stopped there—this was enough to convict McKenzie of contempt—but instead he drew on the volumes of the Heacock proceeding to describe the broader contours of a plot to seize Alaska's gold by foul means, a conspiracy in which Noyes also was an active participant. The court did not accept, he said, the "pretension" that McKenzie refused to obey the writs merely on advice of counsel: "it was intentional and deliberate, and in furtherance of the high-handed and grossly illegal proceedings initiated almost as soon as Judge Noyes and McKenzie had set foot on Alaskan territory, and which may safely and fortunately said to have no parallel in the jurisprudence of this country." Ross did not name any of the Washington participants in the scheme, but in an unmistakable reference to the Credit Mobilier affair, he said that McKenzie, in organizing the Alaska Gold Mining Company, had placed "a portion" of the shares where he thought those shares "would stand him in good stead."

In stating that the Nome affair had "no parallel" in American jurisprudence, Ross might have gone even further than this declaration. For no previous scandal could be said to match this one in breadth, across the branches of government. Credit Mobilier was about corruption in the legislative branch, also an element of the Alaska scandal, but unlike the latter, Credit Mobilier did not involve corruption in the judiciary.

Wall Street had visited upon the country spectacular efforts at manipulating the securities markets, notably the attempt by Jay Gould and Jay Fisk, in 1869, to corner the gold market. But in that instance, the conspiracy touched on the executive branch, with Gould enlisting a brother-in-law of President Ulysses S. Grant as well as an assistant secretary of the Treasury in the scheme, which Grant ultimately foiled. The Whiskey Ring scandal, also during the Grant administration, involved a much greater number of actors than McKenzie's caper. A multistate criminal syndicate operated by Internal Revenue Service agents, Treasury clerks, whiskey distillers, and shopkeepers conspired to defraud the federal government of liquor tax revenues. The courts convicted more than one hundred individuals. But the courts themselves were not part of the scheme. As these examples suggested, the

Alaska scandal had certain unprecedented features in the annals of corruption in America.

For those in Alaska subjected to the reign of McKenzie, Ross offered words of praise: "And it speaks well for the good, sober sense of the people gathered on that remote and barren shore that they depended solely upon the courts for the corrections of the wrong thus perpetrated among and against them." This was an overstatement—McKenzie was lucky to escape Alaska with his life, and as the territorial governor had warned McKinley just weeks before, Noyes remained in physical danger. Still, this was the essential point for the Ninth Circuit, the triumph of rule of law in perilous circumstances, and Ross drove it home: "And it is well, in these days of the rapid extension of our national domain, for all persons, whether residing in remote regions or nearer home, to remember that courts which respect themselves . . . will never tolerate any disobedience of their lawful orders, writs, or judgments, wherever committed within their jurisdictions." As for the boss's punishment, "it is now here ordered and adjudged," he concluded, that McKenzie be imprisoned in the Alameda County jail, across San Francisco Bay in Oakland, for one year, the marshal to "execute this judgement forthwith."

The *San Francisco Call* was exultant: "Justice Ross . . . called things by their true names." Illustrated portraits of a sad-eyed McKenzie, mustache drooping, and a bespectacled Noyes, looking far younger than his age, accompanied the story. As for the man in the dock, the *Call* permitted itself a touch of melodrama. The "scorching words" from Ross "made the Canadian giant writhe in his chair," the paper wrote. "It's rough on me"—that was all the boss had to say on leaving court, Geary, "gray and grave," silent.

THE NEWS THAT MCKENZIE WAS HEADED TO JAIL TRAVELED INSTANTAneously across the wires: "Alexander McKenzie is in North Dakota what Napoleon I was in France—the absolute dictator of all things governmental or judicial," declared the *Seattle Times*, a noisy populist voice, in an editorial applauding McKenzie's conviction. "CLAIM GRAB-BER SENTENCED," was the curt headline in the *Evening Times-Republican* of Marshalltown, Iowa.

"Alexander McKenzie, chief stockholder in an Alaskan mining company capitalized at $15,000,000, slept last night in the Alameda County Jail and will remain there for a year," the *Call* happily informed its readers, the day after the court delivered its verdict, "just the same as though he were an humble laborer, unless . . ."

Chapter 26

"I WILL GO TO THE PRESIDENT"

"UNLESS," THE *CALL* NOTED OF MCKENZIE'S COURT-DECREED JAIL time, "the President of the United States shall see fit to commute his sentence." It was certainly within the power of the president, according to the Constitution, Article II, Section 2, to shorten McKenzie's sentence, to spring him from jail immediately, even to issue a pardon absolving him of his crime. Still, the political pressure seemed to be pushing McKinley in the other direction. With McKenzie's conviction, with the rebuke of Noyes by the Ninth Circuit for overseeing "grossly illegal proceedings," and with the "shocking record" of the conspiracy laid bare by Heacock's probe, McKinley faced suggestions, even outright demands, that he restore order in Alaska. The impeachment process was the remedy provided by the Constitution for removing a federal judge on grounds of misconduct—charges to be approved by a simple majority in the House, followed by a trial in the Senate, with a two-thirds majority required for conviction. Not since 1873 had the House taken this drastic step—in the case of Kansas district judge Mark W. Delahay, impeached on charges of chronic intoxication. Still, nothing in the Constitution barred a president from taking this step unilaterally, before Congress even initiated impeachment proceedings. On the day after the Ninth Circuit rendered its verdict, John Fletcher Lacey of Iowa, the Republican chairman of the House Committee on Territories and the floor manager of the bill that Congress passed the year before to establish a civil code of governance for Alaska, released a blunt statement of undisguised impatience. "The

President has had the case before him for about two months," he said. "Yesterday's decision will, in my opinion, cause some action to be taken. The decision is official; it is a part of the court record, and the judges' utterance relative to Judge Noyes will have great weight. It is not rumor or hearsay, but something on which the president can act. A copy of the decision is now on its way here and will be laid before the attorney general for his information and construction." Serving his fifth term in Congress, a lawyer by training, Lacey was a practical politician, not known for airing in public a difference with his president. McKinley had a serious political problem in the making.

Yet the president did not act against Noyes—not in response to Lacey and not in response to an editorial in the *Washington Post* declaring that unless Noyes was "deaf, dumb, blind and crippled," he must have known how McKenzie "intended to loot the entire neighborhood" in the Alaskan adventure. Beriah Wilkins, the owner, publisher, and editor of the *Post*, was a friend of McKinley's, a fellow Ohioan and Civil War veteran. McKinley overlooked, too, a letter from a Republican friend in Missouri, Republican attorney H. G. Orton, warning of a "great scandal" in Cape Nome: "the people there have no confidence in the integrity of the courts. . . . So strong is this feeling that prospectors—men who buffet the fierce winds of that arctic clime and men having mining claims—dare not develop them." The attorney's son was a junior member of Pioneer Mining's legal team in Nome.

Why was the president hesitating? The *Call* astutely sensed the countervailing powers working on McKinley. These were mighty forces, hidden from public view, and they placed the president, three weeks before the inauguration of his second term, in an excruciating bind.

A TELEGRAM ARRIVED FOR THE MOST IMPORTANT RESIDENT OF THE ALAmeda County jail in Oakland on the third day after his arrival. It was a brief message of reassurance from railroad baron J. J. Hill, who told inmate McKenzie not to worry—he was actively on the case, taking up his friend's matter "strongly in the East." McKenzie wired back thanking Hill for his "kindness." In a letter two days later to Elva, the boss sounded upbeat. "I expect to be in Washington in about three weeks," he said. "My friends are at work and some are working hard." Knowing that the warden might read his correspondence, he had already found a "friend," he told her, through whom he could send letters in secret. It would be best, he added, for her not to write him back. "I will drop you a note when I can."

From the start, Hill was the driver of a campaign to pressure President McKinley into releasing the boss from prison, with a full pardon no less. He spared no effort to make it happen, calling in every favor due him, reaching out to his stable of friends in politics and business, to everyone capable of bringing influence to bear upon the president. He got the word out, from Wall Street to Washington, that here was a cause of the utmost personal importance to him. To help McKenzie was to help him; friends would be remembered for how they responded in this hour. One of the first letters went to his longtime friend John Stewart Kennedy, a Scots immigrant who had amassed a fortune on Wall Street in railroad financing. Kennedy, now seventy-one years old and in retirement, replied that he was off for several weeks to Jekyll Island—the retreat, off the coast of Georgia, that was a haven for figures like J. P. Morgan. But he said that he had shown Hill's letter to the Wall Street banking house J. Kennedy Tod & Co., run by his nephew of that name. Tod's firm was the depository for the stock book of the Alaska Gold Mining Company and a power in its own right. Kennedy said he had asked the firm "to do anything and everything they possibly can" for McKenzie "and this they have promised to do."

Hill was one of America's busiest men. In 1901, just as in every other year of his long climb to the very top of American industry, the immense work of building and tending to his rail empire occupied just about every waking minute. Indeed, he was gearing up for one of the most audacious campaigns of his career, a bid to form, with J. P. Morgan and E. H. Harriman, the most powerful railroad combination the nation had ever seen. One of the few pleasures he permitted himself, as he traveled the rails in his private car, was a meal of pig's feet. The task of obtaining a pardon for a jailed political boss at the center of a national scandal, of arranging, as Hill was seeking, a private meeting with the president on the subject, was incidental to his wider business aspirations. And yet Hill committed to it. Why? He certainly felt a sense of loyalty to a man, a friend, he had known for decades and who had helped him in his business dealings. Hill had not risen to where he was by leaving his friends at the wayside. Still, did loyalty require exertions of this magnitude and urgency? The more compelling explanation, and the one that McKenzie's friends in the Dakotas assumed to be true, was that Hill from the beginning was an undisclosed investor in the "Nome Proposition." He believed in the promise of Alaska and perhaps put down what, for him, was small change. But now that the venture had ripened into a political scandal, Hill conceivably faced personal exposure.

THREE WEEKS PASSED, AND STILL MCKENZIE REMAINED IN JAIL. HILL HAD yet to meet with the president. Hesitant to act against Noyes, McKinley was no less reluctant to address McKenzie's imprisonment. Perhaps, had the furor over the Alaska scandal subsided, he would have been more willing to get involved. But thanks to Senator William Morris Stewart of Nevada, the issue was only becoming more inflamed. One year earlier, in the Senate debate on the Alaska civil code bill, Stewart had thwarted the bid by Hansbrough and Carter to revoke "alien" mining claims in the gold region. Now, during a debate on the Philippines, he declared, "If you go to Cape Nome, you will find that a worse condition exists there than ever existed in any country under Spanish rule." The matter might have been left there, but Hansbrough impulsively sped to the chamber to attest to the integrity of McKenzie, "in every respect an honorable and responsible man," and of Noyes too. Having expertly baited and hooked Hansbrough, Stewart said he could not "allow any whitewashing of Judge Noyes to pass unnoticed" and proceeded to read from an abstract he had assembled of Noyes's handling of the Anvil mining cases. Asked by his colleague William Lindsay of Kentucky, a Democrat, whether Stewart believed that the offenses Noyes had been charged with warranted impeachment, Stewart gave a one-word response: "Undoubtedly." In that case, Lindsay suggested, the "trying" of Noyes ought to await a formal trial by the Senate—should the House send an indictment to the upper body. Stewart, not quite ready to stand down, inserted into the record the full text of the Ninth Circuit's opinion in the matter of McKenzie's contempt of court. A Republican colleague, Nelson Wilmarth Aldrich of Rhode Island, begged him to get off the topic. Aldrich, whose daughter Abby would go on to marry the only son of oil baron John D. Rockefeller in the "wedding of the Gilded Age," advised Stewart to drop "these extraneous private matters," to which the Nevadan tartly replied, "Is it not a matter of public business that a whole country is tied up and robbed?" His outburst won immediate notice in the press, prompting a mine operator in San Francisco to write him a letter the next day: "I was at Nome last season and know from bitter experience the corruption there. . . . And while I am a good Republican I am ashamed of the present administration. If we could remove Judge Noyes and get a square man in his place the Nome section will produce more gold monthly for the next ten years than any other gold field that modern history speaks of."

Carter might have been expected to defend Noyes, but he was now a lame duck, the Montana state legislature having voted to send to the Senate a Democrat to replace him. While the excitable Stewart was out of line in prematurely adjudging Noyes guilty, the bipartisan chorus of objections from his fellow senators to his foray into the Alaska matter spoke to something else—a deep sense of institutional embarrassment. The wretched state of affairs in Cape Nome *following* the passage by Congress of legislation meant to provide for fair and honest governance in Alaska and a California court's harsh condemnation of a judge confirmed to the bench by the Senate just eight months before spoke to the Senate's failure to do its job and to a broader failure of Washington to get right the "public business." It was an awful moment for McKinley to consider leniency for McKenzie.

Fortunately for the president, he had a good excuse for dallying. The boss was giving the Supreme Court one last try, his lawyers filing a petition for a writ of habeas corpus—a petition that, if granted, would have the Court look into the reason for his imprisonment. If the Court could not find a good reason, it could free him from his "unlawful restraint," without McKinley having to do anything. McKenzie knew this was a long shot. "In the event of failure," he wrote Elva on March 6, two days after McKinley's second inauguration, "I will have to go to the President." Nearly three weeks later, the Court spoke. This was speedy for a case like this—a testament to McKenzie's political prominence. But as he expected, the ruling went against him. And this time there was an opinion, authored by Chief Justice Fuller. He addressed the central argument raised by the McKenzie camp—the contention that an order by a federal judge for the appointment of a receiver, in the midst of ongoing litigation, was not subject to appeal. Wrong, Fuller said, as Congress had specifically allowed an appeal to the circuit court of an "interlocutory order" of this sort made by an Alaskan district court— that is, an order given between the commencement and the termination of the trial. So, too, Fuller rejected the argument that Morrow, as a lone judge, lacked the authority, on behalf of the full court, to grant writs of supersedeas requiring McKenzie to return the gold to the Anvil defendants. Precedent suggested otherwise, he said. The Ninth Circuit was on solid ground, Fuller said, in issuing the original writs, on solid ground in commanding McKenzie's arrest for disobeying the writs, and again on solid ground in dispatching McKenzie to jail as fit punishment for criminal contempt. "We hold that the Circuit Court of Appeals had jurisdiction" in Alaska, Fuller wrote for the court, "and was clothed with the power to pass on all questions in respect of the means taken to enforce and maintain it. We are not called on to revise its conclusions on this application. It is enough that, in our judgment, it has not exceeded its powers. Leave denied."

"I have a decision at last, as you may know," the boss wrote Elva two days after the ruling. "My Dear, do not be discouraged—everything will come out right soon. . . . I am well treated and I am comfortable. . . . I expect to see you within thirty days after you receive this . . . and my good name will win out."

The Supreme Court's ruling was unambiguous: there was not the slightest suggestion of unfair treatment of McKenzie. But in the fertile mind of the boss, he still had "many moves to make yet."

Chapter 27

"THE ACCIDENT
IN THE ELEVATOR"

MCKENZIE KNEW THAT ELVA WAS CLOSELY FOLLOWING PRESS COVER-
age of his case, and this concerned him for one particular reason.
In the letter he sent to her just after the Supreme Court went
against him, he made of point of saying, "Do not worry about reports
about me and my health." He was hinting at the plan he was hatching
to obtain his release from jail. The president might have cause to free
him, he figured, if he was said to be ill—badly ill. The "sick prisoner,"
of course, was a familiar jailhouse ruse. But the boss would do better
than that. He needed someone reliable to vouch for his illness. And
all the friends pushing for his release needed to have the story straight.

The tale involved a supposed mishap in an elevator. As McKenzie confided in a second note to Elva, one he must have felt especially sure no one would read before it got to her, "I am setting up in
the pardon papers The Accident in the Elevator and the Doctors are
making certificates. You understand about my health and so forth," he
said reassuringly. His effort began with Dr. Charles L. Tisdale, county
physician for Alameda County, responsible for the health care of the
inmates of the jail. McKenzie complained of ailing from the effects
of an incident some years before in which, he said, he fell nine stories in an elevator in New York City and quite seriously injured a leg.
Dr. Tisdale, for reasons that surely could have stemmed from a financial inducement offered by the boss, accepted the account. On April 1,

Tisdale sent a telegram to Porter James "P. J." McCumber, the junior senator from North Dakota, stating his medical opinion that continued imprisonment posed a threat to McKenzie's life—the effects of the elevator accident were that serious. McCumber was the coordinator in chief of the McKenzie pardon campaign, the main point of contact between the boss in Oakland, J. J. Hill and other sympathetic friends of the boss, and the Executive Mansion and Justice Department. A Republican, he was new to the Senate, sent there by the legislature in Bismarck in 1899 after the McKenzie machine blocked the path to the seat for his main rival, and he was spotlessly loyal, a true friend, both to McKenzie and to Hill.

There was no time to spare, for Hill had a meeting scheduled with the president in Washington on April 4. The magnate was staying at the Netherlands Hotel in Manhattan. On April 3 McCumber sent him a letter there, updating him on the state of play. The senator began with some troublesome news contained in a letter he had just received from McKenzie. The boss, McCumber told Hill, felt sure that the judges of the Ninth Circuit were "onto," in McKenzie's words, the campaign to spring him from jail and none too happy about it. "They will do all they can to prevent me getting a pardon." That said, McCumber continued in his note to Hill, "I have the petition and other papers so arranged that you can go over it easily with the President," and "inasmuch as the application will be rested almost exclusively upon the physical condition of Mr. McKenzie . . . it seems to me that the request for immediate action should have great weight with the President." McCumber closed with a note on McKenzie's condition, as "confidentially" disclosed to him by the prisoner: "he is gradually getting worse [and] the suspense is drawing on his strength very materially and rapidly. He seems to be somewhat depressed and disheartened. Of course he cannot understand just the particulars of the efforts that are being made here." So the boss, it seemed, had the senator genuinely believing in his dire straits, even as McKenzie was secretly reassuring Elva that he was far from suffering in Oakland: "I have two good rooms and I have everything as comfortable as if I were at home."

When Hill arrived at the Executive Mansion, he had with him, for reinforcement, his friend Daniel S. Lamont, vice president of the Northern Pacific and a secretary of war under Grover Cleveland. By McKinley's side for the meeting, almost surely, was his secretary and trusted right-hand man, George B. Cortelyou. Perhaps the new vice president, starting his second month in office, attended. Theodore Roosevelt and McKenzie, after all, went way back. McCumber met with Hill and Lamont before the meeting—or as the senator called it, "their interview with the President"—and just afterward. "Mr. Hill presented the matter most admirably," he wrote in a letter dashed off to Geary, who was tending to McKenzie's legal affairs in San Francisco. "While still impressing the President with the injustice of the sentence, the high character and standing of Mr. McKenzie, his personal acquaintance with him, and his [McKenzie's] standing in his State and the country," McCumber wrote, Hill "brought especially to [McKinley's] attention the absolute danger to the life of Mr. McKenzie; that the effect of that sentence if carried out would result in a judicial murder."

The president's visitors could hope that their testimonials to the boss's "high character" and precarious state of health would be enough to sway him, but, just in case, they offered a third point for consideration. This matter was really about Alaska and the pursuit of gold there, Hill told McKinley. McKenzie had aroused the enmity of rival business clans—the Wild Goose and Pioneer Mining factions—that had an interest in keeping him in jail so that he could not return to Cape Nome for the mining season, starting in a few months. This line, probably taken straight from McKenzie's communications with McCumber, quite likely reflected the boss's sincere view of the matter: he was in prison not because he had flagrantly defied a court but because, and only because, his Alaskan enemies had (temporarily) gotten the better of him.

The president had little patience for the business quarrel. He probably believed that McKenzie truly was ill—how could he know otherwise?—but didn't seem to consider his death imminent. He made it plain to Hill and Lamont that, for McKenzie to have any chance of presidential leniency, the boss had to show contrition to the Ninth Circuit judges, starting with writing them a letter in this spirit. But this was just the first step, McKinley stressed. He would not act without conferring with the judges of the Ninth Circuit.

"Keep Mack in good cheer," McCumber signed off to Geary in the report on the session with McKinley. He attached a rough draft of a letter for "Mack" to sign and send to the San Francisco judges— his best impression of what the president wished for McKenzie to say. The note was a modest improvement on the boss's sworn statement to the Ninth Circuit, back in January, when he took responsibility, just barely, for his conduct in Alaska:

> Honorable Sirs.
> Having been adjudged in contempt by your honorable body
> in disobeying a certain writ . . . and as one who has heretofore
> always rendered obedience to and held respect for the laws of
> the land and the decision of the Courts through which such
> laws must be enforced . . . I desire to assure you that nothing
> was further from my mind than an intent to show disrespect to
> your Honors, to the Court, or to its Process; and further desire
> to express my sincere regrets that in following the course I
> did in the premises, it has placed me in a seeming attitude of
> disrespect or discourtesy towards your Honors or said Court,
> which I most earnestly assure you was most foreign to my mind.
> Very respectfully yours,

McCumber tried to sound hopeful in his note to McKenzie's attorney, but as he could see for himself, from a follow-up conversation with the president after the Hill and Lamont meeting, McKinley needed more convincing. The president promised "fair treatment" in the McKenzie matter, McCumber reported in an update to Hill, now back in New York, but no more than that. "I was unable to induce him to use the wire in communicating with the Judges. . . . He wished some good friend who was also a friend of the court" in San Francisco "would intercede" on McKenzie's behalf. As for the draft of the letter to the judges for McKenzie to sign, McKinley "approved it as being just right."

It was time, Hill and McCumber agreed, to wheel a new piece of artillery into the campaign. The gun was Mark Hanna, now a US senator representing Ohio and still chairman of the Republican National Committee. No one in American politics and business had a closer tie to McKinley. This relationship could be easily misunderstood— McKinley was not a tool of Hanna, as presented in newspaper caricatures. Had that been the case, Theodore Roosevelt would not be vice president, because Hanna vigorously opposed putting him on the ticket. Still, the president retained a high estimation of Hanna's judgment, and Hanna had open access to the Executive Mansion and to top officials in the administration.

Hill felt that he had every right to call on Hanna's services, in the first place in return for his exertions to get McKinley elected in 1896 as one of the largest donors to a campaign that Hanna had managed. "I have practically had to carry the Republican Party through on my own shoulders," he wrote Hanna four months after that election. Now, four years later, he addressed a handwritten note to "My Dear Senator" on the McKenzie matter. After suggesting McKenzie was a victim of business skullduggery and reassuring Hanna that McKenzie would want to do more for the Republican Party when no longer caught up in the affairs of Alaska, Hill added a personal plea on behalf of his friend: "He is so thoroughly good," Hill closed, "that I feel most deeply his suffering for no crime or reason other than the whim of the court. If there is anything you can do in this matter to help it along I will be always grateful to you."

Hill's note surely didn't strike Hanna as unusual: he was accustomed to serving as a bridge between the president and America's richest men. Back in December, he had escorted Andrew Carnegie into the Executive Mansion library for a meeting with McKinley. Hanna's prompt response to Hill showed his dedication to the task. "My Dear Jim," he wrote on April 10, "I have taken an active interest in this case from the

beginning. . . . You have seen the Pres't and he tells me that you presented the case better than any lawyer could do. He is very anxious to
please you and will do all he can consistently to help you in the matter."
Hanna then shifted to an issue vexing both Hill and McCumber. The
McKinley Justice Department, both of these men felt, had no warmth
of heart for either McKenzie or Noyes. That mattered, since McKinley
was relying on input from his attorney general on the McKenzie case.
The good news in this regard was that the department was getting a new
leader, Philander C. Knox, a Pittsburgh attorney. Knox was a favorite of
the bosses and business barons, with Carnegie, a client, recommending
his appointment. Knox "is a personal friend of mine," Hanna told Hill.
"I had him at breakfast this morning and went over the whole matter
in the best way I could from a layman's standpoint, so he gets his <u>first</u>
impression from me [Hanna's emphasis]. I have made an appointment
for Senator McCumber to meet him this afternoon. I will follow it up
and use all the influence in my power to serve you in the matter as I personally feel very kindly to Alex." There was nothing in Hanna's note
to suggest that, as speculated about in the newspapers, he was a promised shareholder in McKenzie's Alaska scheme. Then again, if he was
involved in the venture, that wasn't something he needed to mention.

Hanna's intervention with Knox undoubtedly helped to move
things along. The Justice Department now shipped the McKenzie
"papers"—the materials that the boss's supporters in Washington
were submitting as the basis for a pardon—to the judges in San Francisco for their review. As these wheels turned, Senator McCumber
prepared, under his personal signature, an "Application of Alexander
McKenzie for Pardon" addressed to McKinley. In a typewritten draft
dated April 18, he devoted fourteen pages to the topic. There was no
mention of a plot by "California mining" to keep McKenzie out of
Alaska. He began on a sounder basis, reflecting his training as a lawyer,
with the argument that McKenzie was "convicted for one offence, and
sentenced for another." The conviction, he correctly noted, was for
contempt of court in disobeying a writ. But the jail sentence, he said,
seemed to reflect the Ninth Circuit's belief "that McKenzie entered

into a conspiracy with Judge Noyes to defraud parties of their mining claims." McCumber posed for the president three questions concerning McKenzie. "Has he ever been indicted for a conspiracy? Has he ever been tried for a conspiracy? Has he or Judge Noyes ever had an opportunity to be heard on such a charge?" The answer to all three questions, McCumber said, was no. That was correct as an answer to the first two questions, but the answer to the third was more complicated. During Commissioner Heacock's proceedings, Geary was able to cross-examine every witness called as to the alleged conspiracy. In this sense, McKenzie and Noyes as well had been "heard" from. And more than that, as the Ninth Circuit judges saw the matter, McKenzie's refusal to obey their writs—his contempt of court—arose from his master plot to take control of Alaska's gold fields.

Moving onto shakier ground, McCumber asserted no one had been injured, not "a single dollar" lost due to an act by McKenzie: "He has simply offended a Court." The Ninth Circuit, of course, did not view that sort of "offense" as a matter to be taken lightly—and this clumsy way of stating the matter was bound to make McKinley wince. To the contention of not a dollar lost, thousands of prospectors could raise a cry of objection. Miners pushed off the beach by the judicial ruling of a McKenzie crony, miners like Sam Dunham in Topkuk ordered off their property by a receiver and many others made to lay dormant for fear of a receiver taking their property—these miners had a fair claim of injury. And beyond the immediate hurt suffered by miners was the damage to the economy for which the town of Nome was the hub. McKenzie's arrival chilled investment; the turmoil he wrought rendered the mining season of 1900, in many respects, a lost year. And McKinley knew this from communications from his friends about the Alaska situation.

McCumber saved the status of the prisoner's health for the end of the application. "McKenzie's physical condition alone calls for immediate pardon," he asserted in his plea. The "known facts" were these:

We are compelled to say that a man six feet, four inches, weighing about 220 pounds, falling nine stories in a heavy elevator, with such

force as to drive the femur bone back and downward past the tibia and
fibula bones, tearing through the flesh and arteries . . . which laid him
up for about a year, much of the time in which he was delirious, must
be seriously injured. We are compelled also to conclude that this fall
must have been a most extraordinary shock to the nervous system, and
that it has left its result.

We know a heart dilated and weak, and pulsating to an enormous
extent beyond the normal . . . renders death immanent [sic] at all times,
even without this punishment.

Such was the story the president was told, later recounted by
McCumber to his Senate colleagues as part of his unflagging defense
of McKenzie. Yet, among McKenzie's friends back in the Dakotas,
men who had known the boss for years and who were familiar with his
ways, there was general disbelief. "Several of Alec's closest friends in
North Dakota never heard of the elevator accident and never knew
him to limp or show any signs of its ill effects," Joseph Jackson, a
biographer who knew and largely admired McKenzie, later wrote in
an unpublished manuscript. Jackson added that a former friend of the
boss, who had become a sharp critic, said, "There was an accident
and, although he was not badly hurt, he remained in his hotel several
weeks so he could collect big damages from the insurance company."
McKenzie's oldest daughter, by his first marriage, offered another version of the story at a court hearing on his estate. The daughter, Mary
Barbara, testified that her father did not attend the funeral of her
mother in Saint Paul at the end of June 1897 because, as she understood, he was "recuperating from a compound knee fracture suffered
in an elevator accident in Bowling Green Building" in lower Manhattan. The problem with this version lay in the time frame. In late
June 1897, McKenzie was writing to Elva, of whom Mary Barbara
knew nothing, about a sprained ankle—not his sprained ankle but
Elva's. And he was writing her not from New York City but from
Washington, DC. It might have been that the boss offered his daughter the elevator accident story as an excuse for not attending her

mother's—his first wife's—funeral. The "Accident in the Elevator," as supplied to McKinley in April 1901 as a reason to pardon McKenzie, appeared to be just what the boss suggested it was to Elva at this time—a tall tale. A master trickster was playing a con on the president of the United States.

Chapter 28

"A FREE MAN AGAIN"

THE BOSS WAS AGREEABLE TO SIGNING A NOTE OF CONTRITION FOR HIS contempt of court as McKinley suggested. "I may be out on the 29th," he wrote Elva, on April 20, from Oakland. He was in an especially buoyant mood because, having "fixed" things—his word—with the postmaster, he was now receiving mail from her via a direct channel that evaded the jail's supervisors. But just as the pardon campaign was gathering momentum in Washington, the effort met with a snag. The hitch lay across the bay from the Alameda County jail—in San Francisco. Having dispensed with McKenzie and concluded the contempt proceeding against his attorney, Dudley Dubose, the Ninth Circuit now made plain its intention to deal with the remaining others whose conduct was at issue, most notably Noyes. In a sense, this represented the response of Judges Morrow, Gilbert, and Ross to the McKenzie pardon campaign: unequivocal opposition. It was a bold maneuver on their part, to target Noyes for criminal prosecution, and, as P. J. McCumber complained to James J. Hill, now in Saint Paul, the maneuver gained McKinley's attention. "The principal thing which troubles the President," the senator wrote, is that he "dislikes to pardon one party to this charged offense before there has been any hearing or even opportunity for reply by Noyes. . . . What we most fear now is the delay." McCumber assured Hill that Mark Hanna was doing good work: "He has certainly taken hold of this matter with vigor." Among other steps, Hanna wired a McKinley-appointed judge, John J. De Haven, a former congressman now on the bench for the Northern

District of California, urging him to talk to Morrow in favor of a pardon for McKenzie.

Morrow, though, dug in, explaining his objections to any break for McKenzie in a fifteen-page report, addressed to Attorney General Knox, titled "In the Matter of the Several Petitions, Letters, and Telegrams Presented to the President of the United States on Behalf of ALEXANDER MCKENZIE to Be Relieved from Further Imprisonment." In the first place, he observed, McKenzie had availed himself, in the US Supreme Court, of two opportunities to challenge the contempt charge of the Ninth Circuit, and in both instances the Court had ruled against him. "Obedience to the orders and writs of the Appellate Court was a duty obvious to all the world, except, apparently, to McKenzie and the officials of the District Court," he noted with evident impatience. As for McKenzie's claim that he disobeyed the circuit court on advice of counsel, this was nonsense, Morrow asserted. It was McKenzie, Morrow reminded, who vowed at that time not to give up the gold dust without a fight in which men might be killed. And even now, Morrow pointed out, McKenzie was holding on to gold dust he had collected as receiver and shipped to Seattle: "In other words, he continued at all times in contempt of the authority of the Circuit Court of Appeals down to the time it passed judgment upon his acts." With "these facts so clearly established and not denied, I cannot, consistently with my sense of judicial duty, recommend the pardon of the respondent," Morrow told Knox.

Morrow's unbending posture left the president as the only one who could resolve the matter, one way or another. McKinley was not much given to conducting business through writing letters or wiring telegrams. Especially on a matter of any sensitivity, he preferred a face-to-face conversation, behind closed doors. And he decided the McKenzie issue needed to be handled in this manner. He would not act before speaking personally to the Ninth Circuit's judges, especially Morrow.

A rail journey the president was preparing to take with Mrs. McKinley westward across the country, all the way to the Pacific, presented the opportunity for a face-to-face meeting. The idea was a postinaugural celebration of the start of his second term in office. The convoy would make stops in Memphis, New Orleans, El Paso, and Los Angeles, among other places, before arriving in San Francisco near the end of May. The McKenzie camp didn't like the prospect of leaving the pardon question to fester until the San Francisco visit. On April 28, a Sunday, Hanna called on McKinley at the Executive Mansion to urge speedier action. But the president, just about to depart on his trip, balked. Hanna relayed to McCumber the president's remarks: McKinley said that "he knew Morrow so well—knew him in Congress, and he was his appointee—and he was certain that he could fix it up in 15 minutes with him." Asked by McCumber whether Hanna felt "absolutely sure" McKinley would act on McKenzie, Hanna candidly replied, "I think I am, but the President, you know, is inclined to be dilatory in doing that which he dislikes to do."

The presidential train departed Washington, DC, on the morning of Monday, April 29, and on the following afternoon rolled into Calhoun Street Station in Memphis, greeted by a twenty-one-gun salute and an honor guard composed of Confederate veterans. With the president, traveling in eight cars, were his indispensable staff man George B. Cortelyou, cabinet officials, stenographers and a telegraph technician, and a press contingent including wire service, newspaper, and magazine reporters and a photographer. Railroad interests covered the entire cost of the journey. Frustrated the president had left McKenzie's fate dangling, McCumber asked Hanna whether it would be helpful for Hill to wire McKinley to give him a nudge. Hanna said no—the magnate had already weighed in. McCumber wasn't sure that was the best advice. "It is probably true that the Senator's judgment is better than mine," McCumber told McKenzie in a note written on April 30. He continued, "I cannot but feel, however, that if the President should hesitate after the matter is presented to him—should feel an inclination to avoid it—that a telegram coming from one who has been his friend—a friend when he needed one, and one who had a right to ask for a little favor . . . might not be the turning point." And still other voices, beyond Hill's, McCumber noted, could be enlisted in the cause. "Of course, Mack, I cannot at all put myself in the position of the President," he wrote. "I cannot understand this wonderful delicacy about offending Judge Morrow. I hope the President will act while he is in New Orleans, but if he does not act on it at that time . . . it does seem to me that telegrams from your friends ought to be brought to bear on him. He says he wants to grant this pardon, and if he does want to, any strong influence at a hesitating time ought to be beneficial."

Yet New Orleans came and went, and so did El Paso, with no action from McKinley. As his train headed toward California, the Ninth Circuit again turned its attention to the Alaska scandal. On May 6, the court found Dudley Dubose, in absentia, guilty of contempt, based on his "spirit of resistance" to the panel's orders, as Morrow explained. The attorney was sentenced to six months in the Alameda County jail, to start as soon as the marshal could retrieve him from Alaska. The judges now decided to launch a second fact-finding proceeding under Commissioner E. H. Heacock, to examine, through testimony and affidavits, the conduct not only of Noyes but also of District Attorney Wood, Justice Department examiner Frost, and Geary, McKenzie's second Nome attorney, who had so far evaded prosecution himself, to determine if any of these individuals, too, were guilty of contempt. And beyond adjudicating that question, the plan was to dig still deeper into the scheme; here again, the Ninth Circuit was determined to do the investigative work that Congress and the Justice Department had failed to undertake. Once more, E. S. Pillsbury, the eminent San Francisco lawyer who had questioned witnesses in the contempt case against Dubose, would serve as lead prosecutor. San Francisco's insistence on yet more probing of the affair would no doubt rile most Republicans in Washington, but short of stripping the appeals panel of its jurisdiction over the investigation, Congress could do nothing to halt the inquiry.

In Oakland, McKenzie could only wonder about the impact of his pardon campaign on McKinley. He had rallied both houses of the legislature in Bismarck, as well as the state senate of Minnesota, to petition for his release, but would that really matter to the president?

Based on conversations with Metson, who had visited him in jail, perhaps hoping to pressure him to return the gold due the defendants in the Anvil cases, the boss was convinced that the judges across the bay would do all they could do to prevent a pardon. In fact, as he warned McCumber, he suspected the judges were trying to get Wisconsin senator John Coit Spooner, a Republican and a friend of McKinley's, to advise against one. Spooner had strongly opposed the bid by Hansbrough and Carter to amend the Alaska bill to invalidate the mining claims of aliens.

On May 8 the presidential entourage arrived in Los Angeles. McKinley was the first sitting president ever to visit California. The dread felt by McCumber and Hill mounted as McKinley drew closer to San Francisco. Given McKinley's disposition to "procrastinate," the senator wrote Hill, "if he arrives in San Francisco without having passed upon this case, not only Judge Morrow but every other possible influence will be brought to bear upon him there to induce him not to interfere with the sentence of the court." But a political boss stewing in jail was not the first thing on the president's mind on reaching the city on May 12. His main concern was the suffering of his wife. Ida McKinley was frequently in poor health. On the Texas leg of this trip, she cut her thumb, which swelled with pus and had to be lanced, and she also contracted dysentery. By the time the couple reached San Francisco, she was severely ill, with a high fever, and her husband was rearranging his schedule so he could be at her side. There was talk that death was near.

Still, even as McKinley tended to Ida and fulfilled obligations like launching the battleship *Ohio*, he plunged into the McKenzie matter. The judges, he found, were in an unforgiving mood, especially indignant that the boss still had not returned to the Anvil defendants the gold he had deposited in the Seattle mint. Surely there could be no thought of releasing McKenzie from jail, they told the president, until restitution was made to satisfy the court's orders. It was done, with Wild Goose's attorney, Samuel Knight, certifying to the Ninth Circuit that the defendants had been made whole.

And now McKinley displayed his wiles. No matter how much pressure he faced from Hanna and Hill, from McCumber and from the state legislators of North Dakota and Minnesota, he was not going to act in favor of McKenzie without the assent of the judges, all three of them. He needed, he understood, to protect his political flank, to guard against criticism from the judges, all the more so because the question of whether he had come to San Francisco to release the boss had become fodder for the city's newspapers, the *Chronicle*, the *Examiner*, and the *Call*, and for other papers in California beyond the Bay Area. The situation, in his mind, called for a compromise. There could be no question of a pardon, because Morrow, Gilbert, and Ross wouldn't stand for it—a presidential pardon would suggest that the judges had been wrong to prosecute McKenzie. That left the possibility of commutation—release from prison for time served.

Attorney General Knox supplied McKinley with the out, informing him by telegram from Washington that there was "no merit" to any of the arguments cited by McKenzie's supporters for either a pardon or a commutation—"except the serious ill health of the prisoner." Health, then, it had to be. The Ninth Circuit judges sent a physician of their choice to examine McKenzie, and he reported that McKenzie appeared to be suffering from a bad heart. This affliction seemed to have nothing directly to do with the injuries suffered by McKenzie to his leg in his supposed accident in the elevator—but then again, could it not be said that a faltering heart was a legacy of that trauma? The physician's report was good enough for the judges—at this point, perhaps, having won the point on the pardon, as eager as McKinley to dispose of this nagging business. Morrow, sounding less like a judge than like McKinley's former colleague in the House, told the *Examiner* in an interview, "McKenzie is a very sick man, and his condition appeals to my humanity. That was the only reason that led us to recommend a commutation of his sentence." The newspapers, including the *Call*, widely accepted this story of McKenzie's looming death, the *Call* writing that the prisoner was "too weak to leave the jail."

The boss had to fulfill one last condition—beyond the note of contrition he had already sent to the judges—for his release. He had to give a deposition. All this time, he had managed to avoid answering, under oath, any questions about his role in the affair. Ever the reluctant witness, McKenzie stalled; the deposition, set for May 23, was postponed, as county physician Tisdale testified to the inmate's "nervous condition." Probably the boss was just bargaining for advantage, leaving nothing to chance. On May 24, McKinley, still in San Francisco, wired his approval of the commutation to Knox in Washington. Only then did the deposition go forward. The proceeding began at ten o'clock the following morning, Saturday, May 25, at the Alameda County jail, Commissioner Heacock presiding. Across the bay, at just the same time, the president and Mrs. McKinley, with the McKenzie business finished and Ida now recovered and well enough to travel, took their leave of San Francisco, amid waving hats and handkerchiefs along the streets of the departure route to the train station. At the jail house, Pillsbury's younger law partner, Frank D. Madison, of Pillsbury, Madison & Sutro, appeared for the court, Geary for the defense. Madison began:

> Your name is Alexander McKenzie?
> Yes, sir . . . Can I ask you a question?
> Yes.
> . . . Am I here testifying against myself?
> No.

As Madison tried to explore why the boss had failed to comply with the writs, Geary intervened and told the boss, "You can decline to answer that, if you want to, if you think the answer would incriminate you." McKenzie responded, "I never felt I could at any time have gotten any of that gold-dust without an order of the [Noyes] Court, and I never took a dollar's worth of it without an order."

McKenzie's consistent strategy was to insist that of course he would have restored the gold to the defendants, if only Judge Noyes had directed him to do so. Left unsaid was the general belief in Nome that Noyes was an instrument of McKenzie, not the other way around. McKenzie was asked no questions about the "conspiracy," as the Ninth

Circuit had called it, to corner Alaska' gold, or about his forming of the Alaska Gold Mining Company, or about enlisting Senators Carter and Hansbrough for the passage of legislation to benefit that company, or about working the appointment of Judge Noyes to the gold district judgeship through McKinley. In short, no questions were posed that, through his answers—and he certainly knew the answers—could have put power brokers in Washington at risk. The man who could have explained everything was asked to explain nothing. A plausible explanation for this farce, although never acknowledged outright, was that the Ninth Circuit's judges, who gave the prosecution the job of probing the Alaska scandal, told the prosecution to limit its questions to the boss as part of the pact the judges made with McKinley to bring this affair to an end.

Knox wired the warden at the jail to let McKenzie go. A supposed eyewitness report, picked up by newspapers, described the allegedly sick man, recently too frail even to appear in court for the deposition, "sprinting down the Southern Pacific Railway depot platform in Oakland to catch a train." That was probably an exaggeration: the boss was not a sprinting man. If he knew anything in life, he knew that there would always be another train to catch. In truth, he remained in Oakland on the day of his liberation. "I received my release today," he wrote Elva, in a letter postmarked Oakland, 7:30 p.m. "I am all OK." His plan, he told her, was to go to Seattle in a day or two, to attend to "some business" there. He didn't elaborate on the nature of the business, but perhaps he planned to lay hands on gold, taken from Alaska, that no one else knew about. On his Senate stationery, McCumber wrote Hill in Saint Paul a triumphant note. "While all of Mr. McKenzie's friends performed their labors to the extent of their abilities," he assured, "I am certain that the effort of yourself and your immediate friends were essential factors in securing his pardon."

HIS PARDON? KNOX TOOK CARE TO NOTE, IN HIS OFFICIAL REPORT, THAT the "Action of President" regarding McKenzie was "Sentence com-

muted to expire, May 24, 1901." No pardon was granted, as Mc-
Cumber well knew. Nevertheless, the far-flung McKenzie friendship
network, extending to his longtime cronies in the Dakotas, assembled
a narrative of his jailhouse time and release that presented him in the
best possible light. It was a mixture of truths, half-truths, exaggera-
tions, and outright fabrications. Many newspapers wrote, as did the
Bismarck Tribune, of a "full pardon," knowing, or not, that there had
been no forgiveness of his crime. But the saga took on a life of its own,
as exercises in mythmaking often do. The stated reason for his commutation, ill health, was said to be the artful trick he had played on
the president and the San Francisco judges. And the president, in this
McKenzie-centric view of the matter, was cast as the supplicant. The
main point of McKinley's trek to the Pacific, the story went, was to
attend to the McKenzie matter. "President McKinley crossed the continent to release McKenzie from the Alameda County jail," a friend of
the boss insisted for years afterward. A version of this tale had the two
men secretly meeting, face-to-face, in Oakland—McKenzie somehow
managing to slip out of the jail for the rendezvous and to return undetected. The belief giving life to such tales, widespread in McKenzie
circles, was that the boss had something on the president—that something probably being McKinley's acceptance of a promise of shares in
the boss's Alaska venture. This was very likely the story that McKenzie
told his old friends, the details varying, as reflected in the comments
that his buddy from Fargo made decades later: "McKenzie was arrested.
He pretended sickness, and a priest who was called smuggled out a
letter for him. This letter was addressed to President McKinley and it
informed William McKinley that McKenzie was not going to take the
rap for their partnership project."

McKenzie's allies seemed to know full well that the commutation
based on his reputed illness was indeed a sham. McKenzie lived for
years afterward. As for McKinley's role, it was true enough that he
been extraordinarily attentive to the boss, from naming the judge of
McKenzie's choice to the Alaska seat to cutting a deal with the San
Francisco judges to gain their support for McKenzie's release from jail.

It was also true that he hadn't shown the least interest in an investigation of the Alaska scandal by his Justice Department or Congress. Yet there was no proof, certainly nothing on paper, that the president had entered into a partnership with the boss. Political loyalty, the coin of his realm, just as easily could explain the president's actions. McKenzie and Hill had helped make him president and therefore had a claim on his help. Friends stood by friends—that was how the world worked according to the code of William McKinley, and according to the laws of political survival in the Gilded Age.

EPILOGUE

"The Looting of Alaska"

DESPERATE ARTHUR NOYES TRIED TO ESCAPE THE REACH OF THE Ninth Circuit. He fled Nome, to the jeers of the townspeople, with the idea of making a personal appeal of his innocence before McKinley in Washington. He never got the chance. On September 6, 1901, an avowed anarchist shot the president in the stomach at the Pan-American Exposition in Buffalo, and McKinley died eight days later. In San Francisco, the Ninth Circuit tried Noyes for contempt. He insisted, in an appearance before E. H. Heacock's commission, that he had never been McKenzie's tool, but the court, with the help of incriminating testimony from Wilson Hume, determined that the two had been part of a "corrupt conspiracy," as Judge Ross said, and found Noyes, like McKenzie, guilty of contempt. In a delicately phrased allusion to coconspirators, as in members of the US Senate, Ross said the conspiracy was committed "with others, not before the Court, and therefore not necessary to be named." The judges, though, were split on a fitting punishment for Noyes. Ross favored sending him to jail for eighteen months for his "shocking offenses." Gilbert and Morrow, though, did not think the court had the authority to effectively remove Noyes from the bench by jailing him. He was ordered to pay a fine of $1,000 for his offenses.

Finding that young C. A. S. Frost, sent to Nome as an examiner for the Justice Department only to join the McKenzie ring, "grossly betrayed the interests of the United States which were entrusted to his care," the judges sentenced him to twelve months in prison. For District Attorney Joseph K. Wood, who apologized to the court for his contempt, they ordered a four-month sentence. Frost and Wood joined Dudley Dubose, brought back from Alaska by a US marshal, at the Alameda County jail. Thomas Geary was let off altogether, the judges finding that the attorney had done nothing more than provide his client, McKenzie, with his opinion on the law. His acquittal was a fair indication that the Ninth Circuit was not, as the McKenzie camp maintained, on a mission to exact revenge on everyone aligned against the "California mining" interest in the battle over Alaska's gold.

All told, the testimony and related materials in the matter of Noyes, Geary, Wood, and Frost ran to eleven volumes comprising over three thousand pages of transcripts. Combined with the earlier testimony in the Dubose matter, the Heacock proceedings totaled thirteen volumes of some four thousand pages. In an era of scandals, big and small, none was more finely exposed than this one. In sum, "the story reads like a proconsular scandal of the later Roman Republic," said *Law Notes*, a trade publication for the legal profession.

Theodore Roosevelt, McKinley's successor, had no sympathy for Noyes. On February 24, 1902, his administration removed the judge from office. TR, though, dealt gingerly with McKenzie, who was done with Alaska but still retained clout as a political boss in the Dakotas and a trusted associate of J. J. Hill. In the spring of 1903, McKenzie, in good health, brought a group of fourteen friends to greet the president, on a campaign-like swing through North Dakota, at the railroad depot in Fargo. Several of them, like McKenzie, were former territorial sheriffs, and they reminisced with Roosevelt about the old days. "I was a little fellow then," TR said in good humor, "but I guess I am as big as you fellows now." In the election of November 1904, with North Dakota voting in his favor, Roosevelt won a sizable victory in the electoral college. One month later, the triumphant president sent his annual message to Congress, a substantial section of which was devoted to Alaska. Although he made no specific mention of the Nome scandal, he acknowledged of the territory that "in some respects it has outgrown its present laws, while in others those laws have been found to be inadequate." District attorneys, he said, should be barred from engaging in private practice, while the governor, and no longer the district judges, should have the power to appoint US commissioners. Alaska also should have popular representation in Washington with an official delegate to Congress, he recommended, and what's more, "Alaskan natives should be given the right to acquire, hold, and dispose of property upon the same conditions as given other inhabitants" and be granted "the privilege of citizenship." Finally a president was treating Alaska with care for its social and political welfare and not merely its extractive possibilities.

The Alaska scandal surged back into public consciousness in 1906. Starting with its January edition, *Appleton's Booklovers Magazine*, a monthly, serialized, in five installments, Rex Beach's "The Looting of Alaska: The True Story of a Robbery by Law," altogether an avalanche of words intended to rile. "Alaska is the galley slave of the Union," Beach began. "She has been ruined, rifled and degraded by such practices as have seldom blackened the pages of American corruption." The tale, "a recital of intrigue and pillage originating in the fertile brains of statesmen beneath the shadow of the Washington monument," begged telling, Beach said, "if for no other reason than to show what abuses are possible under our much-touted systems where we are supposedly equal in the eye of God and the law." With McKenzie cast as the archvillain, the January and February editions of *Appleton's* sold out throughout the Dakotas region. The Good Government League of North Dakota reprinted and distributed the articles; a Swedish translation was made. "All this shows that the people at large want, above everything else, the truth," *Appleton's* publisher said in a note appended to the March installment. In April, Harper & Brothers published *The Spoilers*, Beach's fictional, abbreviated version of the story, to national best-selling acclaim. "About all I had to do was add a little imagination, flavor with love interest, season to taste and serve," the author recalled in his memoirs. He turned McKenzie into the character of Alec McNamara, "a gigantic, well-groomed man, with keen, close-set

eyes, and that indefinable easy movement and polished bearing that
come from confidence, health and travel." Told at the outset that his
venture, "the biggest scheme that ever came north, backed by the biggest men in Washington," might be dangerous, the McKenzie figure re-
plies, with a shrug of the shoulders, "We've got the law—or rather, we
ARE the law. Now, let's get to work." *The Spoilers* was adapted into a
play and later several films, the best known of which starred Randolph
Scott in the McKenzie role.

THE MUCK RAKED BY THE LIKES OF REX BEACH GAVE LIFE TO THE MOST
important structural reform, in terms of the framework of government, of the Progressive era: the shift to the direct popular election
of senators. The push to amend the Constitution to strip from state
legislatures the power to select senators was long-standing, backed by
populists and good-government activists. Advocates stressed that this
power enabled bosses like McKenzie, through their control over the
legislatures, to control the appointments of senators and in this fashion
the senators themselves. The arrangement made possible schemes like
the Nome Proposition. The House of Representatives in Washington,
already a people's body, embraced this amendment and tried to shame
the upper body into following suit. Whenever the roll was called in the
Senate, Representative J. Adam Bede of Minnesota quipped, it was to
be wondered of senators "whether they will answer 'present' or 'not
guilty.'" But the Senate refused even to vote on a resolution to submit
to the states, for their consideration, an amendment mandating direct
elections. So the states took matters into their own hands. In 1907,
North Dakota enacted a law permitting voters to express a preference
for senator in a primary—a preference that state legislators could ignore only at their peril. McKenzie saw the future and announced that
he would not seek reappointment as the state's representative on the
Republican National Committee. Finally, with the states on the brink
of forcing a constitutional convention, Congress submitted "direct
election" to the states for ratification, and in 1913, the Seventeenth

Amendment became the law of the land. The Senate "of the people" was certainly not perfect, but nine years later this newly constituted Senate authorized the historic investigation that exposed corruption at the Interior Department in what became known as the Teapot Dome scandal.

MCKENZIE LIVED TO SEE PASSAGE OF THE SEVENTEENTH AMENDMENT. HE died in June 1922, at the age of seventy-two, or perhaps seventy-one, as the precise date of his birth remained a mystery. His body lay beneath the Speaker's stand in the House of Representatives in Bismarck, the casket piled with flowers. Respects paid, he was put to rest, as he wished, next to the remains of his first son, John Alexander. "Alexander McKenzie had a dominating but engaging personality," the *Bismarck Tribune*, striving for balance, said. "Linked with his ambition to develop and build up the state, was an almost equal passion for power, and the exercise of it and to gratify this he naturally delved deep into the field of politics. He made friends that he bound to him by hoops of steel. He made enemies who never forgave or forgot." Only on his passing, with probate of his will, was his marriage to Elva, who had died the month before, discovered, along with the existence of the rest of his second family. McKenzie had "an adventurous career," the *New York Times* said. His estate came to about $900,000—nearly $13 million in 2020 dollars. Some of the wealth he left behind derived from long-standing holdings in Bismarck. Whether any part of the remainder came from Alaska gold, perhaps reinvested in municipal bonds or the like, was a matter for speculation. But surely the possibility could not be dismissed. He had, after all, a channel for getting gold out of Nome, to the US mint in Seattle. The best reason to think that he had made off with gold was his character. First, he didn't consider himself a thief, in the sense that the law did. He thought he had a right to use his wits and connections to lay hands on Alaska's treasure. Second, he practiced deception and gamed the system as a kind of life philosophy. He played a trick on his first wife and the judge overseeing his

divorce in blaming her for irrational jealousy while in truth he was
having a child with another woman. He conned the president, with
his tale of the "Accident in the Elevator," in gaining release from jail.
If people could be fooled, why not fool them? Third, his interest was
never just in amassing political power; above all, he wished to use that
power to amass wealth. That was the point, and in this steady pursuit,
he was a faithful exemplar of his era. His Nome Proposition was true
to the Gilded Age; he fell short not because he made any mistakes
in distributing the shares "where they will do the most good"—he
played his hand rather well in this regard—but because, even in this
age, not everyone was lacking in public spirit and gumption. Although
he mostly had his way with a president, William McKinley, he was
frustrated by the Ninth Circuit Court of Appeals and the US Supreme
Court, by honest opponents in Congress and reformers in his party, by
truth tellers in the press, and by ordinary miners in Alaska who refused
to bow down to him. America proved not as malign or feckless as it was
often said to be. The Gilded Age died not of exhaustion but because
the country willed its demise.

In a way, the Cape Nome affair helped give Alaska a boost in its
long path to statehood, finally granted in 1959. The scandal showed
that the territory could not be effectively managed by a distant over-
seer in Washington—Alaska needed its own institutions of government. Nowadays, Nome is connected to the outside by an airport,
satellite television, a cellular telephone network, and the Internet. Yet
the town and surrounding region help give meaning to the state mot-
to's, "The Last Frontier." Nature has not been tamed; the journeyer
to the tundra is as worried about the presence of grizzlies as were the
intruders of 1900. Wild herds of muskox graze by the roadside. Few
streets in Nome are paved; the mud is everywhere. Guns and liquor
abound. And the search for gold continues. Anvil Creek felt deserted,
to this visitor, on a sunny July afternoon, the waters clear and cold and
running strong, but mining rigs dotted the area beneath the mountain,

the namesake rock formation visible on the summit. Alaskan natives are now claims owners, through the Bering Straits Native Corporation, and there is talk that the motherlode has yet to be discovered. For those from the outside looking for a second or third shot at life, a chance, just maybe, to get rich, Cape Nome is a destination. Dredgers methodically work the ocean floor. Divers pluck nuggets from submerged coastal bluffs—for their daring, they are stars of the Discovery Channel's reality television series *Bering Sea Gold*. The golden sands of the beach still beckon, as they did one hopeful miner, from Maine, who had cycled through past jobs as a clam digger, a bus driver, a bodyguard. His fourteen hours of pan labor in the white-night days of summer typically yielded $200 in gold. An amateur—your author—panned about $10 of dust, more like tiny flecks, yellow sparkles, well less than a thimbleful, in an hour's work. There is no longer a tent city, but some prospectors live in ramshackle trailers, three units to a trailer, the bathtubs used as makeshift sluice boxes. The gold abides, in the earth and, perhaps even more powerfully, in the dreams of treasure seekers, and where there is gold, as ever, there is bound to be mischief.

Acknowledgments

THIS PROJECT RELIED HEAVILY ON ORIGINAL SOURCE MATERIALS, FOUND with the generous help of librarians, archivists, and others, from Alaska to Cape Cod. Thanks to Jack Omelak and Amy Phillips-Chan at the Carrie M. McLain Memorial Museum in Nome. Thanks to Tom Nadolny in Nome for a lesson in pan gold mining. Leon Boardway at the Nome Visitor Center also assisted me. Damon Stuebner and Sandra Johnston at the Alaska State Library Historical Collections in Juneau helped me, along with Rose Speranza and Becky Butler at the Alaska and Polar Regions Collections and Archives, Elmer E. Rasmuson Library, University of Alaska, Fairbanks.

Thanks to Rollins Emerson, archivist for the Ninth Circuit Court of Appeals in San Francisco, and Christina Luini at the Ninth Circuit's library. Thanks to David Frederick, in Washington, DC, for making his files available to me through the Ninth Circuit's library.

John Hallberg and Trista Raezer-Stursa at the Institute for Regional Studies and University Archives at North Dakota State University, Fargo, helped me locate important documents relating to the life of Alexander McKenzie. James A. Davis, Daniel Sauerwin, and Ann B. Jenks at the State Historical Society of North Dakota in Bismarck helped me find materials, including the letters of McKenzie's secret wife, Elva, to her husband. Thanks to Pamela Pierce at the Theodore Roosevelt Center at Dickinson State University, Dickinson, North Dakota.

Jessica Sutherland at the James J. Hill House in Saint Paul guided me on the tour of the home, and I was assisted in my research by librarians at the Minnesota Historical Society in Saint Paul. Carol McAdow, at the Ramsayer Research Library, McKinley Museum, Canton, Ohio, helped me. At the Library of Congress in Washington, DC, I received help from librarians in the manuscript reading room, the law library, the main reading room, and the rare books reading room. I also was assisted by staff at the National Archives. Jesse Bustos-Nelson, in Charleston, South Carolina, helped out on research.

Cheryl Bergeron, Jane Ames, and Linda Huntington at Snow Library in Orleans, Massachusetts, my hometown library, fielded my requests for far-flung materials, including newspaper microfilm reels from Alaska.

This is my second book for Clive Priddle at PublicAffairs; he has been, as always, a wise editor. Thanks, also, for help from Athena Bryan, Iris Torres, Anupama Roy-Chaudhury, Kaitlin Carruthers-Busser, and Jen Kelland at PublicAffairs, and to map designer Patti Isaacs. Thanks to my agent, Andrew Stuart, for advice in shaping the proposal.

My son, Samuel Starobin, and my sister, Leslie Starobin, assisted with research. Thanks to my wife, Nargiza, our daughter, Deora, and Babula for their patience as I took time away from home to gather material for the book. And thanks, Jolly, for your furry companionship.

Bibliographical Note

T HE NOME PROPOSITION, AS ALEXANDER MCKENZIE CALLED HIS scheme, has fascinated several generations of puzzle solvers. The single best source of information on the Nome plot and an invaluable source of material on the Alaska gold rush of this era is the volumes of testimony and exhibits of the Heacock Commission, established by the Ninth Circuit Court of Appeals in San Francisco, to investigate the McKenzie affair. One set of volumes is dedicated to the matter of Dudley Dubose, a McKenzie attorney, and the other set to the matter of Judge Arthur Noyes, McKenzie's chief tool in the conspiracy. These volumes are available online as part of the digitized collection of the Hastings School of Law, University of California.

Newspapers in Nome, including the *Nome Daily Chronicle*, the *Nome Daily News*, and the *Nome Gold Digger*, portions of which are available on microfilm, did their best to track the story as it unfolded in 1900. The *San Francisco Call* dedicated many of its pages, in 1900 and 1901, to the details of the plot as revealed in the courtroom; the coverage can be found on Chronicling America, a digital website of the Library of Congress. Rex Beach, on the scene in Nome in 1900 as a miner, wrote "The Looting of Alaska," a series of muckraking articles published in *Appleton's Booklovers Magazine* starting in January 1906. Waldemar Engvald Lillo, a graduate student, undertook original research for *The Alaska Gold Mining Company and the Cape Nome Conspiracy*, submitted to the University of North Dakota as a PhD dissertation in 1935. Joseph Jackson, an acquaintance of McKenzie, wrote a manuscript, drawing on interviews with primary sources, titled

Bismarck Boomer: The Amazing Career of Alexander McKenzie. The manuscript, dated 1964, remained unpublished; a carbon copy of the typewritten original is in the collection of the Minneapolis Historical Society. Terrence Michael Cole, a graduate student, wrote a chapter, "A Monster Conspiracy," as part of his PhD thesis, *A History of the Nome Gold Rush: The Poor Man's Paradise*, submitted to the University of Washington in 1983. Legal scholar and attorney David C. Frederick drew on archival research for a chapter, "Intrigue at Anvil Creek," in his book *Rugged Justice: The Ninth Circuit Court of Appeals and the American West, 1891–1941* (Berkeley: University of California Press, 1994). Frederick's research files for this chapter are deposited in the archives of the Ninth Circuit Court of Appeals in San Francisco.

Many primary materials relating to the life of Alexander McKenzie, including a cache of letters he wrote to his secret second wife, Elva, can be found at the State Historical Society of North Dakota in Bismarck. Other primary materials, including the record of his divorce from his first wife, Mary Ellen, are in the archives of the North Dakota Institute for Regional Studies at North Dakota State University in Fargo. Documents relating to interactions between James J. Hill and McKenzie, as well as to efforts by Hill and Senators P. J. McCumber of North Dakota and Mark Hanna of Ohio to press President William McKinley to pardon McKenzie, are in the James J. Hill collection of the Minnesota Historical Society.

Notes

Prologue

1   *"One day near the end of February 1900"*: Edward Jesson's bicycle trip across the length of Alaska recounted in "From Dawson to Nome," a diary portion edited by Ruth Reat, in *Pacific Northwest Quarterly* 47, no. 3 (July 1956): 65–74.

2   *"Few men become rich"*: Great Northern flier quoted in Terrence Michael Cole, *A History of the Nome Gold Rush* (PhD diss., University of Washington, 1983), 116.

Chapter 1. Anvil Creek

7   *"A young man stood"*: Jafet Lindeberg's story recounted by him in an interview with Henry Carlisle in *Mining Engineering* (July 1964): 112–113. Other details are in an interview he gave at the age of eighty to Hazel Lindberg (no relation), in Hazel Lindberg Papers, box 3, folder 52, University of Alaska Fairbanks, Alaska, and Polar Regions Collections and Archives.

8   *"The men could not know this"*: The geological characteristics of the Nome gold mining fields detailed in T. K. Bundtzen et al., "Progress Report on the Geology and Mineral Resources of the Nome Mining District," Public-Data File 94-39, State of Alaska, Department of Natural Resources, Division of Geological and Geophysical Surveys, July 13, 1994, http://dggs.alaska.gov/webpubs/dggs/pdf/text/pdf1994_039 .pdf.

9   *"storm-locked gate"*: From poem "Comrades of the Klondike" in Samuel C. Dunham, *The Goldsmith of Nome* (Washington, DC: Neale Publishing Company, 1901), 11.

9   *"native peoples in northern Alaska"*: The term "Eskimo" was commonly in use in this era by settlers and others to refer to native peoples in northern Alaska. See, for example, Edward Sanford Harrison, *Nome*

and Seward Peninsula: History, Description, Biographies and Stories (Seattle, WA: Metropolitan Press, 1905). Chapter 4, "The Native Race," begins, "The Eskimo is the aboriginal race of Seward Peninsula." Nowadays, "Inuit" is a common term of reference for natives of this region, although some natives also use "Eskimo." The term "Inupiat" is also in use to refer to an Alaska native tribe of this area.

9   *"The influx raised"*: Legal issues and status of Lindeberg, Lindblom, and Brynteson discussed in William W. Morrow, "Spoilers," *California Law Review* 4, no. 2 (January 1916): 89–113.

11   *"By power of attorney"*: Anderson's story told in Leland Carlson, *An Alaskan Gold Mine* (Eugene, OR: Resource Publications, 2015), 4–5.

11   *"Anderson, in turn"*: Role of G. W. "Gabe" Price told in Kenneth J. Kutz, *Nome Gold* (Darien, CT: Gold Fever Publishing, 1991), 12–13.

12   *"indigenous to an Arctic Circle region"*: "Lapp" or "Laplander" was the common term of reference at this time for the people now known as Sami, native to the Arctic region, their land stretching across a northern swath of Norway, Sweden, Finland, and Russia.

13   *"No, not even Eskimos"*: Lindeberg interview with Carlisle, *Mining Engineering*, 112A.

13   *"An Eskimo elder"*: Oral history recounted in Jeff Kunkel, *The Two Eskimo Boys Meet the Three Lucky Swedes* (Anchorage, AK: Glacier House Publications, 2002), 15.

13   *"By one account"*: Carlson, *An Alaskan Gold Mine*, 9. In 1902, C. M. Thuland, a Nome attorney for Alaskan natives, asserted that Lindblom originally staked Number Eight Above for the native Constantine Uparazuck and Number Nine Above for the native Gabriel Adams. According to a lawsuit brought by Thuland and a colleague, the pastor P. H. Anderson subsequently defrauded these two natives of their rights to the properties. See June 21, 1902, letter of C. M. Thuland to Washington Posten, in the online archives of the Norwegian-American Historical Association, Northfield, Minnesota., Volume 16, "Life in the Klondike and Alaskan Gold Fields."

14   *"al-ak-shak"*: T. A. Rickard, *Through the Yukon and Alaska* (Seattle, WA: Mining and Scientific Press, 1909), 9.

14   *"The treaty is a wise one"*: *Charleston Daily News*, April 12, 1867.

15   *"Give me fifty"*: Quoted in Warren Zimmerman, *First Great Triumph* (New York: Farrar, Straus and Giroux, 2002), 28.

Chapter 2. What's Yours Is Mine

17   *"The ptarmigan roosting"*: Flora and fauna of Seward Peninsula in Anne Sutton and Sue Steinacher, *Alaska's Nome Area* (Juneau: Alaska Department of Fish and Game, 2012).

17   *"Kirke Requa"*: Kirke Requa's journey recounted in her testimony before the Heacock Commission. See US Circuit Court of Appeals, Ninth Circuit, *In the Matter of Arthur H. Noyes et al.* (San Francisco, CA: Filmer Brothers Co. Print, 1901), 11:2696–2792 (hereafter *In re Noyes*).

18   *"We called it"*: Requa testimony, *In re Noyes*, 2698.

19   *"very tattered"*: Requa testimony, *In re Noyes*, 2702.

20   *"could shoot quite straight"*: Requa testimony, *In re Noyes*, 2709.

20   *"like an animal"*: Carlson, *An Alaskan Gold Mine*, 14.

21   *"Chipps had arrived"*: Chipps's arrival in Alaska recounted in his testimony before the Heacock Commission. See US Circuit Court of Appeals, Ninth Circuit, *In the Matter of the Alleged Contempt of Dudley Dubose* (San Francisco, CA: Published bound transcript of the Ninth Circuit), 1:264–269 (hereafter *In re Dubose*). Background on Chipps in Waldemar Engvald Lillo, *The Alaska Gold Mining Company and the Cape Nome Conspiracy* (PhD diss., University of North Dakota, 1935).

21   *"I located it"*: Chipps testimony, *In re Dubose*, 271.

22   *"to prevent crime"*: Statement of purpose of Law and Order League, Council City, Alaska, April 10, 1899, printed in *Congressional Record—Senate*, April 19, 1900, 4417.

22   *"half-breeds"*: Letter from J. J. Wilson, president, Law and Order League, and A. P. Mordaunt, secretary, May 25, 1899, Council City, to William McKinley, printed in *Congressional Record—Senate*, April 19, 1900, 4416–4417. This letter may never have reached McKinley in the White House.

22   *"The plotters figured"*: The plot recounted in James Wickersham, *Old Yukon* (Fairbanks: University of Alaska Press, 2009), 93–95.

Chapter 3. "Star Mist"

25   *"Soldiers Gulch"*: Cited in Harrison, *Nome and Seward Peninsula*, 52.

25   *"star mist"*: The Nome beach miner Peter L. Trout ventured the "star mist" theory, cited in Cole, *A History of the Nome Gold Rush*, 79.

26   *"poor man's paradise"*: Cole, *A History of the Nome Gold Rush*, 75, citing *The Argus* (Seattle, WA), December 20, 1899.

26   *"poor opportunities"*: Sam C. Dunham, cited in Cole, *A History of the Nome Gold Rush*, 82. Dunham also was an analyst on a mission in Alaska for the Department of Labor; Cole quoting from a report filed by Dunham in 1900.

27   *"prosecuted for trespass"*: Cited in Cole, *A History of the Nome Gold Rush*, 84. This episode also recounted by Harrison, *Nome and Seward Peninsula*, 52–53.

28   *"farce"*: Cited in Cole, *A History of the Nome Gold Rush*, 85–86.

28   *"His courtroom"*: Johnson's time in Nome recounted in Harrison, *Nome and Seward Peninsula*, 53–54.

29   *"I am a rough-and-tumble"*: Interview with Charles D. Lane, *Seattle Post-Intelligencer*, January 21, 1900.

30   *"Born in Marion County"*: Biographical sketch of Lane in Harrison, *Nome and Seward Peninsula*, 197–201.

30   *"bulldog pertinacity"*: F. B. Millar, "The Utica Mine," *The Idler* (March 1902): 723.

31   *"Wherever Lucky Lane goes"*: *San Francisco Call*, April 9, 1897.

31   *"belched forth"*: Lane interview, *Seattle Post-Intelligencer*, January 21, 1900.

31   *"He purchased"*: Lane's purchases of mining claims and investment plans detailed in letter of April 6, 1900, from his wife to Nevada senator William M. Stewart, printed in *Congressional Record—Senate*, April 9, 1900, 3928.

32   *"He was a surly"*: Description of Frances Ella Fitz, who worked in Hubbard's Nome law office in 1900, in Frances Ella Fitz, as told to Jerome Odlum, *Lady Sourdough* (New York: Macmillan Company, 1941), 32.

32   *"to commence and prosecute"*: Cited in a typical agreement between a jumper, Kirke Requa, and Hubbard & Beeman, in exhibit inserted into Requa testimony, *In re Noyes*, 2733–2735.

34   *"We all knew"*: Requa testimony, *In re Noyes*, 2737.

Chapter 4. "Honest, Outspoken and Reliable"

40   *"was to obligate"*: Quote from an unnamed legislator interviewed by McKenzie biographer Joseph W. Jackson, cited in Jackson, *Bismarck Boomer: The Amazing Career of Alexander McKenzie* (unpublished manuscript, 1953), 143 (hereafter Jackson MS). Carbon copy of the original in collection of Minnesota Historical Society, Saint Paul; a photocopy was provided to the author. Jackson, generally sympathetic to McKenzie, interviewed more than one hundred contemporaries of the boss, including members of his family as well as close friends and implacable enemies.

41   *"His information"*: December 17, 1896, letter from J. J. Hill to Mark Hanna in JJH "Letters" collection, Minnesota Historical Society (hereafter JJH papers).

41   *"stooping and bowing"*: May 8, 1912, letter from Charles Fremont Amidon to Theodore Roosevelt, digital collection of Theodore Roosevelt Center at Dickinson State University, Dickinson, North Dakota, 3.

41   *"First as to what"*: May 13, 1912, letter from Theodore Roosevelt to Charles Fremont Adison, Theodore Roosevelt Digital Library, Library of Congress Manuscript Division.

42 *"may never be determined"*: Jackson MS, 14.

42 *"passing through a country"*: Quoted in Colonel Clement A. Lounsberry, *North Dakota History and People* (Chicago: S. J. Clarke Publishing Company, 1917), 1:100. Colonel Lounsberry, a Civil War veteran, founded the *Bismarck Tribune* in 1873 and was an ardent McKenzie admirer.

42 *"read character in their feet"*: Jackson MS, 418.

43 *"No man knows"*: Hamlin Garland, *A Son of the Middle Border* (New York: MacMillan Company, 1920), 309.

43 *"a tall slim"*: Quotation from Lounsberry, Jackson MS, 54.

43 *"absolutely without fear"*: Quotation from longtime McKenzie friend George P. Flannery, Jackson MS, 45.

44 *"When father caught"*: Quotation from McKenzie daughter Jeannette, Jackson MS, 51.

44 *"scout for George Armstrong Custer"*: Cited in biographical entry for McKenzie in *The National Cyclopedia of American Biography* (New York: James T. White & Company, 1945), 32:92. In his unpublished manuscript, Jackson said that McKenzie met Custer at Fort Lincoln but added that the claim that McKenzie served as Custer's scout "has not been confirmed" (Jackson MS, 45).

44 *"he would give anything"*: January 14, 1882, Winnie Pearce letter, printed in Gladys M. Pearce, *Claimed by the Prairies* (unpublished manuscript in Pearce papers at the University for Regional Studies & University Archives at the North Dakota State University in Fargo), 90–91 (hereafter, Pearce MS).

44 *"His keen features"*: Pearce MS, 99.

45 *"He never seemed"*: Pearce MS, 99.

45 *"necessary to protect"*: January 7, 1887, letter from N. G. Orway to James J. Hill, JJH papers.

46 *"the capital in Bismarck"*: Jackson covers this episode in detail in chapter 4 of his unpublished manuscript. Burleigh F. Spalding, a member of the commission and a prominent McKenzie critic, also wrote at length about this affair in his papers, held by the State Historical Society of North Dakota in Bismarck. Spalding bridled at McKenzie's pressure tactics and believed that the boss "never forgot this incident."

46 *"To him we owe"*: *Bismarck Tribune*, cited without date in Jackson MS, 64.

46 *"Alexander the Great"*: From an unnamed South Dakota newspaper publisher quoted in Jackson MS, 62.

47 *"go far"*: January 14, 1882, Winnie Pearce letter, Pearce MS, 90.

47 *"Walk across the state"*: Quoted in William R. Hunt, *Distant Justice* (Norman: University of Oklahoma Press, 1987), 104.

47 *"appreciating the power"*: This observation was made by a McKenzie critic, Edith Wakeman Hughes of Bismarck, quoted in Robert P.

Wilkins, "Alexander McKenzie and the Politics of Bossism," in *The North Dakota Political Tradition*, ed. Thomas W. Howard (Ames: Iowa State University Press, 1981), 37.

47   *"X is an honest man"*: Quotation from Angus Fraser, North Dakota friend of Alexander McKenzie, from interview with Fraser, May 1953, in G. Angus Fraser Papers, manuscript collection of Institute for Regional Studies and University Archives at North Dakota State University, Fargo (hereafter Angus Fraser papers).

47   *"His brawny right arm"*: Recollection of *Grand Forks Herald* newspaper publisher George B. Winship in his unpublished memoirs, made available to McKenzie biographer Jackson, cited in Jackson MS, 100–101.

47   *"A gang of men"*: The crime occurred at the office of William Porter Moffit, known as Colonel Moffit, publisher of *The Settler* in Bismarck. The incident is recounted in Jackson MS, 145.

48   *"'duties' of all American citizens"*: Theodore Roosevelt, "Address to Citizens of Dickinson," July 4, 1886, Dickinson, Dakota Territory, in digital library of Theodore Roosevelt Center, Dickinson State University.

49   *"One man never disappointed"*: Said by J. J. Hill to McKenzie friend George P. Flannery, cited in Wilkins, "Alexander McKenzie and the Politics of Bossism," 37.

49   *"Be sure Alex McKenzie"*: April 23, 1904, telegram from J. J. Hill to son Louis Hill, JJH papers.

49   *"Hill held personal stock"*: Richard White, *Railroaded* (New York: W. W. Norton & Company, 2011), 156.

50   *"Alaska awakens"*: Address by J. J. Hill, June 1, 1909, Seattle, JJH papers.

50   *"Men in our day"*: Hill, June, 1, 1909, Seattle address.

50   *"extreme cruelty"*: McKenzie's divorce papers, including his "Complaint for Divorce," the response of his wife, Mary Ellen, to the complaint, and "Findings of Fact and Conclusions of Law" by Judge William B. McConnell, District Court, Cass County, North Dakota, in records collection of Institute for Regional Studies and University Archives at North Dakota State University, Fargo.

51   *"She is willing to take $15,000"*: September 27, 1889, letter from McKenzie to Elva, in Alexander McKenzie Family collection of papers held by the State Historical Society of North Dakota in Bismarck (hereafter E. McKenzie letters). The collection contains a large cache of letters from McKenzie to Elva, who became his wife.

51   *"the babies"*: August 5, 1890, letter from McKenzie to Elva, E. McKenzie letters.

51   *"She must have conceived"*: McKenzie's divorce records apparently never came to public light during his lifetime or afterward. The author

came across them in Cass County archives held in a library at North Dakota State University, Fargo, and is revealing them, to his knowledge, for the first time.

51   *"The ruby ring"*: Recounted by Jeannette McKenzie, McKenzie's eldest daughter by his marriage to Elva, on his death in June 1922, to the *Minneapolis Tribune*; story reprinted by *Fargo Forum*.

Chapter 5. The Nome Proposition

53   *"I have been so busy"*: January 13, 1900, letter from McKenzie to Elva, E. McKenzie letters.

54   *"situation of the country"*: E. M. Walters testimony, *In re Dubose*, 756.

54   *"He told me"*: E. M. Walters testimony, *In re Dubose*, 757.

55   *"Walters agreed to deed"*: Walters possibly exaggerated in pegging the value of his shares at $475,000. Robert Chipps testified that Walters received $300,000 in promised stock.

55   *"most trusted"*: Jackson MS, 67.

56   *"the gang that today controls"*: *Grand Forks Herald* piece cited in Jackson MS, 146.

57   *"a Republican leader"*: *Washington Post* comment published in *Nome News*, May 4, 1901.

57   *"plumb & strong"*: Reminiscences of Carter family sister Julia Anne in Thomas Henry Carter papers, Library of Congress, Manuscript Division, Washington, DC (hereafter Carter papers).

58   *"old man"*: Walters testimony, *In re Dubose*, 769.

58   *"It was not his own"*: Walters testimony, *In re Dubose*, 761.

58   *"I never had"*: January 20, 1900, letter from McKenzie to Elva, E. McKenzie letters.

58   *"new Eldorado"*: Paul F. Travers, "Some Notes on Nome, Alaska," *Engineering and Mining Journal* 69, no. 4 (January 27, 1900): 105.

Chapter 6. "Where They Will Do the Most Good"

60   *"have the laws fixed"*: Walters testimony, *In re Dubose*, 762.

60   *"A mine is a hole"*: This Mark Twain quote appeared in the *Detroit Free Press* in 1881, and variations appeared elsewhere; for a compilation of sources, see "A Gold Mine Is a Hole in the Ground with a Liar at the Top," Quote Investigator, https://quoteinvestigator.com/2015/07/19/gold-mine/#return-note-11680-3.

61   *"for the mere taking"*: Russell H. Conwell, "Acres of Diamonds" pamphlet in *Life-Changing Classics* (Boiling Springs, PA: Tremendous Leadership, 2004), 5:15.

62   *"a thin, worried"*: Fitz, *Lady Sourdough*, 8.

62   *"an enormously big man"*: Fitz, *Lady Sourdough*, 8–9.

62   *"he said it belonged"*: Chipps testimony, *In re Dubose*, 224.

63   *"where they will"*: Ames used this phrase in an 1868 letter to investor
      Henry S. McComb; quotation in Oakes Ames, *A Memoir* (Cambridge,
      MA: Riverside Press, 1883), 27.

Chapter 7. "Turning Alaska Over to the Aliens"

65   *"Aliens"*: Hansbrough Amendment printed in *Congressional Record—
      Senate*, March 26, 1900, 3307.

65   *"I think the amendment"*: Carter, *Congressional Record—Senate*, March
      26, 1900, 3310.

65   *"any alien"*: This provision in Section 72 of the Alaska code bill as re-
      ported by Carter's Committee on Territories to the Senate, is cited in
      Lillo, *The Alaska Gold Mining Company and the Cape Nome Conspiracy*,
      57. In defending the Hansbrough Amendment on the Senate floor,
      Carter said such language permitting alien title to mining claims in
      Alaska "was copied from the Oregon code" and "crept into this compi-
      lation" crafted by the committee "and escaped attention, so far as the
      members of the committee are concerned, I believe."

66   *"Lindeberg was an alien"*: There was a technical issue relating to the
      claims of Lindeberg and many of the Lapps. As advised by a US com-
      missioner of education, Dr. Sheldon Jackson, these aliens in good faith
      had made their US citizenship declaration before Judge L. B. Shep-
      hard, a US commissioner, acting as a kind of justice of the peace, in
      Saint Michael. Technically, they should have gone before a clerk of a
      federal court, as noted in Lillo, *The Alaska Gold Mining Company and
      the Cape Nome Conspiracy*, 113.

66   *"He is moving"*: March 16, 1900, *Bismarck Tribune* report cited in Jack-
      son MS, 190.

67   *"uplift and civilize"*: Quoted in John B. Judis, *The Folly of Empire* (New
      York: Scribner, 2004), 45.

67   *"These Laplanders"*: Pettigrew, *Congressional Record—Senate*, April 25,
      1900, 4664.

67   *"statement of facts"*: Pettigrew did not name his former constituent;
      the statement was inserted into *Congressional Record—Senate*, April
      25, 1900, 4664.

68   *"I believe"*: Pettigrew, *Congressional Record—Senate*, April 25, 1900,
      4664.

68   *"Mr. President"*: Carter, *Congressional Record—Senate*, April 17, 1900,
      4310.

68   *"the world is indebted":* Carter speech in his Library of Congress papers, typed on Pioneer, Rent and Collection Company stationery.

68   *"by poor men":* Carter speech in his Library of Congress papers.

69   *"Hard Pan List":* Cited in Margaret Leech, *In the Days of McKinley* (New York: Harper & Brothers, 1959), 441.

69   *"Gold, gold, gold!":* Cameron County (Pennsylvania) *Press,* April 19, 1900.

69   *"I am somewhat":* Nelson, *Congressional Record—Senate,* April 18, 1900, 4373.

70   *"the benefit of reindeer":* Hansbrough and Nelson exchange, *Congressional Record—Senate,* April 9, 1900, 3932.

70   *"a dreary waste":* Nelson, *Congressional Record—Senate,* April 18, 1900, 4372–4373.

70   *"good authority":* Teller, *Congressional Record—Senate,* April 9, 1900, 3933.

70   *"In ninety-nine cases":* Teller, *Congressional Record—Senate,* April 18, 1900, 4376.

71   *"follows in the wake":* Bate, *Congressional Record—Senate,* April 20, 1900, 4474.

71   *"That is good":* Stewart, *Congressional Record—Senate,* April 20, 1900, 4474.

71   *"I choked him":* William Morris Stewart, *Reminiscences of Senator William M. Stewart, of Nevada,* ed. George Rothwell Brown (New York: Neale Publishing Company, 1908), 60.

71   *"the boys":* Stewart, *Reminiscences,* 82.

72   *"Now, the question":* Stewart, *Congressional Record—Senate,* April 9, 1900, 3928.

72   *"a letter from Mrs. Lane":* April 6, 1900, letter from Mrs. Lane to Stewart, printed in *Congressional Record—Senate,* April 9, 1900, 3928.

72   *"an affidavit attesting":* Affidavit of A. N. Kittilsen, MD, April 6, 1900, inserted by Stewart into *Congressional Record—Senate,* April 9, 1900, 3928.

72   *"an affidavit sworn by Hubbard":* Affidavit of April 6, 1900, inserted by Hansbrough into *Congressional Record—Senate,* April 9, 1900, 3930.

73   *"They have a jumper":* Bate, *Congressional Record—Senate,* April 20, 1900, 4474.

73   *"a personal interest":* Hansbrough referred to a Seattle, April 1, 1900, clipping from an unnamed newspaper featuring an interview with an Alaskan attorney, Kenneth M. Jackson. He said he had been advised that Jackson was representing Charles Lane. Jackson was representing some claims holders whose claims had been jumped but probably was not representing Lane. Hansbrough, *Congressional Record—Senate,* April 9, 1900, 3931.

73 *"I have no interest"*: Hansbrough, *Congressional Record—Senate*, April 9, 1900, 3931.

73 *"adroitly written"*: Bate-Hansbrough exchange, *Congressional Record—Senate*, April 20, 1900, 4471–4472.

73 *"honorable inducements"*: Bate, *Congressional Record—Senate*, April 20, 1900, 4472.

74 *"there is a monster conspiracy"*: Hansbrough, *Congressional Record—Senate*, April 30, 1900, 4844.

74 *"a retroactive law"*: Stewart, *Congressional Record—Senate*, May 1, 1900, 4894.

74 *"I never worked"*: May 12, 1900, McKenzie letter to Elva, E. McKenzie letters.

74 *"horde of Chinese"*: Green, *Congressional Record—House*, May 22, 1900, 5878.

74 *"We desire"*: King, *Congressional Record—House*, May 22, 1900, 5877.

75 *"It could probably be shown"*: Mark Twain, *Following the Equator* (Hartford, CT: American Publishing Company, 1901), 98.

Chapter 8. "But the Chain's McKinley Gold"

78 *"would be friendly"*: Hume deposition, *In re Noyes*, 387.

78 *"a large number of wealthy"*: Hume deposition, *In re Noyes*, 388.

79 *"puny President"*: Pettigrew remarks in Robert W. Merry, *President McKinley* (New York: Simon & Schuster, 2017), 401.

79 *"My Papa's watch"*: Jackson MS, 257–258.

79 *"treasure land"*: Speech of Washington State attorney James M. Ashton, from text of official proceedings of Republican National Convention, Philadelphia, June 1900, 133, https://archive.org/stream/12threpub naticon00blumrich/12threpubnaticon00blumrich_djvu.txt.

80 *"He made his name"*: Introduction by Terrence Cole to Wickersham, *Old Yukon*, xii.

81 *"I knew him intimately"*: Noyes testimony, *In re Noyes*, 2226–2227.

82 *"a new country"*: Noyes testimony, *In re Noyes*, 2229.

82 *"later said that he thought"*: Chipps testimoney, *In re Dubose*, 236.

82 *"Alaskan miner"*: Noyes testimony, *In re Noyes*, 2243.

83 *"a gentleman"*: May 15, 1900, letter from Hansbrough to McKinley, in archives of Ninth Circuit Court of Appeals, San Francisco, from files given to Ninth Circuit by David C. Frederick, author of *Rugged Justice: The Ninth Circuit Court of Appeals and the American West, 1891–1941* (Berkeley: University of California Press, 1994). Frederick obtained the Hansbrough letter and many other documents from the collection of the National Archives (hereafter Frederick files).

83   *"If he did"*: Noyes testimony, *In re Noyes*, 2234.

84   *"shunted to"*: Cole introduction to Wickersham, *Old Yukon*, xvii.

84   *"Tremendous pressure"*: June 8, 1900, entry in James Wickersham diary in Alaska State Library, Historical Collections, Juneau.

84   *"partnership project"*: Recollection of Angus Fraser, in Angus Fraser papers.

85   *"My purse"*: Said to McKinley by Chicago businessman and newspaper publisher Herman Henry Kohlsaat, in Merry, *President McKinley*, 91.

85   *"by reputation"*: Wood testimony, *In re Noyes*, 2609.

85   *"my political backer"*: Wood testimony, *In re Noyes*, 2609.

Chapter 9. "Tents, Tents, Tents"

89   *"Eat, sit"*: Cited in Cole, *A History of the Nome Gold Rush*, 125–126.

91   *"you can hear"*: September 24, 1901, entry in James Wickersham diary in Alaska State Library, Historical Collections, Juneau.

91   *"Tents, tents, tents"*: Lanier McKee's arrival in Nome, June 20, 1900, in Lanier McKee, *The Land of Nome* (New York: Grafton Press, 1902), 27.

92   *"in the worst days"*: E. C. Trelawney-Ansell, quoted in Lael Morgan, *Good Time Girls* (Fairbanks: Epicenter Press, 1998), 165.

93   *"Well, here I am"*: June 22, 1900, Sherzer letter to Clara Miller, in Kutz, *Nome Gold*, 25–27.

93   *"kind of bookkeeper"*: Walters testimony, *In re Dubose*, 763.

94   *"Cape Nome was a rough place"*: June 22, 1900, letter from miner William Ballou to brother Walt, quoted in Morgan, *Good Time Girls*, 164.

94   *"It is to be hoped"*: June 28, 1900, *Nome Daily News*, cited in Kutz, *Nome Gold*, 205–206.

Chapter 10. "Alert, Aggressive, and Busily Engaged"

95   *"With the discoveries"*: Wolcott speech, Republican National Convention, Philadelphia, official proceedings, 39.

97   *"stood open-mouthed"*: Wickersham, *Old Yukon*, 4.

97   *"On comparing"*: Wickersham, *Old Yukon*, 3–4.

97   *"founded on gold"*: August 8, 1900, speech by James D. Richardson, chair of Democratic National Committee, Military Park, Indianapolis, Indiana, in *Official Proceedings of the Democratic National Convention Held in Kansas City, Mo., July 4th, 5th, and 6th, 1900* (Chicago: M. Lellan Printing Co.), Appendix, 202, https://archive.org/stream/official00demo/official00demo_djvu.txt.

98   *"contemptible"*: Said by the Knights of Labor over Gould's Texas and Pacific holding, in White, *Railroaded*, 337.

Chapter 11. Big Alex Enjoys a Meal

101   *"supposed"*: Chipps testimony, *In re Dubose*, 227.

101   *"Nome's Streets"*: *Nome Daily News*, July 18, 1900.

101   *"in paying quantities"*: *Nome Gold Digger*, July 18, 1900.

102   *"down the drain"*: For Hume's account of these dealings with McKenzie, see Hume deposition, *In re Noyes*, 385–397.

103   *"we were compelled"*: Hume testimony, *In re Noyes*, 315.

103   *"we believed"*: Hume testimony, *In re Noyes*, 319.

103   *"smeared with blood"*: Fitz, *Lady Sourdough*, 38–39.

104   *"a large man"*: *Nome Daily News*, July 21, 1900.

105   *"hereby authorized"*: "Copy of Order Appointing Receiver," in US Supreme Court decision on Alexander McKenzie petition for habeas corpus, *In re Alexander McKenzie*, 180 U.S. 536 (1901), https://supreme.justia.com/cases/federal/us/180/536.

107   *"he had known"*: Hume testimony, *In re Noyes*, 252.

107   *"Just as soon"*: S. R. Calvin testimony, *In re Dubose*, 741.

108   *"The boss grabbed"*: From Harrison, *Nome and Seward Peninsula*, 63.

Chapter 12. The Lawyers Resist

109   *"The assignee is"*: *Nome Gold Digger*, July 25, 1900.

111   *"He immediately fined"*: From "Men, Mines and Markets," *Copper, Curb and Mining Outlook* no. 2 (June 14, 1916): 17.

112   *"I had been raised"*: January 18, 1932, Metson letter to Lillo, in Lillo, *The Alaska Gold Mining Company and the Cape Nome Conspiracy*, 331.

114   *"Your people"*: Metson testimony quoted in Gilbert opinion of Ninth Circuit Court of Appeals in the *Noyes et al.* case; see "Opinions and Judgment," *In re Noyes*, 13.

114   *"old friend"*: Metson testimony, *In re Noyes*, 732.

114   *"stayed his temper"*: Confrontation with McKenzie recounted by Metson, *In re Noyes*, 732–734.

115   *"Order Enlarging"*: Cited in Gilbert opinion of Ninth Circuit Court of Appeals in the *Noyes et al.* case, in "Opinions and Judgment," *In re Noyes*, 14.

115   *"a broad-minded"*: *Nome Daily News*, July 25, 1900.

Chapter 13. "Clean Money"

118   *"Give me a barnyard"*: Quoted in John David Ragan, *The Explorers of Alaska* (Broomall, PA: Chelsea House Publishers, 1992), 96.

119 *"roulette wheel"*: Lindeberg's loss attested to by Dietrich Hellman, in interview quoted in J. L. Campbell, *Cape Nome, Alaska: The Poor Man's Diggings* (Chicago: J. L. Campbell, 1900), 20.

120 *"The machinery"*: Lane detailed plans in interview with the *Seattle Post-Intelligencer*, January 21, 1900.

121 *"The money"*: Harrison, *Nome and Seward Peninsula*, 199.

Chapter 14. The Battle of the Beach

123 *"I want you"*: McKenzie told this to S. R. Calvin; in Calvin testimony, *In re Dubose*, 737.

123 *"I felt"*: Walters testimony, *In re Dubose*, 781.

124 *"so crooked"*: October 7, 1901, entry in James Wickersham diary in Alaska State Library, Historical Collections, Juneau.

125 *"drinking very hard"*: Pinkerton Detective Agency report of Asst. Supt. C. W., January 31, 1890, 56, in Angus Fraser papers.

125 *"worst boodler"*: February 10, 1890, Pinkerton report, 73, in Angus Fraser papers.

126 *"You had better"*: J. C. Barton testimony, *In re Dubose*, 914.

126 *"If I had known"*: McKenzie told to J. C. Barton, in Barton testimony, *In re Dubose*, 915.

126 *"with intent to commit"*: Stevens ruling, printed in *Nome Gold Digger*, August 1, 1900.

127 *"BEACH LAND NOT FREE"*: Headline, *Nome Gold Digger*, August 1, 1900.

128 *"meant the practical"*: *Nome Daily News*, August 1, 1900.

128 *"grasping corporations"*: Jones speech covered in *Nome Daily News*, August 2, 1900.

129 *"draft resolution"*: resolution printed in *Nome Daily News*, August 2, 1900.

130 *"Come up and enlist"*: *Nome Gold Digger*, August 1, 1900.

130 *"Some five hundred"*: *Nome Daily News*, August 1, 1900.

130 *"Well, here we are"*: August 2, 1900, Will McDaniel letter to Mrs. J. J. McDaniel, in "Letters from Alaska, 1899–1905" collection of McDaniel letters held in Carrie M. McClain Memorial Museum, Nome.

131 *"Condemning Men"*: *Nome Daily News*, August 2, 1900.

Chapter 15. "We Sleep with Our Revolvers"

133 *"Every penny"*: Hume quoted in *Nome Daily News*, August 3, 1900.

134 *"it will be"*: Hubbard to E. M. Walters, Walters testimony, *In re Dubose*, 784.

135   *"many rich"*: Hubbard to Kirke Requa, Requa testimony, *In re Noyes*, 2785.

135   *"I had confidence"*: Requa testimony, *In re Noyes*, 2788.

135   *"This is the little lady"*: Requa testimony, *In re Noyes*, 2783.

135   *"a villain"*: Requa testimony, *In re Noyes*, 2789.

136   *"Men up here"*: July 27, 1900, letter from Sherzer to Miss Clara Miller, in Kutz, *Nome Gold*, 38.

137   *"more murderers"*: August 7, 1900, letter from Vawter to Griggs, quoted in Hunt, *Distant Justice*, 109.

137   *"Fred Welsh"*: August 14, 1900, letter from Frost to Griggs, *In re Noyes*, 1259.

138   *"Compared with Nome"*: August 6, 1900, letter from Frost to Griggs, Frederick files.

138   *"The way of transgressors"*: Quoted in Stan Sauerwein, *Soapy Smith: Skagway's Scourge of the Klondike* (Canmore, Alberta: Altitude Publishing Canada, 2005), 132.

139   *"uneasiness felt as to its safety"*: Testimony of bank manager Whitehead, *In re Noyes*, 2810.

Chapter 16. The Taking of Topkuk

142   *"I will not only appoint"*: Barton testimony, *In re Dubose*, 920–921.

143   *"all the money"*: McCormack to J. C. Barton, Barton testimony, *In re Dubose*, 918.

144   *"Ragged and half starved"*: Sam C. Dunham, "The Yukon and Nome Gold Regions," *Bulletin of the Department of Labor*, Washington, DC, July 1900, 858.

144   *"procurers"*: Dunham, Yukon and Gold Regions report, 859.

144   *"We have a sub-receiver"*: Dunham poem "A Greeting to the Swedes," in *The Goldsmith of Nome*, 69.

145   *"The sentiment"*: Robert McKillican testimony, *In re Dubose*, 940.

145   *"secured many valuable claims"*: *Nome Gold Digger*, August 8, 1900.

Chapter 17. "The McKenzie Evil"

147   *"all the claims"*: August 16, 1900, letter from Sherzer to Miss Clara Miller, in Kutz, *Nome Gold*, 45.

148   *"It was launched"*: Pioneer Mining attorney Metson acknowledged the loan, not paid back so far as he knew, under cross-examination by a McKenzie attorney; see *In re Dubose*, 584.

148   *"the miner against"*: *Nome Daily Chronicle*, August 16, 1900.

149   *"wise men"*: *Nome Daily Chronicle*, August 20, 1900.

150   *"not a ghost"*: *Nome Daily News*, July 25, 1900.

150   *"NO TURNING BACK"*: *Nome Daily News*, August 14, 1900.

150   *"They discussed it"*: Robert McKillican testimony, *In re Dubose*, 940.

151   *"the only man"*: *Nome Daily Chronicle*, August 20, 1900.

151   *"THE McKENZIE EVIL"*: *Nome Daily Chronicle*, September 10, 1900.

151   *"it is to the interest"*: *Nome Daily Chronicle*, August 20, 1900.

152   *"he would take care"*: Hume testimony, *In re Dubose*, 277–278.

152   *"I have been intending"*: August 20, 1900, Noyes letter to Griggs, Frederick files.

153   *"'alien' claims in Alaska's gold fields"*: *Evening Times*, September 4, 1900.

Chapter 18. "The Law Is Supreme"

159   *"Morrow was born"*: Morrow biographical sketch in Oscar Tully Shuck, ed., *History of the Bench and Bar in California* (Los Angeles: Commercial Printing House, 1901), 655–656.

160   *"Why, I used"*: Shuck, *History of the Bench and Bar in California*, 656.

161   *"has no entangling"*: February 25, 1897, letter from J. M. Walling to McKinley, Frederick files.

161   *"perfect impartiality"*: February 19, 1897, letter from Barclay Henley to McKinley, Frederick files.

161   *"Christian civilization"*: From published address by Morrow, "The Service of Lawyers in Wartime and Their Obligation to Promote Patriotism," in the proceedings of the annual session of the California Bar Association in San Jose, June 7, 1918 (San Francisco, CA: Recorder Printer and Publishing Co., 1918), 16.

161   *"You know, we expect"*: Morrow, "The Service of Lawyers," 15–16.

162   *"It is written"*: Morrow toast, October 13, 1911, printed in the *Chicago Legal News* 44, no. 21 (December 30, 1911): 168.

162   *"The Asiatic tramp"*: Morrow as congressman quoted in Kelly Lytle Hernandez, *City of Inmates: Conquest, Rebellion, and the Rise of Human Caging in Los Angeles, 1771–1965* (Chapel Hill, NC: University of North Carolina Press, 2017), 68.

162   *"He is a man"*: Shuck, *History of the Bench and Bar in California*, 656.

164   *"entirely surcease"*: Copy of writ printed in US Supreme Court decision on Alexander McKenzie petition for habeas corpus, *In re Alexander McKenzie*, 180 U.S. 536.

164   *"in a lecture"*: Morrow lecture, delivered before the Law Association of the School of Jurisprudence at the University of California, November 19, 1915, printed in "The Spoilers," *California Law Review* 4, no. 2 (January 1916): 89–113.

165   *"we say the law"*: Morrow, "The Spoilers," 113.

Chapter 19. "Breakers like Race Horses"

167 *"I have seen"*: Davis telegram cited in *San Francisco Call*, November 6, 1900.

168 *"Morrow, in defending"*: Morrow cited an amendment to the original Circuit Court of Appeals Act of 1891, the revision made by Congress just three months before, in June, on the same day the Alaska code was passed. It appears that the opponents of McKenzie's effort to rig the judicial process in Alaska anticipated the possible need for the Ninth Circuit in San Francisco to act as a check on the new district court with jurisdiction over the gold fields.

169 *"The breakers"*: September 3, 1900, Will McDaniel letter to family in California, in the "Letters from Alaska, 1899–1905" collection of McDaniel letters held in Carrie M. McClain Memorial Museum, Nome.

169 *"increased in fury"*: September 10, 1900, Will McDaniel letter to family in California, with this line written on September 5, 1900, five days before the letter was finished, in the "Letters from Alaska, 1899–1905" collection of McDaniel letters held in Carrie M. McClain Memorial Museum, Nome.

169 *"They gaped"*: Storm described in September 10, 1900, Will McDaniel letter to family, as well as in *Nome Daily Chronicle*, September 5 and 7, 1900, and in *Nome Daily News*, September 7, 1900.

Chapter 20. "The Ring Is Broken"

171 *"The Ring Is Broken"*: *Nome Daily Chronicle*, September 14, 1900.

171 *"the great majority"*: *Nome Gold Digger*, September 19, 1900.

172 *"We learned today"*: Dunham poem "A Greeting to the Swedes," in *The Goldsmith of Nome*, 68–70.

172 *"We'll save"*: Fitz, *Lady Sourdough*, 41.

173 *"I am not prepared"*: McKenzie, *Nome Daily News*, September 14, 1900.

173 *"We have not determined"*: Beeman, *Nome Daily News*, September 14, 1900.

174 *"the popular idea of Nome"*: *Nome Gold Digger*, December 19, 1900.

174 *"I can do nothing"*: Knight testimony quoted in Gilbert opinion of Ninth Circuit Court of Appeals in the *Noyes et al.* case in "Opinions and Judgment," *In re Noyes*, 15.

175 *"What do we care"*: Hubbard remarks cited in *San Francisco Call*, November 6, 1900.

175   "layman": McKenzie remarks cited in "Application of Alexander
      McKenzie for Pardon," prepared by Senator P. J. McCumber for
      McKinley, April 18, 1901, 7; document in JJH papers.

175   "void": Geary testimony quoted in Gilbert opinion of Ninth Circuit
      Court of Appeals in the Noyes et al. case, in "Opinions and Judgment,"
      In re Noyes, 34.

176   "He is putty": Vawter affidavit, August 31, 1901, cited in In re Noyes,
      2803. McKenzie denied making that statement in his affidavit, Octo-
      ber 4, 1901, In re Noyes, 2804.

176   "It must be prevented": Frost testimony quoted in Gilbert opinion of
      Ninth Circuit Court of Appeals in the Noyes et al. case, in "Opinions
      and Judgment," In re Noyes, 44.

176   "I told him": Vawter testimony, In re Noyes, 529.

Chapter 21. "Stand Aside!"

177   "vigilance committee": Van Orsdale testimony, In re Noyes, 1577.

177   "serious state of affairs": Van Orsdale testimony, In re Noyes, 1579.

178   "the interest of peace": Van Orsdale testimony, In re Noyes, 1579.

178   "very cautiously": Van Orsdale testimony, In re Noyes, 1580.

179   "I certainly do advise": Jackson testimony, cited in Morrow opinion for
      Ninth Circuit Court of Appeals, In re Dubose, May 6, 1901, 109 Fed.
      971, No. 632, 4.

179   "void": Vawter testimony, cited in Gilbert opinion of Ninth Circuit
      Court of Appeals in the Noyes et al. case, in "Opinions and Judgment,"
      In re Noyes, 40.

179   "To hell with": Frost quoted in Hunt, Distant Justice, 111.

179   "still too sick": Nome Daily News, September 15, 1900.

179   "My Dear Major": Noyes letter of September 15, 1900, in Gilbert
      opinion of Ninth Circuit Court of Appeals in the Noyes et al. case, in
      "Opinions and Judgment," In re Noyes, 20.

181   "apologized for": Nome Daily Chronicle, September 15, 1900.

181   "like stealing it": September 29, 1932, Metson letter to Lillo, in Lillo,
      The Alaska Gold Mining Company and the Cape Nome Conspiracy, 336.

181   "Wait till": September 29, 1932, Metson letter to Lillo, in Lillo, The
      Alaska Gold Mining Company and the Cape Nome Conspiracy, 336.

181   "day's work": January 18, 1932, Metson letter to Lillo, in Lillo, The
      Alaska Gold Mining Company and the Cape Nome Conspiracy, 331.

182   "gun play": September 29, 1932, Metson letter to Lillo, in Lillo, The
      Alaska Gold Mining Company and the Cape Nome Conspiracy, 336–337.

182   "I am an American citizen": Quoted in Beach, "The Looting of Alaska,"
      540.

182   *"It looks as tho'"*: September 29, 1932, Metson letter to Lillo, in Lillo, *The Alaska Gold Mining Company and the Cape Nome Conspiracy*, 337.

Chapter 22. "The Supreme Court Will Knock Them Out"

183   *"McKenzie is ruined"*: *Nome Daily Chronicle*, September 15, 1900.

184   *"Aren't you afraid"*: Quoted in Beach, "The Looting of Alaska," 545.

184   *"In the first place"*: Vawter testimony, cited in Gilbert opinion of Ninth Circuit Court of Appeals in the *Noyes et al.* case, in "Opinions and Judgment," *In re Noyes*, 17.

186   *"shotguns and Winchesters"*: In Harrison, *Nome and Seward Peninsula*, 65.

186   *"A detective retained by Frost"*: Discussion of Frost's use of detectives in Gilbert opinion of Ninth Circuit Court of Appeals in the *Noyes et al.* case, in "Opinions and Judgment," *In re Noyes*, 41–45. Details also in *Nome Gold Digger*, March 6, 1901.

186   *"I have done nothing"*: *Nome Gold Digger*, September 26, 1900.

187   *"I come among you"*: *Nome Gold Digger*, October 10, 1900.

187   *"As long as this regime"*: *Nome Gold Digger*, October 10, 1900.

188   *"I have had considerable trouble"*: October 12, 1900, Noyes letter to Griggs, Frederick files.

189   *"a detective accused Metson"*: Affidavit of detective Charles Herron summarized by Hansbrough in *Congressional Record—Senate*, February 26, 1901, 3056.

Chapter 23. "The Game Is All Up"

192   *"to attach the person"*: The Ninth Circuit's order for McKenzie's arrest printed in US Supreme Court decision on Alexander McKenzie petition for habeas corpus, *In re Alexander McKenzie*, 180 U.S. 536.

193   *"writ of attachment"*: Metson testimony, *In re Dubose*, 87.

194   *"The game is all up"*: Requa testimony, *In re Noyes*, 2796.

194   *"I don't know"*: Testimony of Deputy US Marshal George Burnham, cited in Gilbert opinion of Ninth Circuit Court of Appeals in the *Noyes et al.* case, in "Opinions and Judgment," *In re Noyes*, 37.

194   *"As soon as"*: Hume affidavit, June 18, 1901, *In re Noyes*, 416.

195   *"Mr. Geary told me"*: Metson testimony, cited on page 9 of "Report of the Honorable William W. Morrow . . . in the Matter of the Several Petitions, Letters, and Telegrams Presented to the United States on Behalf of Alexander McKenzie . . ." submitted by Morrow to Attorney General Philander C. Knox, April 19, 1901; copy of report in Alaska State Library Historical Collections, Juneau.

195   *"Gatling gun"*: Metson testimony, *In re Dubose*, 525–526.

195   *"I have come to you"*: Requa testimony, *In re Noyes*, 2788–2789.

196   *"sons of bitches"*: Burnham testimony, cited in Gilbert opinion of Ninth Circuit Court of Appeals in the *Noyes et al.* case, in "Opinions and Judgment," *In re Noyes*, 37–38.

196   *"the men from"*: *San Francisco Call*, November 6, 1900.

196   *"I never did"*: October 15, 1900, Noyes letter to Hansbrough, inserted by Hansbrough into *Congressional Record—Senate*, February 26, 1901, 3055.

197   *"When you know me better"*: Johnson testimony, *In re Noyes*, 2991–2992.

197   *"Exit Mephistopheles"*: *Nome Weekly Chronicle*, October 20, 1900.

198   *"if you can find"*: Burnham testimony, *In re Dubose*, 948–949.

198   *"I had done nothing"*: September 29, 1932, Metson letter to Lillo, in Lillo, *The Alaska Gold Mining Company and the Cape Nome Conspiracy*, 339.

199   *"There's a smooth"*: Dunham poem "Homeward Bound," in *The Goldsmith of Nome*, 75.

Chapter 24. "Now Alaska Has a Scandal"

203   *"inning"*: McKenzie quoted in *San Francisco Call*, November 6, 1900.

204   *"real fortunes"*: Gray Brechin, *Imperial San Francisco* (Berkeley: University of California Press, 2006), 31.

205   *"the honest"*: Spreckels as characterized by the *Call* before he bought the paper, in *San Francisco Call*, May 7, 1896.

205   *"tales that savor"*: *San Francisco Call*, November 6, 1900.

205   *"big political pull"*: *San Francisco Call*, October 31, 1900.

205   *"a matter of courtesy"*: *San Francisco Call*, November 9, 1900.

206   *"I have had"*: November 30, 1900, McKenzie letter to Elva, E. McKenzie letters.

208   *"My lot has been thrown"*: December 31, 1864, entry by E. S. Pillsbury in extract of "diary of E.S. Pillsbury," available from HaithiTrust Digital Library, https://babel.hathitrust.org/cgi/pt?id=uc1.31822043023506&view=1up&seq=3.

209   *"I met him every day"*: Chipps testimony, *In re Dubose*, 323.

209   *"Now Alaska Has a Scandal"*: *Washington Sentinel*, November 17, 1900.

210   *"Colleagues found in him"*: Representative Clarence C. Gilhams of Indiana, in *Abraham L. Brick (Late a Representative from Indiana) Memorial Addresses, Sixtieth Congress, Second Session, House of Representatives, February 14, 1909, Senate of the United States, February 27, 1909*, ed. United States. 60th Congress, 2nd session, 1908–1909 (Washington, DC: Government Printing Office, 1909), 37.

210   *"innuendo and insinuation"*: Text of Carter resolution in the *Washington Post*, December 18, 1900.

211   *"Open Letter"*: December 18, 1900, Carter pamphlet in Carter papers. Carter's Montana accuser was Wilbur F. Sanders.

211   *"alleged Alaska scandal"*: Carter "Open Letter" pamphlet, Carter papers, 19.

212   *"but it is understood"*: Reported in *Nome News* (now published twice weekly), March 23, 1901.

212   *"a surprise"*: Seattle *Post-Intelligencer*, December 25, 1901.

212   *"trying to besmirch"*: December 28, 1900, McKenzie letter to Elva, E. McKenzie letters.

Chapter 25. "High-Handed and Grossly Illegal"

213   *"all objections"*: "Answer of Alexander McKenzie," January 16, 1901, provided to Ninth Circuit Court of Appeals, "In the Matter of Alexander McKenzie for Contempt," copy of answer in *In re McKenzie* in Law Library, Library of Congress, Washington, DC.

213   *"That said"*: "Answer of Alexander McKenzie," 3.

213   *"it was never"*: "Answer of Alexander McKenzie," 7.

214   *"We admit the fact"*: Geary in January 28, 1901, trial of McKenzie by Ninth Circuit Court of Appeals, in *In re McKenzie*, 35, in Law Library, Library of Congress, Washington, DC.

214   *"personal services"*: *In re McKenzie* trial, 92–93.

214   *"shocking record"*: Ross opinion for Ninth Circuit Court of Appeals, February 11, 1901, on page 783 of *Tornanses v. Melsing et al.*, *Kjellman v. Rogers*, Nos. 634, 636, 106 Federal Reporter, downloaded from Westlaw.

215   *"high-handed and grossly illegal"*: Ross opinion, 789.

216   *"And it speaks well"*: Ross opinion, 789.

216   *"rapid extension"*: Ross opinion, 789.

216   *"true names"*: San Francisco *Call*, February 12, 1901.

216   *"Canadian giant writhe"*: San Francisco *Call*, February 12, 1901.

216   *"absolute dictator"*: Seattle *Times*, February 13, 1901.

217   "CLAIM GRABBER SENTENCED": *Evening Times-Republican*, February 12, 1901.

217   *"humble laborer"*: San Francisco *Call*, February 12, 1901.

Chapter 26. "I Will Go to the President"

219   *"commute his sentence"*: San Francisco *Call*, February 12, 1901.

220   *"about two months"*: Lacey statement in the *Minneapolis Journal*, February 12, 1901.

220   *"deaf, dumb, blind"*: *Washington Post* editorial printed in *Nome News*, May 8, 1901.

220   *"great scandal"*: January 18, 1901, Orton letter to McKinley, Frederick files.

220   *"strongly in the East"*: February 13, 1901, Hill telegram to McKenzie, JJH papers.

221   *"kindness"*: February 13, 1901, McKenzie telegram to Hill, JJH papers.

221   *"I expect to be"*: February 15, 1901, McKenzie letter to Elva, E. McKenzie letters.

221   *"to do anything"*: February 18, 1901, Kennedy letter to Hill, JJH papers.

222   *"if you go to Cape Nome"*: Stewart, *Congressional Record—Senate*, February 26, 1901, 3050.

222   *"an honorable and responsible"*: Hansbrough, *Congressional Record—Senate*, February 26, 1901, 3055.

222   *"allow any whitewashing"*: Stewart, *Congressional Record—Senate*, February 26, 1901, 3056.

223   *"trying"*: Lindsay, *Congressional Record—Senate*, February 26, 1901, 3059.

223   *"matter of public business"*: Stewart, *Congressional Record—Senate*, February 26, 1901, 3062.

223   *"I was at Nome"*: February 27, 1901, letter from W. L. Leland to Stewart, Frederick files.

224   *"In the event of failure"*: March 6, 1901, McKenzie letter to Elva, E. McKenzie letters.

224   *"interlocutory order"*: Fuller opinion for Supreme Court, March 25, 1901, *In re Alexander McKenzie*, 180 U.S. 536 (1901).

224   *"Fuller rejected the argument"*: Fuller cited in *In re Claasen*, 140, U.S. 200, a case decided by the Supreme Court in 1891, in which New York criminal defendant Peter J. Claasen was deemed subject to a writ of supersedeas issued by just one member of a multimember panel.

224   *"We hold that"*: Fuller opinion for Supreme Court, March 25, 1901, *In re Alexander McKenzie*, 180 U.S. 536 (1901).

224   *"I have a decision"*: March 27, 1901, McKenzie letter to Elva, E. McKenzie letters.

225   *"many moves to make yet"*: March 27, 1901, McKenzie letter to Elva, E. McKenzie letters.

Chapter 27. "The Accident in the Elevator"

227   *"health and so forth"*: March 27, 1901, McKenzie letter to Elva, E. McKenzie letters.

227   *"I am setting up"*: April 11, 1901, McKenzie letter to Elva, E. McKenzie letters.

228   *"prevent me getting"*: McKenzie cited in April 3, 1901, P. J. McCumber letter to Hill, JJH papers.

228 *"I have two good rooms"*: April 11, 1901, McKenzie letter to Elva, E. McKenzie letters.

229 *"Mr. Hill presented"*: April 4, 1901, Geary letter to McCumber, JJH papers.

230 *"Keep Mack in good cheer"*: April 4, 1901, Geary letter to McCumber, JJH papers.

230 *"Having been adjudged"*: April 5, 1901, McCumber letter to Hill, with a copy of correspondence sent the day before by McCumber to Geary, JJH papers.

230 *"fair treatment"*: April 7, 1901, McCumber letter to Hill, JJH papers.

231 *"I have practically"*: March 1897 letter from Hill to Hanna, quoted in Steven H. Gittelman, *J. P. Morgan and the Transportation Kings* (Lanham, MD: University Press of America, 2012), 73.

231 *"My Dear Senator"*: April 9, 1901, Hill letter to Hanna, JJH papers.

231 *"My Dear Jim"*: April 10, 1901, Hanna reply to Hill, JJH papers.

232 *"typewritten draft"*: April 18, 1901, McCumber pardon application draft in JJH papers.

234 *"Such was the story"*: McCumber, *Congressional Record—Senate*, February 5, 1902, 1323.

234 *"Several of Alec's"*: Jackson MS, 244.

234 *"recuperating from"*: McKenzie daughter's statement on page 1 of transcript of hearing on Alexander McKenzie estate, Burleigh County Clerk of Court, North Dakota, in McKenzie papers, State Historical Society of North Dakota.

234 *"McKenzie was writing"*: McKenzie's first wife, Mary Ellen, died on June 27, 1897; the funeral was held in Saint Paul. On June 26, McKenzie wrote to Elva with concern for her health. The letter was postmarked Washington, DC, June 26. He wrote her again on June 28, the letter postmarked Washington, DC, and again on July 3, the letter postmarked Washington, DC. E. McKenzie letters.

Chapter 28. "A Free Man Again"

237 *"I may be out"*: April 20, 1901, McKenzie letter to Elva, E. McKenzie letters.

237 *"The principal thing"*: April 20, 1901, McCumber letter to Hill, JJH papers.

238 *"In the Matter"*: "Report of the Honorable William W. Morrow . . . in the Matter of the Several Petitions, Letters, and Telegrams Presented to the United States on Behalf of Alexander McKenzie . . ." submitted by Morrow to Attorney General Philander C. Knox, April 19, 1901.

238 *"Obedience to the orders"*: Morrow report on McKenzie pardon campaign, 7.

238 *"In other words"*: Morrow report on McKenzie pardon campaign, 14–15.

239 *"he knew Morrow so well"*: Hanna's remarks to McCumber conveyed to McKenzie in April 30, 1901, McCumber letter to McKenzie; a copy of this letter was sent by McCumber to Hill in a letter of this same day. JJH papers.

239 *"It is probably true"*: April 30, 1901, McCumber letter to McKenzie, JJH papers.

240 *"spirit of resistance"*: Morrow opinion for Ninth Circuit Court of Appeals, *In re Dubose*, May 6, 1901, 109 Fed. 971, No. 632, 4–5.

241 *"if he arrives"*: May 3, 1901, McCumber letter to Hill, JJH papers.

242 *"no merit"*: Knox telegram to McKinley quoted in Jackson MS, 259.

242 *"McKenzie is a very sick man"*: Morrow remarks to the *San Francisco Examiner* cited in Jackson MS, 254.

242 *"too weak to leave"*: *San Francisco Call*, May 26, 1901.

243 *"nervous condition"*: Tisdale testimony, *In re Noyes*, 116.

243 *"Your name is"*: Madison and McKenzie exchange in *In re Noyes*, 127–128.

243 *"I never felt"*: McKenzie testimony, *In re Noyes*, 134.

244 *"sprinting down"*: In the *Washington Post*, February 3, 1902, "a reliable eyewitness" was said to have "observed" McKenzie "sprinting down" the railway platform. South Carolina senator Benjamin Tillman inserted the *Post* story into the *Congressional Record—Senate*, February 3, 1902, 1235.

244 *"I received my release"*: May 25, 1901, McKenzie letter to Elva, E. McKenzie letters.

244 *"While all of"*: May 31, 1901, McCumber letter to Hill, JJH papers.

244 *"Action of President"*: "Annual Report of the Attorney General of the United States," Department of Justice, 1901, 294.

245 *"full pardon"*: *Bismarck Daily Tribune*, May 25, 1901, cited in Jackson MS, 261. The *Tribune* said that McKinley gave McKenzie a "commutation of sentence, which amounts to a full pardon."

245 *"President McKinley crossed the continent"*: An unnamed friend of McKenzie, quoted by Jackson in Jackson MS, 252.

245 *"McKenzie was arrested"*: Fraser interview, in Angus Fraser papers.

Epilogue

247 *"corrupt conspiracy"*: Ross concurring opinion, *In re Noyes*, 46.

247 *"grossly betrayed"*: Gilbert opinion for the court, *In re Noyes*, 45.

248 *"the story reads"*: *Law Notes*, April 1901, 3.

248 *"I was a little fellow"*: Theodore Roosevelt quoted in James F. Vivian, *The Romance of My Life* (Fargo, ND: Prairie House, 1989), 36.

248   *"Although he made"*: Theodore Roosevelt address to Congress, December 6, 1904, American History from Revolution to Reconstruction and Beyond, http://www.let.rug.nl/usa/presidents/theodore-roosevelt/state-of-the-union-1904.php.

249   *"Alaska is the galley slave"*: Rex E. Beach, "The Looting of Alaska," *Appleton's Booklovers Magazine* 7, no. 1 (January 1906): 3.

249   *"About all I had to do"*: Rex Beach, *Personal Exposures* (New York: Harper & Brothers, 1940), 30.

249   *"a gigantic"*: Rex Beach, *The Spoilers* (Scotts Valley, CA: CreateSpace, 2015), 30.

250   *"We've got the law"*: Beach, *The Spoilers*, 32.

250   *"whether they will answer"*: J. Adam Bede, "Side-Stepping the Vice-Presidency," *Leslie's Monthly Magazine* 58 (September 1904): 508.

251   *"a dominating but engaging"*: *Bismarck Tribune*, July 1, 1922.

251   *"an adventurous career"*: *New York Times*, June 30, 1922.

Index

Page numbers preceded by *ph* refer to photographs or their captions in the photo spread section.

Paul Starobin is author of *Madness Rules the Hour: Charleston, 1860 and the Mania for War*, praised by the *New York Times* as a "fast-paced, engagingly written account" of the hysteria that descended on Charleston, South Carolina, on the eve of the Civil War. He has been a frequent contributor to *The Atlantic* and is a former Moscow bureau chief for *Business Week*. He has written for other publications, including the *Wall Street Journal*, *Washington Post*, *Los Angeles Times*, *Politico*, *City Journal*, *National Geographic*, and *Smithsonian*. He lives with his family in Orleans, Massachusetts.

PublicAffairs is a publishing house founded in 1997. It is a tribute to the standards, values, and flair of three persons who have served as mentors to countless reporters, writers, editors, and book people of all kinds, including me.

I. F. STONE, proprietor of *I. F. Stone's Weekly*, combined a commitment to the First Amendment with entrepreneurial zeal and reporting skill and became one of the great independent journalists in American history. At the age of eighty, Izzy published *The Trial of Socrates*, which was a national bestseller. He wrote the book after he taught himself ancient Greek.

BENJAMIN C. BRADLEE was for nearly thirty years the charismatic editorial leader of *The Washington Post*. It was Ben who gave the *Post* the range and courage to pursue such historic issues as Watergate. He supported his reporters with a tenacity that made them fearless and it is no accident that so many became authors of influential, best-selling books.

ROBERT L. BERNSTEIN, the chief executive of Random House for more than a quarter century, guided one of the nation's premier publishing houses. Bob was personally responsible for many books of political dissent and argument that challenged tyranny around the globe. He is also the founder and longtime chair of Human Rights Watch, one of the most respected human rights organizations in the world.

·   ·   ·

For fifty years, the banner of Public Affairs Press was carried by its owner Morris B. Schnapper, who published Gandhi, Nasser, Toynbee, Truman, and about 1,500 other authors. In 1983, Schnapper was described by *The Washington Post* as "a redoubtable gadfly." His legacy will endure in the books to come.

Peter Osnos, *Founder*